Living with London's Olympics

Palgrave Studies in Urban Anthropology

ITALO PARDO is Honorary Reader in Social Anthropology at the University of Kent, U.K. Dr. Pardo, a well-known specialist in urban anthropology, is the author of several books and peer-reviewed essays.

GIULIANA B. PRATO is Honorary Senior Research Fellow in Social Anthropology at the University of Kent, U.K. Widely published in anthropology, she serves as Chair of the Commission of Urban Anthropology, as Head of the Council of Commissions and as a member of the Executive Committee of the IUAES.

Living with London's Olympics: An Ethnography
Iain Lindsay

Contents

List of Figures and Tables	vii
Series Preface	ix
Preface	xi
Prologue	xv
List of Abbreviations and Acronyms	xix
Introduction In Pursuit of Olympic Gold	1
Chapter 1 The New(Ham) World	5
Chapter 2 The 2012 Transition: Process and Politics	23
Chapter 3 Newham Divide and Document	37
Chapter 4 Life in the Shadow of the Olympic Torch	63
Chapter 5 Employment and Capital Gains	79
Chapter 6 The Rings of Exclusion	97
Chapter 7 Securitization: The Olympic Lockdown?	107
Chapter 8 Big Game Hunting: Baiting the Hooks	119
Chapter 9 Going for the Gold: The All-Consuming 2012 Ethos	135
Chapter 10 Conclusion: Extinguishing the Olympic Torch	149

Notes	165
References	181
Index	199

Living with London's Olympics
An Ethnography

Iain Lindsay

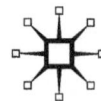

LIVING WITH LONDON'S OLYMPICS
Copyright © Iain Lindsay, 2014.

Softcover reprint of the hardcover 1st edition 2014 978-1-137-45672-4

All rights reserved.

First published in 2014 by
PALGRAVE MACMILLAN®
in the United States—a division of St. Martin's Press LLC,
175 Fifth Avenue, New York, NY 10010.

Where this book is distributed in the UK, Europe and the rest of the world, this is by Palgrave Macmillan, a division of Macmillan Publishers Limited, registered in England, company number 785998, of Houndmills, Basingstoke, Hampshire RG21 6XS.

Palgrave Macmillan is the global academic imprint of the above companies and has companies and representatives throughout the world.

Palgrave® and Macmillan® are registered trademarks in the United States, the United Kingdom, Europe and other countries.

ISBN 978-1-349-49855-0   ISBN 978-1-137-45321-1 (eBook)
DOI 10.1057/9781137453211

Library of Congress Cataloging-in-Publication Data

Lindsay, Iain, 1981–
   Living with London's Olympics : an ethnography / Iain Lindsay.
     pages cm.
   Includes bibliographical references and index.

     1. Olympic Games (30th : 2012 : London, England) 2. Olympics—Social aspects—England—London. 3. Ethnology—England—London. I. Title.

GV7222012 L55 2014
796.48—dc23   2014020500

A catalogue record of the book is available from the British Library.

Design by Newgen Knowledge Works (P) Ltd., Chennai, India.

First edition: November 2014

10 9 8 7 6 5 4 3 2 1

Figures and Tables

Figures

3.1	Carpenters' Residents Memorialized	48
4.1	Burns, Hambleton, and Hoggett's Ladder	77
5.1	The Froud Community Center	83
5.2	We Have Work…	94
6.1	Café Lympic	98
6.2	Ringing in the Customers	99
8.1	The Shoal	126
8.2	Viva Las Newham…	130
8.3	Electric Avenue	131
8.4	Eating Out	131
10.1	One Day to Go	162
10.2	Olympic Screening	162

Tables

3.1	2005 Carpenters Estate Occupation Levels	45
3.2	2011 Carpenters Estate Occupation Levels	45

Series Preface

Half of humanity lives in towns and cities, and that proportion is expected to increase in the coming decades. Society, both Western and non-Western, is fast becoming urban and mega-urban. Cities are identified as hubs of cultural and ethnic interaction as well as challenging settings for future sustainable development. Clearly, studying urban settings and the attendant complex social, economic, and political dynamics is timely and of great importance. It is indeed reasonably argued that the future of the social sciences, and of anthropology in particular, will inevitably be urban-bound.

Given the disciplinary commitment to an empirically based analysis, Anthropology has a unique contribution to make to our understanding of our rapidly changing and increasingly complex urban world. It is in such a belief that we have established the *Palgrave Studies in Urban Anthropology* series. Books in the series consist of high-quality contributions from anthropologists and other social scientists engaged in empirical research across the world. The topics covered set the agenda concerning new debates and chart new theoretical directions, encouraging reflection on the significance of the anthropological paradigm in urban research and its centrality to mainstream academic debates and to society more broadly. As Editors, we aim to promote critical scholarship internationally. Volumes published in the series expand knowledge on the state of the art and on methodological and theoretical developments in this important field, showing the relevance of ethnographic research in understanding the socio-cultural, demographic, economic, and geo-political changes of contemporary society.

Italo Pardo
and
Giuliana B. Prato

Preface

This book is an attempt to communicate a view of urban life that played out during the seven highly transitory delivery years of the 2012 London Olympic Games. The fieldwork was carried out predominantly in the London borough of Newham, an East London neighborhood at the heart of the 2012 Olympic-related urban renewal, and was conducted throughout Olympic delivery. This cycle began on 6th July 2005, when the London Olympic bidding committee won the right to host the 2012 Olympic Games, and culminated seven years later; at which point London's Olympic venues had been built on time, team GB had won an unprecedented medal haul and no significant security incidents had occurred. These results justified a positive evaluation of the 2012 Games and global attention turned to the forthcoming mega-events in Brazil in 2014 and 2016.

Following the resplendent closing ceremony, the necessary period of legacy evaluation officially began in earnest. Because of the nature of Olympic analysis, accounts of transition are often dominated by assessments that focus on before and after evaluations that compare and contrast the post-event delivery outcomes and pre-event promises. This book presents an altogether different account, offering the reader the opportunity to follow the implications for local life during Olympic delivery. The discussion follows the French sociologist Pierre Bourdieu in considering that "one cannot grasp the most profound logic of the social world unless one becomes immersed in the specificity of an empirical reality" (1993a, p. 271). Through ethnographic inquiry, what follows contrasts the rhetoric and reality of 2012 Olympic delivery in the hope of providing a contextual analysis that addresses this under-researched topic.

Pre-Olympic Newham presented the observer with a difficult decision—whether to buy into the 2012 Olympic delivery rhetoric and dismiss this area as a chaotic, deprived and anarchic place whose way of life was thankfully doomed to extinction thanks to Olympic regeneration, or to ask whether there was a rationale for its deprived outlook that might suggest different conclusions. This study combines Auge's concept of *non-place* (1995), Lefebvre's theorizing on space (1991), and Bourdieu's thinking tools to look at the diversified location that was pre-Olympic Newham. I address issues of inclusion, exclusion, power relations, ideology, and identity, arguing that the relatively short time frame of Olympic delivery needs to be understood taking into account the segregation between "Olympic" and "non-Olympic" Newham. Furthermore, rhetoric and reality diverged during a delivery period that was oriented towards the needs and goals of Olympic migrants from different backgrounds, as opposed to enhancing the lives of those living in a community that was advertised as rife with crime, poverty and deprivation.

The analysis offered here moves beyond the view that the Olympic delivery milieu disseminates capitalistic norms and values and shifts the focus towards everyday realities of rationality and self-interest. In Newham, the micro-level outcomes of such broader delivery processes facilitated a re-negotiation of place-identity and place-ownership that fostered an environment oriented towards attracting a future affluent population whilst vilifying the pre-Games community. I conclude that such attempts to re-mold Newham into a post-Olympic utopia where, to follow the Newham council strap line, prosperous and educated families "live, work and stay" are based upon the short-sighted assumption that creating an aesthetically pleasing entertainment location is tantamount to creating a desirable location for sustainable family life. Focusing on the micro-level sheds new light on the way in which hosting the Olympic Games influences opportunity, morality, and individual choice and on how and why these are translated into action or inaction.

Through a detailed examination of how people negotiate their lives in this complex and changing environment, the discussion identifies the deep-rooted significance and dichotomies of sport-led urban regeneration, the symbolism of personal identity, and the attendant diverse implications. The interactions between the local community and Olympic deliverers profoundly informed the actors' sense of themselves, their urban setting, and their identity, and the way in which these inter-related. The fact that so much modification is condensed into a relatively short seven-year Olympic delivery window ensures a period of hyper-regeneration, wherein existing norms and values are contested, modified, and in some cases erased entirely. During this period, the civic choices and beliefs of the inhabitants of these contested realms underline the problematic character of event-led urban reclamation for the host communities.

Mega-event media coverage during delivery indicates that such reclamation projects are strongly oriented to community enhancement and usually profess to have much local-level support. However, the reality "a new broom does not necessarily sweep clean" (Pardo 1996, p.xii) appears to be an inevitable victim of the Olympic delivery rhetoric, only to re-emerge anew in post-Olympic legacy evaluation. The 2012 Olympic Games promised to deliver the systematic improvement of this part of East London, referred to as "London's Gash" by those tasked with its eradication. Rhetoric aside, the ethnographic account offered here brings to light the implications of such policies for local people who lived there throughout. Such an account of delivery reality is unprecedented and I suggest that unless the process of change is understood, the conclusions on the destination will be incomplete. Time will tell whether the London 2012 urban reclamation was a success, and much will depend on the methodology used to assess the situation. I hope that the present account of Olympic delivery will contribute to future discussion by providing a valuable contextualization.

In the following pages, I seek to demonstrate that the empirical investigation of the implications of sports-driven urban regeneration need not be limited to a "before and after" comparative analysis. A major objective of this study is to encourage a serious questioning of existing models of mega-event bureaucracy and relations of power, of overly structured analyses of social relations, and of the class analysis approach to contemporary sports-driven urban reclamation projects. Drawing upon a critical reading of modern social theory, the discussion follows Pardo (1996) to build towards a demonstration of how documenting the micro-level processes and implications of Olympic delivery allows controlled speculation on the processual relationship between agency and structure. I shall therefore argue that, because this level of analysis carefully avoids a deterministic view of culture, organization, and power, it brings to light critical processes, dichotomies, and inconsistencies of sports-driven urban regeneration.

Over the years, I have enjoyed much assistance from many people, to all of whom I am immensely grateful. Throughout the fieldwork, Dr. Gary Armstrong provided invaluable support, challenge, advice, and thought-provoking discussion. The construction of the final text also benefitted greatly from Dr. Armstrong's and Dr. Monica Degen's criticism and feedback. I have presented this research widely at workshops and conferences and am indebted to participants who provided constructive criticism and advice. Particular gratitude must be expressed to Dr. Italo Pardo and Dr. Giuliana Prato of the Commission on Urban Anthropology. Dr. Pardo's advice, support, and guidance during various conferences and beyond have helped me enormously in writing the final text and in my development as an academic.

It would be remiss of me not to mention the diverse people from beyond academe who have allowed me to conduct the research itself. Those who opened doors, encouraged, forewarned, facilitated, and populated my networks, willingly engaged in conversation, and included me in all things "Olympic" are all highly valued contributors to this final text. My research would not have been possible without such cooperation and generosity. Necessarily, the majority of these people will have to remain unnamed (or be given pseudonyms); anonymity was offered to all as either a courtesy or a necessity, depending on the context. I am extremely grateful to all the aforementioned and hope that my debt of gratitude is in some small way repaid by this book, which would not have been possible without their help. Thank you.

Prologue

Squashed, jostled, pushed and pulled, I was engulfed in a crowd that surged as one through the exit doors of an overcrowded, early morning Central line train arriving at Stratford underground station. Stratford, located to the North West of the London Borough of Newham, was to host the main public transport entry points to the 2012 Olympic Park. However, on this 2009 winter morning, there was no indication that this truly unremarkable tube-station was going to be the portal to what was being sold as the Golden Games. There was no sign of the plush carpets that the Olympic top brass had walked upon months earlier during their inspection visit, or of the harmonic sounds by the consummate orchestra that had serenaded them through the rat run of gray walkways leading to the stadium of impending Olympic deliverance. At this time, the streets in this part of London were definitely not paved with Olympic gold.

This morning, Stratford station was a quintessential London commuter-processing mechanism, impossible to differentiate from many other stations on the network. The customary fight-for-ground amongst the commuting hordes was being played out as usual, with incalculable numbers of the faceless competing for woefully inadequate carriage space. One individual, for reasons unknown, fell afoul of the automated barriers—ideally negotiated through a quick swipe of an electronic ticket, much to the collective irritation of the impatient pack biting at his heels, eager to board a carriage in the virtually futile pursuit of the scarcest of London's resources—a seat on a rush hour tube. Outside, long snaking queues for the ATMs and ticket machines demarcated the approach, while those with somewhere to be had to slalom through the crowds using unscripted, unpredictable maneuvers to negotiate a quick passage, tinged with anger and annoyance at the randomness and lethargy of the others.

For those directed to the 2012 site, alighting at Stratford ensured a swim against this human tide. If one believed all that one was told, one would expect to be met by a multitude of smiling, happy locals thrilled to host the Olympics. However, such an idealistic notion would quickly disappear in the harshness of a Stratford reality marked by the apparent business-as-usual chaos, as the customary throng of East End people went about their daily lives. Theirs was a Stratford where one lived and survived; the Olympic dream was not on their minds.

On the paved concourse outside the station, amid a throng of commuters, stood a large bus depot—the terminal of 45 routes that served the area. Form seemed to mimic function at this depot. It was marked by what appeared to be a multitude of upturned large white umbrellas, but were officially individually lit "inverted conics" offering protection from the elements. A dated shopping center built in the early 1970s stood to the left, attempting to outlast the three dilapidated 23-story council-built high-rise tower blocks that stood on the opposite side of the railway tracks, to the right. The Olympic Park development lay behind the station, easily observable from any of the aforementioned locations. By the summer of 2012, the Park was to dominate the neighborhood physically and metaphorically. However, at this moment in time, the development was conspicuous only by the lack of deference paid to it; it was simply a run-of-the-mill, albeit sizeable, building site.

Conversely, the rest of the Stratford cityscape crackled with the energy of contradiction. The most cursory of examinations revealed a number of diversities—rich/poor, old/young and a confusion of races, cultures, accents, and dress styles. In this urban thrall, construction workers in high visibility bibs and work-soiled clothing jousted with suit-wearing city types and liveried shop assistants. Black youths in their late teens seemingly oblivious to the discipline of the quasi-efficient queuing system ambled along in baggy jeans that showed too much of their underpants and hinted at an MTV-oriented US stereotype of black gang allegiances. Groups of chatty teenage girls, of various skin shades, took the opportunity to scream, shout, or laugh—their noise punctuating the silence of the hunched-shouldered pensioners making their way to the shopping center.

Newspaper sellers, coffee vendors and concession stands speckled the area, though not for long. Such enterprises had been told that one day soon their business permits would be discontinued, hinting at what it meant for a place to become, in planners' parlance, an "Olympic City". Contests of sound and smell took place all around. The guttural murmur of the crowd amidst the smell of fresh coffee, urine, stale lager, and cheap aftershave saw life, both oral and aural, compete for air space. Few spoke native English. This was a neighborhood of the working classes that seamlessly combined well-established and emerging occupational cultures. Exponential change would unfold here in the following few years, as the Olympic delivery took shape. This neighborhood was in a sense marked out for a quick death, but a better life was promised for those who remained.

As an ethnographer, I began to try to explore the themes that underlined my research, namely, to document life in the shadow of the Olympic Games during the 2012 delivery.

Abbreviations and Acronyms

AGM	Annual General Meeting
AM	Aston Mansfield
BOA	British Olympic Association
CARP	Carpenters Against Regeneration Plan
CLC	The City of London Corporation
CLO	Community Legal Observer
CLT	Community Land Trust
COF	Citizen's Organising Foundation
DCLG	The Department of Communities and Local Government
DCMS	The Department for Culture, Media and Sport
ETOA	The European Tour Operators Association
GLA	The Greater London Authority
HMIC	Her Majesty's Inspectorate of Constabulary
IAF	Industrial Area Foundation
IF	International Federations (IOC)
IMD	The Index of Multiple Deprivation
IOC	The International Olympic Committee
IPCC	The Independent Police Complaints Commission
LC	London Citizens
LDA	The London Development Agency
LLDC	The London Legacy Development Corporation
LOCOG	London Organising Committee for the Olympic Games
MOD	The Ministry of Defence
MPS	The Metropolitan Police Service
NEET	Not in Education, Employment or Training
NHPS	The Newham Household Survey Panel
NI	National Insurance
NMP	The Newham Monitoring Project

NOC	National Olympic Committees
NVSC	The Newham Voluntary Sector Consortium
NYPP	The Newham Youth Providers Partnership
ODA	The Olympic Delivery Authority
ONS	The Office of National Statistics
OPLC	The Olympic Park Legacy Company
ORN	The Olympic Road Network
OSD	The Olympic Security Directorate
NL	The UK National Lottery
SWF	Save Wanstead Flats
TBAG	Tower Block Action Group
TELCO	The East London Citizens Organisation
TFL	Transport for London
TMO	Tennant Management Organisation
TOP	The Olympic Partner Programme
UCL	University College, London
UEL	The University of East London
UVG	The Urban Villages Group
WCC	The Worshipful Company of Carpenters
YOT	The Youth Offending Team

INTRODUCTION

In Pursuit of Olympic Gold

The attraction of the Olympic Games, as a sporting event with its memorable ever-ready athletic performances, is easily understandable. World records in sport are *enthralling*. The Games and the narratives they provide are *enchanting*. Their public, the teeming mass of common humanity, rejoices and commiserates with those undergoing athletic rigors. However, the prevalent belief of those spouting the benefits of an after-Games "*legacy*" appears less fundamentally sound. This issue has surrounded the Games over the past 40 years. For decades, as in 2012, the promised benefits to the host communities have been expected to be felt from the very beginnings of the Olympic delivery in the shape of jobs in construction, skills-training related to the building and servicing of Olympic venues, and the transformation of Olympic locales for the benefit of the local community.

Bearing this in mind, the goal of this research was to investigate the realities and implications of Olympic delivery, particularly from the perspective of the local hosting community. The ethnographic method would help to address both the rhetoric and the reality of Olympic delivery. The objective was to add to the knowledge of sports-led regeneration and development by exploring the delivery phase of the 2012 Games. The key aim was to offer an empirical account of a transition—essentially a "before and during" study—with no other ulterior motive than that of providing a first-hand account of the process and impact of Olympic delivery. Surprisingly, such a process had never been studied ethnographically. This lacuna—extending to other aspects of Olympic research—provoked Olympic scholar John MacAloon (1992) to criticize Olympic researchers for their general failure to employ ethnographic methods.

Olympic delivery amplifies Spanish sociologist Manuel Castells's suggestion that a distinctive feature of contemporary society is the decoupling of the sense of community from the sense of place (Castells, 1991). This decoupling in Newham is defined and explored in the discussion that follows, evidencing what Bourdieu (1984) would call *hysteresis*, the essential features of which were

> the mismatch between habitus and field, the time dimension associated with it—how habitus is out of synch with field...differential responses of organisations and individuals lead to the dislocation and disruption of habitus which occurs in any field change...Often it is those already well endowed with economic and symbolic capital who are able to achieve desirable dominant positions within the new field structures. (Hardy, cited in Grenfell 2008, pp. 133–148).

If we consider that Castells' de-coupling of community and place is a distinctive feature of contemporary society, then the application of Olympic delivery *hysteresis* symbolizes an attempted sports-driven reclamation of the relationship between place and community. For some in the regenerated Olympic locales, the outcome was a reconfiguration of the social cues that informed daily life. This resulted in identities being consistently negotiated and renegotiated during Olympic delivery. Consequently, in the areas that may best be defined as "Olympic" Newham, Olympic delivery was a tale of two cities—Newham's past and Newham's future—and of two narratives—one historical and the other projected. One was a relic, informed by those that possessed knowledge on how to exist in a pre-bid Newham. The other was a vision, symbolized by a media-promoted idealistic post-Games utopia, which was yet to be. What seemed real during this particular time, in this particular place, was a sense of an inevitable—if unknown—transition; where everything was up for negotiation and re-ordering.

When, in 2003, it became apparent that London would be bidding to host the 2012 Games (in the East side of the city), few Londoners seemed to take the bid seriously. It was widely assumed that Paris, the long-time favorite (whose odds fluctuated between 1–3 and 4–9 during the bidding process),[1] would win the beauty contest and be awarded the right to host the 2012 Games. During the bidding campaign, a clear dichotomy began to emerge between local perceptions and the media representations. The Olympic bidding team[2] claimed that the demographics described as "East London communities" universally "backed the bid."[3] To many observers such claims appeared far from the reality, which should perhaps not have been entirely unexpected. Olympics critic Lenskyj had previously stated that the Olympics industry had the power to "promote the illusion of unequivocal support on the part of host cities and countries" (Lenskyj 2004, p. 152).

So, the 2012 Olympic bid simply did not seem to resonate with the communities that were, some eight years later, to host the world's premier sporting "Mega-Event." Moreover, members of the communities located in the proposed Olympic settings appeared, for the most part, disinterested; and those who did express an interest were largely opposed to the event. The Games were not for them; in their own words, they were not "Olympic People." One apparently unifying factor was the belief that London was most unlikely to win the bid. In truth, most people who were interviewed in 2004—2005 had more pressing concerns and decisions to make. The East of London was high on poverty and deprivation indexes, and the people who lived there appeared to be too busy surviving to worry about the ramifications of hosting the Olympics. Most showed indifference to the matter; what to have for dinner that evening was more pressing. While opinions about the Games were multi-faceted, as opposed to simply two-sided, the *leitmotif* was disinterest.

However, when in 2005 the unexpected happened and London won the bid, everything changed. The present effort to document this change examines both the people subjected to the ramifications of building the Olympic structures and infrastructure in their communities and the political merry-go-round that winning the bid brought to these areas. While this research proceeded, there were changes in national and local government policies; London Mayors and UK governments were elected; the demographic composition of the population in East London changed; a post-2008 world economic crisis impacted upon the domestic purse; inner-city riots, various protests, and many other social and cultural events took place. Meanwhile, the 2012 Olympic delivery continued; unabated and largely unchallenged.

In what follows we will see street gangs of black youths, originally from some 20 countries, and Albanian domestic cleaners fight against well-heeled Anglo-Saxons and Oxbridge scholars for access to a variety of opportunities. Freedom and rights clash with security and restriction. Market traders compete with high-end retail outlets; low-end bookies with high-end casinos; chicken shops with expensive restaurants. In this transitory time and in this transitory place, everything was up for Olympics-related negotiation. In these areas, the Olympics-driven re-definition of identity began its journey along the same inclusive lines described earlier, but for many local residents, it meant descending into apathy, ambivalence, segregation, securitization and prohibition of access, before finally coming full circle and re-joining the pro-Olympics ranks as the time for the Games approached. The analysis begins with an overview of the London borough of Newham.

CHAPTER 1

The New(Ham) World

In introducing the London borough of Newham, I will draw on a combination of statistical data and first-hand accounts to provide an indication of everyday life in this complex, unique, and diverse urban setting. What follows explores the composition of the borough: its peculiarities and dichotomies. I shall consider how hosting the Olympics was intended to transform Newham, and who was involved in such a project at the local level.

Newham: A Place to Live, Work, and Stay?

Data from the 2001 British census and additional data from the Office of National Statistics (ONS) emphasize Newham's diversity and population growth, which have attracted media attention:

- Newham is the most ethnically diverse district in England.
- In 2001 the population numbered 243,737 (a rise of 10.2% from the 1991 census).
- Newham has the highest fertility rate in the country (the 2009 figures show an average of 2.87 children per woman, compared to the national average of 1.95).[1]

Statistical data also shows that Newham residents have a lower life expectancy and a higher rate of premature mortality than anywhere else in Britain. The local health issues are typical of situations of poverty and deprivation and show no signs of abating. The data released by the Newham

Council[2] indicates that those experiencing poor health are far less likely to be in employment, resulting in lower incomes, poorer housing conditions, and reduced access to opportunities. In correlation, they indicate that employment is a key element in improving long-term health, which would suggest that those who fall into the poverty trap would have an incredibly difficult time getting out of it.

The London borough of Newham and the City of London are just 5 miles apart. They are, however, separated by two London Underground zones and are, to all intents and purposes, two worlds apart economically, socially, culturally, and in as many other categories as one can fathom. In stark contrast with the affluence evident in the City, Newham presents many characteristics that would indicate why this borough would be receptive to widespread Olympic regeneration. According to the 2007 Index of Multiple Deprivation,[3] this is one of the most deprived areas in the UK. In 2008, the Newham Household Survey Panel (NHPS)[4] recorded that, after housing costs were taken into consideration, the poverty rate was more than double the London average (45.3% as opposed to 22.1%). These figures emphasize a correlation between poverty and ethnicity, the highest levels of poverty being recorded among Asian Bangladeshis (61%) and Asian Pakistanis (59%); at 33%, poverty among white people was also well over the London average. Poverty among black people was recorded at 22%.

Newham's deprivation was spread throughout the borough, as opposed to the centralized pockets of deprivation observable in other locations.[5] The visibly high levels of deprivation that permeated the borough were reflected in the public perceptions gathered from across London's 32 boroughs. This survey of opinions illustrated the negative connotations attached to the borough by those who were intimately familiar with it. For example, in 2008, Newham residents reported the lowest levels of satisfaction with their local area, the highest levels of anti-social behavior, and the second lowest levels of "community cohesion" in London.[6] These concerns were reflected in Newham's housing situation; for example, in 2009, it was reported that "over twice as many private houses in Newham were designated unfit for living within (15% compared to 6% in London) and 50% of social housing stock in Newham was below Decent Homes Standard."[7] At the same time, the demand for housing increased; in 2010, 33.5% of households were on the Newham's housing register, a 10% increase on the figures reported in 2000.[8] These findings indicate the scale of Newham's Olympic regeneration and illustrate the challenges faced by public services such as policing and health provisions during the Olympic Games and beyond.

The League of Nations

One of the most significant characteristics of this borough is that there is no majority/minority population. According to the *Annual Population Survey 2008*, published by the Office for National Statistics (ONS), 64.6% are "non-white." The primary ethnic groups are white and Asian but we need further sub-division to appreciate fully the diversity of this borough. Of the 39% classified as white residents, 32.6% defined themselves as "British."[9] Of the 38% classified as Asian, 13.9% were Pakistani, 10.2% were Indian, 7% Bangladeshi and the remaining 5.1% were "Asian other." Additionally, in 2001, 20% of Newham's population was classified as black; 12.4% of these were African, 6.5% Caribbean and 1.1% "Black other." Add to such diversity, 1.6% Chinese and 2.6% people of other ethnicity. As is exemplified by the remarks of a Newham Community Worker, the white British are considered an ethnic minority group in Newham, with specific events designed to cater for them. "Most places you go in Newham," he said, "have visual reminders of the diversity of the borough. The minorities posters provided by Newham council are usually full of smiley and happy blacks and Asians. As a result of these constant visual reminders the white working class feel under threat and increasingly more marginalised and foreign. They often feel like they have lost their place in society, which has been gradually whittled away by other groups that attain greater social prominence. Less than one third of the community are white indigenous or white working class, and these tend to be much older than the rest of the borough. Their numbers are decreasing all the time as they die or move out of Newham to be closer to their children who moved out of the borough years earlier" (Fieldwork Interview, April 2010).

This aging white, working-class population had a sound basis for their feelings of marginalization, their numbers dwindling as a result of what Hobbs called "white flight" (1988). As the *Local Economic Assessment 2010 – 2027*, published in October 2010, summarized:[10]

- The population of Newham is rising, and is projected to continue to rise significantly.
- Newham has a very young and highly diverse population.
- Newham has high levels of population churn compared to London as a whole.
- Newham is a highly deprived borough with especially high rates of deprivation affecting children and older people.
- Poverty in Newham is high and life expectancy is lower than the London average.

White people were a waning Newham group and were conscious of their ever-diminishing social standing. They may be seen as a lost—certainly, an aging—generation whose history was becoming less and less recognized. As a consequence, some were attempting to preserve their cultural history, which is exemplified in the following excerpt from my fieldwork notes of June 2011:

> Newham's older, white working class had a desire to get together to tell stories and reminisce about their shared histories but often they lacked the ability or location to do so. As a result, community centres, such as the Froud centre in Manor Park created programmes that kick-started this basic human function. They granted permission for this to occur in schemes such as a lunch club for these people. These meetings are not simply about a nostalgic mourning of the past, although much reminiscing does take place. Rather, these programmes attempt to help white people to feel less marginalised in today's Newham. They do this by involving young people from the diverse community into these meetings. These young people voluntarily cook for the old people, serve them, and eat with them. They listen to the old people's stories in an attempt to bridge the gaps between the present and the past. They are creating an environment for informal learning to occur.
>
> I attended one such event. The walls of the cafeteria where the event was held were covered with black and white photos taken in Newham in the past; the faces were too white, there were ships of all shapes and sizes in the docks and the images hinted at a lost magical past the way photos tend to do. Buddy Holly and Chuck Berry provided the soundtrack for the twenty or so old white pensioners to shuffle into the room, all wearing heavy coats and hats despite the warmth of the summer's day radiating through the large windows. These pensioners searched for their names on the two long tables at the center of the room. The tables were nicely set and the imagery was reminiscent of the stereotypical Christmas dinner setting. Each table sat around 15 people, and the pensioners were interspersed with gaps that would be filled by the dozen young people who either helped them to their seats or were in the kitchen helping with the cooking. "Bangers and mash" (sausages and mashed potatoes) was a particular favorite it seemed, having been chosen over fish and chips or a lamb roast at the end of the group's last meeting, weeks earlier.
>
> After the food had been served and eaten, the plates were cleared and the space became filled with contented, comfortable, and lively conversation. Conversation-prompts permeated the scene; in addition to the photographs

that charted various decades of modification and transformation of the lived environment, there were collections of magazines, catalogues and adverts that prompted discourse about fashion, technology, culture, and iconography through the ages. As the barriers between the old and young, the white British and the diverse Newham representatives decreased, the conversations became increasingly jovial and light-hearted. To give an example, Mary, an 80-year-old lady, recounted for all who cared to listen: "I was married for 62 years. I fell in love with my Dave because he had a nice motorbike. When I met him, I told him to take me for a ride on the back of his bike, we rode for a while and he took me out to the countryside. It was such fun that when we got to a field I let him have a feel." The day culminated with a sing-a-long to East End Music Hall tunes such as "Roll-out-the-Barrel," which prompted further conversations between the old and the young about the origins and historical resonance of the terms "Lucifer" and "fag," and how "during the war the bastard German snipers would shoot the British if they saw a cigarette being lit," which arguably proved one of the most effective anti-smoking campaigns to date. With that, it was time to return to the present; on went the overcoats and the pensioners shuffled out onto the busy and diverse Newham streets.

Indigenous white people formed a segment of contemporary Newham. Establishing what proportion of Newham's populace this group exactly represented proved to be challenging. The composition and density of the population in Newham is a complex issue. In 2008, a Greater London Authority (GLA) report raised the estimated population of Newham to 265,688.[11] However, both the figures produced by the GLA and the earlier census appeared problematic because of significant numbers of unregistered peoples living illegally in the borough. In September 2011, two new Task Forces were initiated by Newham Council to tackle the growing menace of what was referred to as "super sheds"; best described as "ramshackle illegal buildings in gardens, often housing people living in squalor."[12] These shanty-style dwellings were tracked through the use of aerial photography and infrared imagery. The borough officials were also attempting to cut down on all forms of slum landlord practice, which included breaking up family homes into tiny residential units that contained no communal space.

A 2009 study by Mayhew[13] attempted to account for residents ignored by the official figures, including those living in the borough for less than one year. This study estimated that the Newham population was 270,100.[14] Arguably, the figures generated by this study are more accurate than the official figures quoted earlier, because they are based on administrative data sets (such as school rolls, council tax records, and GP registrations).

However, the study does highlight the fact that there are many "sleepers" that could not be included in the figures. Accordingly, it suggested that in 2008, there were over 15,000 "unconfirmed citizens" living at unregistered Newham addresses, estimated to be predominantly young males who had recently arrived in the UK. More recent population estimates suggest that as many as 320,000 people now live in Newham (Bagehot 2012). [15]

In this regard, Newham was emblematic of what the anthropologist Gordon Mathews described as "low-end" globalization, which he defined by differentiating it from the globalization involving big brands and huge corporations. He argued that a low-end globalization was typical of informal economies; it spoke to those seeking a better life in foreign countries through such opportunities as temporary work, asylum, or work in the sex industry. Mathews argues that this kind of globalization is dominant in much of the developing world (2011, p. 13). It would appear to be pertinent to Olympic-delivery Newham. What follows is an indication of living with "low-end" globalization, which in some parts of Newham has become synonymous with criminality. For some Newham residents life is governed by fear of such criminality.

The City of Dreadful Night?

Newham's crime figures, in parallel with the escalating population, are high and rising. According to a report published in October 2010 by the local charity, Aston Mansfield,[16] Newham saw an increase in recorded crime in 10 of the 15 crime categories. Crimes that increased in Newham but not London-wide between the years ending in November 2009 and 2010 were:

- Homicide
- Burglary (residential and total)
- Gun crime (a 52% increase, compared to an 8% decrease across London)
- Motor vehicle crime
- Violence against the person

As the following example from my fieldwork notes indicates, these crime statistics contributed to the way everyday life in the borough unraveled. Marta, 21, and Laura, 28, were two single female Hungarian economic migrants who moved to Newham in 2010 from a small Hungarian town, in the hope of having a better and more interesting life in London. They arrived in the UK on an early morning, after a three-day coach ride across Europe. On arrival, they quickly moved into a small, one-bedroom, rented apartment, which had been arranged through a family contact; it was basic but seemed to have all they needed. They were happy to finally be there and were ready to get to know the area; they were soon to discover the day/night dichotomy of Newham. Looking out of their window into the street outside, they were met with the unmistakable sight of prostitutes walking up and down, soliciting their wares; these streets were theirs to work from 10:00 pm until early morning. This was a new reality to the Hungarians. They were ambivalent about such occupation of public space, but understood that for some women this was a way of life and that was how things were. What was more unsettling for the pair was the diversity of the borough, which they were completely unprepared for, coming from a mono-cultural Hungarian province. Newham was indeed very foreign to them, and it took them a long time to adjust.

Their adjustment was predicated on a fear of crime, and their views and rituals were emblematic of such fear. All of their views regarding the appeal and vibrancy of Newham life revolved around their daytime encounters, which they referred to in reverent tones, proselytizing about the dynamic multiculturalism and the inclusive friendliness of the area. Their negative impressions of the area revolved around its nighttime alter ego, which they referred to as "life in the shadows." They saw this nighttime environment as being populated by unknown figures that threatened their existence. These faceless spectral figures lurked in the shadows; they occupied the street corners, alone or in groups, marking their territory through fear and intimidation. These fears became manifest in the Hungarians' daily lives, and they made their best to be home before nightfall. If either were to be out in Newham after dark, they would arrange for the other to leave the deadbolt unlocked in order to minimize the time that the returnee would spend unlocking their front door.

The statistics and the example given above are indicative of Newham's "*slow rioting*," whereby the lack of tangible economic opportunities becomes manifest in the form of endemic crime, collective destitution, and internal social decay (Curtis 1985). The fear of crime was very real for the Hungarians, as it was for many long-term residents, and this fear was based not only upon the imagined but also upon first-hand personal experience. Statistical evidence is telling. For example, in September 2010, Newham recorded the third highest number of knife crime offences in London. The *Safer Newham Crime and Disorder Reduction Partnership Performance Report 2010/11* shows that, compared with the previous year, from April to August 2010, serious knife crime increased by 13.1%, gun crime by 130%, and serious youth violence by 9.9%. *Newham's Borough Command Unit Strategic Assessment* in February 2010 reported that the level of violence against the individual was 9.9 offences per 1000 population, the worst in a group of 15 similar areas despite a downward trend in violence against the individual over the past 5–6 years.

This report noted that nearly one-third of "most serious violent crimes" involved a young offender (10–19 years olds) and nearly one in four involved a youth victim. Similarly, 54% of robbery offences involved a youth offender. In 2008–9, with a 25.8% increase from 2006–7, the number of first time entrants to the Youth Justice System (under 19s) was the second highest in London. The Youth Offending Team (YOT) caseload by ethnic group (December 2009—March 2010) showed that young black males made up the highest proportion of young offenders. The reality behind these statistics is addressed in the following section, which begins with a black youth (aged 17) involved in Newham-based Street Crime.

Street Life: Day and Night Dichotomy

As the demographics of the borough outlined earlier indicates, for the disaffected youth of Newham, life was bleak. Some of these youth, who populate Newham's nighttime economy, might be appropriately described as the urban "underclass."[17] This term denotes a segment of the (mostly) black American poor characterized by behavioral deficiencies and cultural deviance (Auletta 1982; Sawhill 1989; Wacquant 2008), although it has previously been applied to the British context (Murray 1990). To use the term "underclass" means venturing into contested terrain. Here, I will not engage in an in-depth exploration of this complex issue. I will only indicate that my choice to use this term is explained by the requirements of the narrative (description, context, and clarity) rather than by theoretical extrapolation. The applicability of the urban "underclass" concept to this Newham context can be demonstrated through gender-differentiating exemplifications, whereby young males have been described as aggressive, criminally inclined "gang-bangers" and young females as benefit-reliant, lazy "welfare mothers" (for a deeper explanation of these expressions, see Wacquant 2008, p. 44). Newham had its variation of both, as the following account of the reality of life among Newham's "underclass" shows.

Ashley, a black youth aged 19, said, "Here life for kids is hard, man. No one looks after the kids round here, not their parents, no one. So when they need food or something it's the "olders" [elder male peers] that look after them. They are nice to them and they do look after them. The reality is the "olders" treat everyone well. If kids are homeless, they give them shelter, a job; it's a nice life. They feel accepted, protected. Some kids are kicked out of their homes when their mums move in a new man and they don't get on with them. The mums choose the man over the son. So they enter the "road life" [Street Crime in peer-group collectives]. In the road life, the young kids look up to the older ones, they see the clothes they wear and the respect they get. They look up to them, so they go robbing [theft from the person] to get money and buy clothes. People think they spend it on drugs but they don't. A bit of weed [marijuana] but that's for relaxation, everyone needs that... The fact is the "crews" [peer group collectives] treat the communities well. They help people out, you'll hear Mr. X, oh he gave money to so and so, he's a good guy, because really, they want to be good. That's the reason why they get away with so much, when something happens, no-one talks to the police. Not because of fear, but because of loyalty." He carried on saying, "What would you do if you were walking down a street and you saw twenty hoodies? [Young black men often wear hoods to conceal their heads and faces from CCTV surveillance cameras] Be honest, would you keep walking towards them?... No?... Then you're a victim. We know that just by looking. We're like dogs, we can sense it. Your body language, your walk quickens, don't know what to do with your hands, you pat your pockets, walk in zig-zags, cross the road. You're a victim... That's good. We do it [robbing] because we're bullies. Imagine you've been bullied all your life. You feel bad about yourself. You want to make others feel bad to make yourself feel better. It doesn't really help though. The media create this image that it's all unsafe, of knife crime, but it's not all like that. The truth is the "road way" is a nice life. You get treated well, you get money. Everyone understands you, they know what you're going through. You get respect."(Private Interview, February 2012).

As the examples of this section indicate, in Newham there was a constant re-negotiation of place between day- and night-time. Although all residents believed in the legitimacy of power, fundamentally, many believed more in the legitimacy of those that wielded it, which was always a situation-specific context. Bourdieu (1987) regards this symbolic power as a "world-making" power, due to its capacity to impose a legitimized vision of the social world. As sociologist Charles Taylor suggests, "The *person* of real practical wisdom is marked out less by the ability to formulate rules than by knowing how to act in each particular situation" (1999, p. 41). In an environment where fear of criminality has become normalized, negotiating criminality becomes an aspect of everyday life. One option was avoidance, as illustrated by the case of the Hungarians Martha and Laura. The following example is more tellingly appropriate to those growing up within the borough. Shahid, a relatively diminutive Bangladeshi boy aged 23, went to school in Newham and became part of a "post-code" gang from a location appropriately named Warrior Square. Shahid told his story of growing up in the territory of a black street gang that habitually victimized people of various ethnicities who were not part of their group. As a consequence of feeling marginalized and victimized, those of diverse Asian origins banded together in solidarity against this black gang, in order to protect themselves and ensure the most basic fundamental human right—safe passage in one's own neighborhood. The dynamics of inter-racial gang rivalry were complex and often superseded by confrontations with other gangs from various proximities. Membership into these protective groups often comes at a cost. For Shahid, this cost materialized in the need to prove himself worthy of membership through an assortment of violent and criminal acts that contributed to the statistics that made Newham notorious (from a private interview, May 2011).

Assessing the implications and causes of crime and criminality is well beyond the remit of this study, and acquiring a working knowledge of Newham's "gang" culture would require a specific investigation. However, taking this issue into account helps to profile the role of crime and criminality in the everyday life of Newham in the attempt to understand the size of the task that is required to heal the systemic local problems and to consider whether Olympic delivery may contribute to address what is a fundamental East London issue. This cultural and social problematic is exemplified by the following example, extracted from my fieldwork notes of November 2011, of a Bangladeshi street gang that eschewed traditional sociological norms to create their own sub-culture.

The Manor Park "Massive" collective was a collection—or a gang—of second or third sons from Bangladeshi families. The core of this collective included 12 members, with an additional 12–15 associates and hangers on between the ages of 15 and 18; all were local Newham people. In their family structures, these second and third sons were considered less worthy than their older brothers were, in that they were all NEET (Not in Education, Employment, or Training). None, however, had signed on to receive unemployment benefit. To all extents and purposes, they were invisible to their families and to society at large. Although this group had no leader, one member, Ali, was clearly dominant. Ali had arrived in Newham aged 10 and had ceased attending school at the age of 13. His oft-stated ambition was to drive a big car and "have" lots of women, both of which he was ultimately successful in accomplishing. Ali was outwardly very aggressive and threatening to all, regardless of familiarity, and was heavily involved in street robbery. He was loath to pigeonhole his earning abilities; throughout his involvement with this gang, his criminal activities included supplying and delivering drugs to punters on a pushbike and occasional burglaries of East London homes and businesses.

As a group, this gang claimed a specific territory and occupied the same street most nights of any given week. They established norms, reputation, and status through their actions and made money for their members through a variety of illegal means. Basically, they created for each other what was missing in their lives; belonging, respect, and the feeling that someone was looking out for them. Ali had attained dominance in the group as a result of his actions and involvement in criminality. He had a reputation based on the fear that he was prepared to do anything, no matter the consequences, if someone had "disrespected" him or his cohorts. This was perhaps best exemplified by his shooting someone in the face with a shotgun because his victim had acted in a way that he saw as "disrespectful." Ali was involved with the gang for a number of years until they eventually grew older and went their separate ways. Some went to prison, some moved away, some turned to drugs. One member was shot in the legs and fled in fear for his life. Only three managed to gain employment; one as a traffic-enforcement officer, one as a council caretaker and the third as a cook. Ali managed to avoid prison and got involved into deeper criminality. His main source of income remains selling drugs from his grandfather's grocery store. He could be considered an entrepreneur of sorts who regularly turns his hand from selling drugs to buying and selling stolen cars and stripping down vehicles into parts for sale. Ali would do anything for money—and women—but most importantly, Ali would do anything to accumulate the cultural capital that equates to power in his quotidian context.

Changing Places: The Churn of Newham

If Ali were to leave, others would replace him. Migration is one of the most significant aspects of Newham in terms of community definition and identity. This was highlighted by a 2007–2008 Report by Mayhew Harper and Associates,[18] according to which the borough had an incredibly high churn of population. The word "churn" refers to the movement of residents in and out of the borough. In 2007–2008, almost one fifth of the Newham population (19.5%) either left or entered the area. Such churn is evidenced in National Insurance (NI) registrations, which in the UK are necessary for legal employment. In 2007–2008, more foreign nationals registered for NI numbers in Newham than anywhere else in the UK. Of these, 15% were Indian, 14% Polish, 11% Romanian, 9% Lithuanian, 7% Bangladeshi and 4% Bulgarian. The Mayhew report estimated that 12,000 people entered the borough from outside the UK, with an average stay of 14 months. Furthermore, the GLA predicted that between 2006 and 2031 Newham would experience a population increase of 46.6% as a result of urban regeneration, which translates into an increase two and a half times that of the London average.[19]

In relation to housing, population churn, and community composition, the findings of the 2008 London Borough of Newham *Newham Household Panel Survey* (NHPS) notably emphasized the association between migration and poverty. The new households sampled were significantly more likely to be below the poverty line than those that had been previously sampled, indicating a decreasing trend in upward mobility. More precisely, after housing costs were taken into account, a longitudinal sample of households found that in 2008, 38.1% of existing NHPS respondent households were below the poverty line, compared to a staggering 74.7% of newly sampled households. The 2008 NHPS concluded that this difference meant that those moving into the borough were much more likely to be poorer than existing households were. Complementary evidence from the Newham Economic Development Strategy (2010a, 2010b)[20] suggests that people who leave Newham are more highly skilled and generally better off than those who arrive. This meets the view of a community worker, who stated that "the one clear unifying fact that unites most of Newham is a want to move away. Most people see Newham as a staging post, a temporary home." This situation is exemplified by the following account, extracted from my fieldwork notes of July 2010. Sarah and Joe are white, in their 50s. They have raised two children in Newham who, now grown up, have moved to Essex for work. Sarah and Joe continue to live, now alone, in the same 3-bedroom mid-terraced house in the nondescript Newham street where they raised their family. The house next door is identical. It is inhabited by fifteen young Eastern European men. According to Sarah and Joe, these young men are pleasant enough and do not cause them any real problems other than they make a lot of noise, "as young men do," and often drink in the garden until late at night. This, the couple comments, is the way of life in the area and they can either put up with it or move out. They have open copies of the property section of the Romford Recorder (a local East London/Essex newspaper that listed properties outside of Newham) on the coffee table. Somewhere east was the land they once knew.

The Ends Justifying the Means: Newham's Socialist Gentrification

As the examples given above illustrate, Newham residents are highly diverse. Consequently, life in the borough is somewhat unique compared to the rest of the UK. Yet there is a common thread that links all parts of this society together. Consider the following evaluation of the place by the *Economist Bagehot column*:

> "It is no coincidence that Newham both elected Britain's first Labour MP, Keir Hardie, and is home to much of the Olympic Park. The docks, and the dirty industry they spawned, made it a poor place. That is why it was receptive to socialism, and also why land prices are low enough that businesses could be turfed out, and the Olympic facilities built, at a reasonable cost... In a borough with a three-quarters ethnic-minority population (more than anywhere else in the country)... [Sir Robin Wales, Newham's mayor] shares the essential Newham characteristic, in that he is an immigrant... was elected mayor in 2002, and re-elected in 2006 and 2010—with 68% of the vote. All 60 councillors are Labour... Newham is a place of arrival... Living in Newham is still fairly cheap: many of its houses are in multiple occupancy (the record, says the council, is 38 people in one property). In contravention of the planning regulations, many of its gardens have been filled with breezeblock sheds to house the latest arrivals... The borough is funded by central government on the basis that it has 242,000 people, but the council reckons it has 300,000, and the police think the tally is 320,000—especially tough, when the council's discretionary grant from the government is coming down from £310m to £240m over three years. It is hardly surprising that Newham is weighed down by debt, and its financial position is deteriorating. Gentrification is not a word that a Labour politician would ever use to describe his plans, but that is what Sir Robin's look like. He wants to reduce the churn in Newham and turn it into a place where people buy houses, settle down and raise children... Plans for the future of the Olympic Park, which imply a high proportion of family homes, sit comfortably with his aims for the borough."(Bagehot 2012, p. 26)

Clearly, one unifying factor in Newham is its endemic social issues. Sir Robin Wales tried to deal with some families that did not fit in his vision of Newham by moving such "aberrations" to other parts of the country, which in 2012 led to him being accused of "social cleansing" ahead of the Olympics. It was alleged that Newham had contacted a housing association in Stoke-on-Trent, some 140 miles away from East London, confessing that it could no longer afford to accommodate in private housing the tenants on its waiting list. Sir Robin admitted to this on BBC Radio 4's Today program, adding that Newham's housing officers had actually written to hundreds of organizations throughout the UK to try to find homes for its poorest families.[21]

Hosting the 2012 Olympic Games was seen as a political, economic, and cultural catalyst that would generate an unprecedented momentum for the regeneration of Newham. The notion that the 2012 Olympic Games would prove a panacea to solve Newham's social issues was outlined by Jack Straw—who was Secretary of State in 2005—in the aftermath of London's surprise victory in the race to host the 2012 Olympic Games. In his statement, Mr. Straw declared, "London's bid was built on a special Olympic vision. A vision of an Olympic Games that would not only be a celebration of sport but a force for regeneration. The Games will transform one of the poorest and most deprived areas of London. They will create thousands of jobs and homes. They will offer new opportunities for business in the immediate area and throughout London."(Jack Straw, House of Commons, July 6, 2005).

As I have highlighted earlier, there appeared to be a ubiquitous conviction that the 2012 London Olympic bid would be a panacea to make East London healthy—literally, socially, and economically. Supported by the media rhetoric, the Newham Mayor, Sir Robin Wales, perpetuated this assumption at the local level. This use of the Olympics for significant urban overhaul revolved around the belief that Olympic hosting would provide the potential to instigate a critical regeneration. For those wishing to buy into this utopian premise, the concept of Olympic "legacy" provided the justification for the expectation of a "better" Newham. However, this view was based upon the assumption that everybody shared the same view of what constituted a "better life" and that all had the ability to take advantage of the opportunities presented therein. Such an assumption, I shall argue, has proved to be groundless.

Theorizing Places and Faces: Lefebvre and Auge Meet Bourdieu

In preparing this research, I realized that the East London borough of Newham was the best location in which to undertake my investigation of Olympic delivery simply because the vast majority of the Olympic regeneration and events would occur within its borders. The local communities were given voice through two single-site ethnographies: one on the boundaries of the Olympic Park (from now on, *Stratfordland*), the other on the direct vicinity of the ExCeL[22] complex (from now on, *ExCeLland*). Additionally, I adopted a secondary method of data collection, which I call *spoking*,[23] in order to complement, and indeed at times contradict, the findings of these two ethnographic enquiries. This enabled the data collection to extend to various locations in Newham—encompassing an area that I have called the Olympic-delivery *Dispersal Zone*.

We have seen that contemporary Newham is a culturally and ethnically diverse location *par excellence*. This diversity has a long history. The demographics and annals of this London borough emphasize Newham as a traditional first port of call for many migrants. This has led to the area being home to a vibrant potpourri of ethnicities, which, crucially, has contributed to the lack of a dominant identity. Newham is consistently referred to as one of the most ethnically diverse places on the planet, with over 300 languages spoken (Newham Language Shop 2005).[24] This is a community of interrelated parts with no majority minority. Here, a myriad of diverse cultural practices have existed for decades which have combined to create a unique urban mosaic that is constantly changing, due to the high-churn of the borough's population. Most importantly, over the past 20 years, there has been no dominant "host" society into which smaller migrant groups may assimilate. Therefore, theories of race relations and the dualism of the immigrant-host model were of questionable applicability in defining this situation.

Contemporary Newham might be best defined as having a holistic acceptance of difference, or at the very least a tolerance of difference given the absence of a dominant race, ethnicity, culture, age segment, or spoken language; granted, most locals speak English, but the *Lingua-Franca* would best be described as *English-Creole*. It thus provides an interesting embodiment of what Lefebvre (1991) would define as a *strange entity*. Pre-Olympics Newham was a community that, though "real" and with a defined boundary, lived with little sense of ownership of place; a community where the underlying belief was that life is a transitory (because of low place ownership and immigration) and frequently nomadic experience. At times, this view appeared to be saturated with the belief that, here, one had little or no control over one's own destiny. As Lefebvre argued, "Any 'social existence' aspiring or claiming to be 'real', but failing to produce its own space, would be a strange entity, a very peculiar kind of abstraction unable to escape from the ideological or even the 'cultural' realm. It would fall to the level of folklore and sooner or later disappear altogether, thereby immediately losing its identity, its denomination, and its feeble degree of reality" (1991, p. 53).

The absence of a tangible, definable place-identity and the observably "feeble degree of reality" combined—ironically—to make Newham an ideal prospective Olympic host. Shared local customs and a consensus around social mores, which are the keystones of identity and are the elements that bond people to a place, were absent in Newham. That is not to say that Newham had no cultural fabric, far from it; there was, however, little evidence of the association between place and identity. In this regard, the application of Auge's (1995) *"non-place"* hypothesis has a degree of resonance. To consider Newham a *"non-place"* is to contrast this locale to other constructions of "place." This is a standard anthropological concept perhaps best defined as a "concrete and symbolic construction of space" (Buchanan 1999, p. 394). That which we call "place" has been considered as a unifier in many fields, including environmental psychology (Russell and Ward 1982) and human geography (Cloke, Philo, and Sadler 1991).

By contrast, Auge insinuated that if "place" is to be defined as relational, historical, or concerned with identity, then a space that cannot be defined in these terms must be considered a "non-place." Although Auge's research predominantly focuses on shopping malls, airports, and the like, the underlying principles he argued for could be applied to the Newham context. In this regard, Newham's diverse, deprived community lacking a holistic identity, a shared history, and even a shared relational culture may be defined as residing in a "non-place."

Notions of culture and place are crucial to any study that seeks to identify the dominant value systems of an area. Notions of shared language, religion, traditions, and customs are integral to culture and place. This constitutes a locale's cultural history and is synonymous with place. Places however are complex things. As Stokols argues, they are fixed, empty and un-dialectical backgrounds to—or containers of—social action; they are dynamic arenas both socially constituted and constitutive of the social (1990). Uncovering and delineating dominant cultural systems, beliefs, and practices that holistically link identity and place in Newham was not easy. Equally difficult would be to apply a rigid theoretical view to this complex research setting.

Some argue that the sense of belonging attached to place is not an aspect of place identity but is a necessary basis for it (Korpela 1989, p. 246). Olympic-delivery Newham was, however, what some might define as a "potpourri of memories, conceptions, interpretations, ideas, and related feelings about specific physical settings" (Proshansky, Fabian and Kaminoff 1983, p. 60). The idea of Newham as the Olympic city-in-waiting had, thus, to be sold to the people living there in the absence of a dominant sense of place identity.[25] Furthermore, this most diverse, deprived, and transitory of communities was representative of what Sennett (2006) calls the "icon of the global age"; that is, migration, whereby people live with the prevailing belief that it is "not the time to settle down, but move" (p. 10). The question is whether cultural significance and place identity are relevant to this inquiry, or are even possible in this location.

In this regard, Olympic-delivery Newham was—perhaps subtly— enforcing the transition of the borough away from a "strange entity" and a "non-place" toward something else. This something else was a borough that was to be re-branded and injected with something called "culture," where a collective identity was intended to be delivered in hermetically sealed,

Olympically inspired instalments. This transitional period (2005–2012) saw Newham become something that Lefebvre (1991) would conceptualize as a *differential space*. For a new space to be produced this *differential space* is, according to Lefebvre, an essential transition. Within this "differential space" the functions, elements, and moments of social practice are restored (or indeed created) (1991, p. 52). This theoretical perspective suited a definition of Newham as did the idea of it being for so many of its dwellers a "non-place," evidencing a "very peculiar type of abstraction" that aspired to be real but was incapable of creating a holistic identity (Lefebvre 1991, p. 53). As a whole, Newham was a place that lacked inclusion; but this absence was not feared because it was never missed. In this regard, Auge's mechanisms of the "non-place"[26] exemplified much of this borough. Olympic delivery was meant to transform this locale into a particularly potent "differential place" and to modify parts of this "strange place." One might argue that such delivery only enhanced the sense of differentiation and strangeness.

This is an intriguing topic that this study aimed to address. To this end, frameworks from the works of theorists such as Lefebvre, Auge, and Bourdieu were deconstructed, merged, and applied to this milieu in a pragmatic manner. The work of each of these theorists can, of course, be directly applied to many contexts. Taken separately, however, their theoretical insights were insufficient to understand adequately the complexities of Olympic-delivery Newham. What was missing was a bottom-up perspective of life during Olympic delivery, and this required additional theorizing and a combined theoretical approach.

It became abundantly clear that this research's aim to separate Olympics rhetoric from reality was not simply about objective notions of place; it was crucially about people, their subjective experience of the place they lived in and the Olympic-related transitions their lives might undergo. This search for guidance on how to adequately theorize Newham's Olympic delivery from the bottom-up led to the application of Bourdieu's theoretical framework to my research. Bourdieu argued that all sociological inquiry should begin with real, empirical data and that such material should be analyzed using a specific set of conceptual "thinking tools" that would act as a guide to discovery and understanding. I applied this approach to Newham's three aforementioned research zones. According to Bourdieu's three-tiered methodological approach,[27] in order to accomplish any such search for discovery and understanding, the researcher should

1. Analyze the position of the field vis-à-vis the wider context.
2. Map out the objective structure of relations between the positions occupied by agents within the field.

3. Analyze the *habitus* of these agents; notably the systems of dispositions they have acquired by internalizing deterministic socio-economic predilections.

We can take this argument further. The methodology that I have just outlined offered a theory of research practice whereby Bourdieu's key concepts only make sense when they are applied to practical research, which then emphasizes the theoretical value of what he argued (Grenfell 2008, p. 219). Bourdieu's notion of *habitus* is best understood as the internalized generative and durable dispositions that guide perception, representation, and action in human beings (Bourdieu and Wacquant 1992). This is in large part the product of social position structuring an individual's earliest experiences. It follows that similar conditions of existence result in common *habitus* and oppositional conditions of existence result in a conflicting idea of *habitus* (ibid). Therefore, *habitus* is a constant social re-negotiation that can only be maintained through exchange, and evolves through continual experiences and exchanges, which subtly transforms the individual's way of being (King 2000). With this in mind, the impact that Olympic-delivery transition and its implications might have upon agents who are involved through choice or circumstance must be considered in relation to the 2012 Olympics bid. To include such subject matter in this study is to provide valuable contextualization for the analysis of those who often go unrepresented in Olympic delivery discourse.

CHAPTER 2

The 2012 Transition: Process and Politics

Let us begin the analysis of the transition from Olympic bid to delivery by considering the direct implications of the decision to select London as the host of the 2012 Olympics. By the mid-noughties, what was once a far-fetched pipe dream had become very much a reality. The former perception of the bid explained some people's lack of interest throughout the bidding phase. Preeti, a 32-year-old Indian-born lifelong Newham resident, typically stated, "I didn't see the point in going to the meetings [community consultations] I didn't think we'd get 'em [Olympic Games] and I had better things to do than waste my life in a draughty hall listening to people talk about something that probably wouldn't happen" (Fieldwork notes, January 2008).

When London won the competition to host the 2012 Olympics, the bid indicated that the Games would be used to regenerate East London and facilitate a number of post-Games legacies that would be credited to hosting the Olympics and to the virtues of Olympism. This prospective regeneration was outlined by the London mayor in bid-time politicking; it was emphasized only to help a stuttering, failing bid that lagged behind Paris. The delivery of London's idealized utopian vision of Olympic urbanity was defined, constructed, and protected through a course of actions that resonated with urban sociological notions of "cleansing space" (Sibley 1995; Fussey et al. 2011). This process was mitigated by the spatial action of the Olympic Games, with all aspects of Olympics-related infrastructure, regulation, and securitization, defined as necessary precursors to event implementation (Smith 1996).

Those tasked with urban regeneration increasingly appear to see hosting the Olympics as a once-in-a-lifetime opportunity, for both the large-scale redevelopment and rebranding of a city, and for advertising a particular urban geography to an international audience (Burbank et al. 2001). The Olympic Games have become synonymous with the processes and enhancement of globalization. Indeed, the International Olympic Committee's (IOC) primary objectives undoubtedly promote Cobden's definition of globalization (cited in Ferguson 2003). Richard Cobden, a nineteenth-century promoter of peace and free trade, postulated that globalization was an economically determined phenomenon in which the free exchange of commodities and manufacture would unite humankind in the bonds of peace. Conversely, opponents of such globalizing processes may categorize the motivations of hosting the Olympics as Machiavellian exemplars of the voracity of international capitalism. So, where does London 2012 stand in this debate?

Olympics hosting, I shall argue, supports the generalized view that increasing global economic openness and flows of international capital raises the living standards of the affected geographical areas. This facilitates the processes of gentrification[1] and encourages the homogenization of landscape, which is central to the globalization/glocalization[2] schemas (Harvey 1989; Albrow 1990; Robertson 1992; Sassen 2001). Bauman stated that being local, which can be inferred to be interchangeable with non-gentrified, in a globalized world was a sign of social deprivation and degradation (1998, p. 2). The question is whether the parts of East London earmarked in the bid were "ready" for Olympic gentrification and whether those intended to benefit from the project would want to live and work in a post-Olympics East London landscape.

London 2012: The Road to Newham

Neil Fraser's 2012 pseudo-historical publication *Over the Border: The Other East End* opens with a summary of London's 2005 Olympic bid victory celebration. The prose resonated deeply with many local people's views, which I recorded throughout my research, and which is worth quoting at this juncture. He wrote, "This story starts with some people celebrating the fact that London was awarded the right to host the 2012 Olympic Games. Images of these people in Trafalgar Square show lots of cheering faces and flags and branded clothing, to remind us, in case we aren't paying attention, that celebrating the spectacle is somehow patriotic. Or something like that. People waved flags because they were given flags, and cheered because it is part and parcel of the spectacle these days, for those lucky to be part of it.

This was history. Very small history—it was after all just the result of a vote, of a selection of men and women who had been wined and dined at various cities around the world and then pressed a button to say who they thought should get to host the Olympics. And the winner was London. More specifically, it was Stratford. Those cheering and waving flags in Trafalgar Square weren't celebrating a victory for Stratford—indeed it is debatable whether it was a victory at all." (Fraser 2012, pp. 1–2).

As I have said, the focus of my research was the impact that the delivery of the 2012 Olympic Games would have on the local community. The latter was not exemplified by the crowds that gathered in Trafalgar Square. It was indeed imperative to delineate how and where to find Olympics-related "local people." This required stepping away from the macro-level outcomes, which revolve around the nation-state perspective and intimate that "hosting the Olympic Games can provide one of the most powerful platforms for any nation. Governments spend billions of dollars every year managing their national image around the world. They seek to influence how they are perceived by other nations. National images, they know, affect political and economic relationships. Whether it is to increase tourism, change foreign and domestic policy, attract investment or aid, or boost international trade, the goal of national image management is to cast the nation in a more favorable light... It is no coincidence that the Games have become an international showcase" (Payne 2005, p. 167–168).

Clearly, Michael Payne's assertions as former head of the marketing division for the IOC are correct; the outcomes of the Olympics can, and should, be evaluated at the national and international levels. The experiential perspective of Olympic delivery provides an illustration of the wider implications of hosting the Olympics. Consequently, the quest for definition turns away from a national perspective on Olympic delivery outcomes in favor of defining the impact on the community.

In 2006, Sir Robin Wales, the New Labour mayor of the host borough of Newham, spoke at a community event, addressing the forthcoming hosting of the 2012 Games. He argued that the hosting offered "a means of reducing deprivation in our [Newham's] community. The Games offer an exceptional opportunity to dramatically change our society." He thus intimated that this opportunity to recalibrate the borough would not—really—be possible without an Olympic-related regeneration.

This re-branding narrative has been prevalent since the beginning of the reign of Juan Antonio Samaranch (1980–2001) who, upon becoming president, stated that the IOC was missing a great opportunity: to brand the Olympic venues and competition sites with Olympic imagery. Accordingly, he developed an Olympic brand. During his presidency, he developed a program, called *Look of Games,* which reinforced the unique nature of the event. By the Sydney 2000 Games, Samaranch's last as president, the *Look of Games* project had become one of the key success factors of the Games. Samaranch was quoted saying that a $300 million stadium is not complete until the *Look of Games* has been applied. Why throw the world's greatest party and not bother to get dressed? (Payne 2005, p. 168).

Newham mayor, Sir Robin Wales publicly and consistently advocated his desire to change Newham dramatically through the hosting of the 2012 Olympics. He stated that London was unlike any other host city because, in his opinion, for the first time in history the Olympics were being used to transform a deprived area completely. He believed that the regeneration of Newham was the primary reason why London had won the Games in the first place.[3] Consequently, procedures for systematically modifying Newham as an Olympics host became intertwined with the issue of addressing its deprivation levels; this narrative became increasingly more prevalent as the delivery of the 2012 Olympics progressed.

Sir Robin's beliefs provided a succinct example of the primary motivations for a city to enter the bidding process. Burbank et al. (2001) outlined these motivations, arguing that the desire to host the Olympics is underpinned by two factors that are central to the entire process. They are "the existence of an established growth regime in the city... (and secondly) a desire to create or change the city's image" (p. 7). The *Look of Games* place branding superseded the variety of established forms of identity, and was undoubtedly intended to rebrand Newham. This process benefited the coalitions of interest that took advantage of this place rebranding. These coalitions included politicians, such as Newham's mayor, planners, real estate developers, and business leaders, who used the Olympic Games in accordance with their professional interests. They attracted new flows of capital and direct investment through the Olympic delivery-related regeneration of specific areas. These transformations supported various forms of business development and employment creation and enhanced the image of Newham as a place in which to *live, work and stay.*[4]

Newham's regenerative narrative suggested that the 2012 Olympics would instigate a wholesale modification of the borough. This belief was best exemplified by the OPLC Olympic Legacy event hosted by the London School of Economics in 2009, which emphasized the perceived pre-Games bleakness of the area vilifying the borough and its residents as "London's Gash."

By thus referring to the area, Altman effectively denigrated all that came before the Olympics as worthless and—arguably—vilified all those that lived there. This was then contrasted against utopian visions of the future, the delivery of which deeply inferred a different Newham and a different post-Games local population. Such presentations typified the traditional tactics employed during Olympic-delivery; they perform a masking effect diverting attention away from reality toward a utopia (Essex and Chalkley 1998). This kind of vilifying narrative is discussed by Echanove and Srivastava (2010) who, in relation to New York City's urban regeneration policy, maintain that the policy makers and planning departments that delivered its regeneration disregarded the local communities' wants and needs. They warn that ignoring local actors comes at a high cost for policy makers because more often than not they result in an urban development that leaves much to be desired from a community-use perspective. Echanove and Srivastava argued for a paradigmatic shift in urban planning, suggesting that in an age of information there should no longer be a dependence upon the "master-planner's map" and the one-way PowerPoint presentations that pass for "community involvement" in urban planning (2010, p. 145–146). Interestingly, the kind of paradigm shift they advocated was—to a certain degree—visible during the 2012 Olympic bidding process. Arguably, this resulted from the belief that hosting the Olympics is an award that is bestowed only after a nation in general, and a local community specifically, publicly display their openness to Olympicization.[5] This vision must be sold to the public and must appear accessible to all, dovetailing nicely with ideals of both Olympism and "community inclusion." This value of perceptible "inclusion" and implicit public support was underscored by the former IOC Vice-President Kevan Gosper, who stated that "public support is very high on the list of priorities; it is, for example, the first thing I look at in a bid" (Bose and Grant 2005).[6] Fundamentally, because a host is only selected after demonstrations of widespread public support, all objections and objectors will have—ideally—been minimized and marginalized at the outset of the Olympicization process. Olympics-bid-time community consultation events indicate an opportunity for continued dialogue throughout Olympics delivery. This was an effective tool for minimizing community objections, particularly when considering that at that time hosting the Olympic Games was, for most, merely a pipe dream. Once a bid becomes a reality, however, Olympics delivery is supported by a plethora of laws and regulations, such as the *London Olympic Games and Paralympic Games Act* of 2006,[7] which helps lubricate whatever actualities are to be faced.

With the foregoing in mind, let us now turn our attention to an evaluation of Olympics delivery actualities. Analysis begins with the consideration of how one might define the Games in relation to their impact on the local context. The political act of modifying the visual landscape of this area, particularly as it was associated with disparity and deprivation, carried undertones of the liberation and reclamation of space that were emblematic of punitive revanchist techniques (Smith 1996, 1998; Wacquant 1999). Olympics delivery outcomes routinely projected future visions of an enhanced Newham landscape that created, and then emphasized, a contrast between the old and the new. They acted as an indicator of what was to come and ensured that the post-Games utopia would not be compromised visually through associations with potentially stigmatizing visions of pre-Olympics Newham.

Olympic Positivism: Outcome or Agenda?

It seems obvious that an Olympics host and its citizens will feel the effects of hosting considerably more extensively than the rest of the country, both through the upheaval caused by the delivery process and through Games-time disruption. The parody of Olympics bidding necessitates that for the host communities the reality in the aftermath of the national celebrations, during the preparations for the Olympic Games and during the Games the promised "*legacy*" amounts to seven years of what might best be called "upheaval." During this period of time, some residents will be moved, voluntarily or otherwise, from their homes and from the area where they have spent their entire lives. For others, the main impact will be experienced through local traffic and transport disruption. Local services will not be exempt, as officials must relinquish some of their authority to the unelected quangos responsible for Olympic delivery. Moreover, Olympic delivery will subject local people to intense policing and security regimes, particularly during the Games, which will significantly affect their lives. Simply put, everyday life will be altered significantly as a result of becoming an Olympic host. The question becomes, from a host-specific perspective, what generates positive attitudes toward hosting the Games?

According to sports economist Holger Preuss (2004), there are numerous reasons that motivate cities to stage the Olympics. They provide a unique opportunity for politicians and industry to follow hidden agendas, including the improvement of infrastructure for sport, housing, communication, and traffic policies. Additionally, Preuss states that political, cultural, ecological, and social issues related to the Olympic Games ensure that Olympic hosting is a complex multi-dimensional project. He identifies the use of the Olympic Games as a vehicle to reach political consensus in terms of national trade (Seoul 1988) and infrastructure construction (Athens 2004 and Barcelona

1992). He also illustrates the opportunity offered by the Games to showcase ecologically sustainable technology (Sydney 2000) and to stage cultural presentations intended to boost post-Olympic tourism (Sydney 2000 and Barcelona 1992). These are examples of the contents that have filled the IOC's "metaphorical empty flask" (Wamsley 2004, p. 232). An important question is how best to consider the contents of the 2012 instalment.

Ultimately, the 2012 Olympics were identified with the geographical prefix of London, not of the UK or England. This adds validity to the argument that the impact of the Olympic Games should be considered primarily in relation to its relevance to the host city's dynamics, particularly when the host is considered a global city. In terms of relevance to my research, the question now becomes, is the prefix "London" sufficient to delineate adequately the community that will be affected by the hosting of the 2012 Olympic Games?

London 2012?

The answer to the above question begins with the consideration of what exactly constitutes "London." London as a whole is a significant landmass that encompasses 32 boroughs, collectively referred to as Greater London. These boroughs are sub-divided into inner and outer London, which makes problematic any holistic-orientated classification of London. Inner London encompasses twelve boroughs (Camden, Greenwich, Hackney, Hammersmith, and Fulham, Islington, Kensington, and Chelsea, Lambeth, Lewisham, Southwark, Tower Hamlets, Wandsworth, and Westminster), outer London the remaining twenty.

London is never fully divisible, and the sheer diversity of borough demographics in contemporary Greater London ensures London's categorization as a "dual city"; that is, a city where the growth of the highly skilled and highly paid financial and business services sector is mimicked, in symbiotic differentiation, by the growth of the low skilled, low paid service sector, which coincides with the decline of the skilled middle-income groups in industry and manufacturing (Mollenkopf and Castells 1991). Historically, London has been divided by poverty, class, ethnic, and racial divisions, with the poorer, more deprived neighborhoods encircling the ever-expanding more affluent center dominated by the City of London.[8]

As over six centuries ago the City of London began to evolve into a hub of global capitalism, the East End followed a parallel, paradoxical path. As Dench, Gavron, and Young (2006) illustrate, initially the East supplied food to the emerging urban community to the West. Then, as the City focused increasingly on the pursuit of profit, the less valuable and more polluting trades were relocated eastwards. As the City became wealthier and more important, its contrast to the East became more pronounced. Together, they became the hub of the British imperial trading system. They were inextricably linked and yet encapsulated contradictory narratives of the same story: one clean, wealthy, and powerful, the other dirty, poor, and powerless. In the pursuit of wealth, the City bought, sold, and financed, whereas East London took, stored, and transported. This unequal partnership transformed East London into the largest impoverished urban enclave in the world and was "abandoned entirely to the working class" (Sanders 1989, p. 91). It has, by and large, remained thus.

East End Games?

The 2012 Games took place in the 2.5 square-kilometer Olympic Park, spanning across five Olympic Boroughs. Four of these were in East London, traditionally the home to the London working classes; they were Newham, Waltham Forest, Tower Hamlets, and Hackney. The fifth was the borough of Greenwich, in South London.[9] Consequently, from the start it was reasonable to predict that the 2012 Olympics would not impact upon London as a whole; the event would be primarily an East London affair with some impact in the West End, where the five star hotels are located. This assumption defined the boundaries of my community-centered research, shrinking its confines to a five-borough perimeter.

Clearly, the 2012 Games might be expected to impact significantly upon these five boroughs during the delivery phase and beyond, in terms of the Olympics-related regeneration. East London boasts fertile ground for the expansion of London; such a potential was made visible in a presentation by the OPLC in 2009, which encouraged anyone interested in the future expansion of London to "look east." Unsurprisingly, the Olympic regenerators were not the first to see such a potential. East London has long been at the heart of urban renewal schemes and initiatives and for many years, it has been earmarked for widespread development (Imrie, Lees, and Raco 2009).

A 2007 report by the Department of Communities and Local Government (DCLG) described the Olympic area as "particularly deprived with Newham, Hackney, and Tower Hamlets continuing to exhibit very high levels of deprivation" (DCLG 2007a, 2007b, p. 40). On the basis of over 50 different indices of deprivation, England's three most deprived local authority areas were the Olympic Boroughs of Hackney, Newham, and Tower Hamlets (respectively); the fourth East London Olympic Borough, Waltham Forest, ranked fifteenth (DCLG 2007a and 2007b; but see also footnote 9 above).

As University of East London (UEL) academic Gavin Poynter (2009) argues, East London's regenerative potential led to the area becoming "a laboratory, a site of social experiments in community development that incorporates a mix of wealth and poverty, high and low rise and social inclusion and exclusion" (p. 132). Poynter advocates that it was in this context that London's bid for the 2012 Olympic and Paralympic Games was conceived, which led to the west Newham location of Stratford being identified as the prime location for the Olympic Park. He argues that the IOC's selection of London's bid revolved around a focus on the regeneration of an area marked by cultural diversity and social deprivation. This view holds a modicum of resonance with what we have discussed so far.

As I have noted, the 2012 Olympic Games were to impact predominantly upon the East of London. However, it would be problematic to categorize the five Olympic boroughs as indicative of the community impact of Olympic hosting. These five Olympic boroughs were to experience Olympic delivery in different ways, with Newham being considered the Olympic borough that would experience Olympic delivery most severely. The conclusion that Newham was the location most appropriate to explore the community impact of Olympic delivery was based on two major reasons.

First, most of the Olympic infrastructure, including the Olympic Park, would be built within its boundaries. Newham also contained the ExCeL,[10] the London City Airport and a host of other Olympic and quasi-Olympic related infrastructures at various stages of development (including the Westfield Stratford City shopping complex). Therefore, this location promised to bring out reactions to the introduction of Olympics-related restrictions and of behavior modification tools, such as borough-wide Olympic regulations. These restrictions and regulations included, amongst many others, dispersal zones, parking restrictions, and road closures. Olympic delivery necessitated the intense securitization of parts of the borough. This, alongside the changes engendered by the development of the infrastructure, amounted to a widespread altering of the aesthetic, symbolic, and cultural capital of the borough, which introduced significant modifications in terms of identity and behavior. The second reason why, out of the five host boroughs, Newham could be considered the most appropriate location to carry out my ethnographic study of Olympic delivery was that this borough had undergone systematic vilification, demonization, and denigration during Olympic bidding and delivery. Newham was considered the absolute embodiment of East London's "Gash," which according to OPLC chair, Andrew Altman, needed to be healed by the Games. This view was based on statistical evidence, according to which Newham ranked highly in the various constituents of the index of deprivation that can be considered as precedent to regeneration (see Armstrong, Hobbs, and Lindsay 2011). These two considerations combined to ensure that if there was an ideal location to explore the community impact of 2012 Olympic delivery, then Newham was surely such a place.

The Quest for Life in the Shadows

Life in the shadows cast by the Olympic torch began with securing positions in Newham's third sector. The nature of these positions required that the researcher should fulfil a number of roles that would facilitate the fieldwork; for example, working in a community center on the Carpenters estate and representing community organizations in Olympic discourse with Olympic delivery agencies. At the initial stages, the research methodology involved "putting the hours in" in the field, hoping to become soon a "familiar face." Therefore, I participated in clearing out cupboards in community centers, sweeping floors with those on community service orders, supervising bouncy castles at Islamic religious functions, overseeing sport events, working in youth clubs, and much more. These actions, in addition to a willingness to say "yes" to every opportunity to build relationships no-matter the task, helped me to develop a complex, inter-woven string of networks through the snowball method.

According to Poplin (1979, p. 275), this kind of research should attempt to describe the research community as "a totality and see the manifold and complex interrelations of its parts." However, in the ultra-diverse, multi-linguistic setting of Newham, this approach proved problematic, even before Olympic migration, as I began to engage in linguistic and cultural interplay. A key initial question was how best to approach the task of field-research in this highly diverse and generally deprived location. As van Maanen (1979) suggests, ethnography is infinitely more than a single method and can be distinguished from participant observation in that it has a broader aim of achieving an analytical description of a culture (p. 539). In this setting, the initial ethnographic question was how to find out what it means to be a member of the Newham community and how best to understand and describe such a community.

Befitting an area of high deprivation, parts of Newham were high in the Metropolitan Police Service (MPS) rankings of street robbery across London; Stratford was top of the tree.[11] The MPS crime mapping statistics also demonstrated that Stratford far exceeded many nearby wards in terms of overall crime ratings and crime count.[12] Internet guides to living in London upheld common views describing Stratford as a "place to avoid living in" if one could do so, adding that it had "become quite dangerous over the last couple of years. A lot of street gangs have taken over the area."[13] Consequently, to gain a holistic view of Newham life the validity of these claims had to be explored and a research methodology appropriate to this location needed to be devised. The most appropriate course of action was to borrow research techniques from other ethnographers who had worked in similar settings. Initially, I tried to apply the investigative techniques outlined by the Marxist sociologist Sudhir Venkatesh's in his 2008 publication *Gang Leader: For a Day*. While Venkatesh's approach was a rehashing of William Foote Whyte and the Chicago School's methods, he attributed it to the advice he received from a gang member while investigating the social implications of Chicago's "Corner Boys" culture. This gang member urged him not to "ask stupid questions. What you need to do is hang out with people" (Venkatesh 2008, p. 4). Ventakesh's approach resonated with Elijah Andersons' view (1999) that in doing research in "poor" neighborhoods, and particularly in impoverished inner-city communities, mutual respect, acceptance, and sensitivity to a particular way of living are essential to one's survival and research. Drawing on this wisdom, in 2008 I began a period of purposive osmosis in the belief that simply by "hanging out" I would eventually uncover implicit knowledge provided, of course, that the "hanging out" would be done in a promising research setting and in a respectful, sensitive manner that promoted mutual respect. This, however, was easier said than done.

I spent ever-increasing amounts of time in Newham in the hope of acquiring the inside knowledge that is synonymous with being "a native." I negotiated access to local "community events," including focus groups, community meetings, coffee mornings, and so on. The feeling that things were going reasonably well lasted until I stopped scrutinizing my field notes and attempted a degree of analysis. Disturbingly, the findings proved to be vacuous. While assessing poorly attended Community Focus Groups, uninspiring interviews, and apathetic questionnaires, I decided that I needed to achieve greater depths of knowledge. My initial desire to understand this community's shared cultural history was soon replaced by the realization that, here, there was no shared cultural history. Insightful knowledge would emerge from questionnaires, interviews, or focus groups, or indeed, from "hanging out" on the off chance that clarity would appear spontaneously. There was a need for greater involvement over a continuous and significant period of time. While discussing the value of interviews for my research, Mo, a local 38-years-old Pakistani-born Muslim suggested a better approach to community-oriented research. He said, "It's pointless [the interviews]. I mean, it's important for you to know stuff but it's not important for anyone you're asking. There's been so much [research, media interest, consultations, etc.] and nothing's happened. Old people might want to talk to you because they haven't got anything better to do but no one else. We're busy and nothing ever changes, our ideas aren't ever used and, that's it, it's pointless. A waste of time."

Retrospective analysis revealed that this view was echoed in many early interviews. A feeling of resentment toward "research" was prevalent. The initial belief that people would be open to interviews, perhaps even grateful to have a forum where they could air their opinions and be asked what they thought, proved very naïve. Moreover, an insurmountable perception gradually emerged; that is, that all researchers were simply transient outsiders who were only interested in self-promotion and self-benefit, or had ulterior motives such as working for the police, benefits agencies or some other authority. When a researcher is confronted with such allegations, the elephant in the room is that there is a certain amount of clarity and truth to this perception. Another example of this skepticism is given by a conversation with T, a black youth who was working in the area to fulfil his community service as part of his conviction for transporting stolen goods. After a few weeks of small talk and relationship building, I outlined my research task and he warned me to be careful for the "only whites asking shit in these ends are the feds blood."[14] The strength of this lowly opinion of academic research was underlined in another interview, where retired docker, Derek, commented, "No, but what do you do? What's your job? I know you're asking questions about what's happening but what's the point of all of this? What's it for? Do you have a real job?" (Derek, white, 58).

In addition to those who questioned my purpose as a researcher, the research itself, or both, there was the underlying perception that the community views regarding the Olympics was a topic that had already been researched to death during the Olympic bidding process. All the community consultations, community-orientated research, and media interest had ultimately left community members skeptical of the purpose of research participation; so, woe betide anyone making the mistake of asking them to participate again. The widely publicized euphoria regarding the impending Olympic benefits that the media presented in the immediate aftermath of the victorious bid seemed to apply to a different population. Perceptions of the futility of research, dismissed colloquially as "tick box exercises" prevailed whenever the term Olympic "research" was mentioned. This attitude was possibly best summed up by a conversation with Phil, another local resident. He remarked, "It's just a big waste of time...We were told that we'd get jobs from the Olympics but we haven't. It's the Poles[15] that got 'em. All you're doing is asking about what's going on. How's that going to help me?

If you want to know about what's happening, go to town just don't waste my time. What's the point of you asking questions all the bloody time?" (Phil, white, 42, Taxi driver).

Clearly, Phil did not feel that Olympicization had delivered any of the expected social or economic benefits to his community, at least not of the anticipated nature or scale. Olympicization was disposing of, or at least altering, a lived reality and replacing it with a conceived city; it was a one-sided process that, in Phil and indeed many other local residents, generated anger and fed their resentment of the subject and of those seeking local opinions. The seemingly endless stream of researchers, media people, and other interested parties that engulfed the area meant that this community was now suffering acute research fatigue.

Opening Newham's Gates

In such a situation, any new research would be prejudged by the merits of previous researchers. Perceived absence of integrity, honesty, planning or considerate exit strategy in such former research would make the lives of those who came later considerably difficult. People who had performed the role of informant for others had been usually cast aside, once their views had been given, and had no idea how what they revealed would be used or what good laying themselves bare had done to anyone, making these residents disillusioned and reluctant to engage with any new research.

This sort of experience strengthened the need to see informants not merely as a means to an end but, instead, engage them in a co-dependent relationship wherever appropriate knowledge was pooled. Also, actively seeking ways of "paying" for information[16] stood me in good stead for the duration of my study and helped to break down initial barriers. Such "payment for information" brings to mind Wray-Bliss' (2002) argument that accounts of empirical methods are generally limited to minimal, technical descriptions which rarely extend beyond listing formal tools, duration of field work and some brief background information. Wray-Bliss also commented on critical interpretive research making the point that the researcher was interdependent with the researched rather than independent of them, which raises ethical concerns on the researcher's ability to be critical about situations that s/he has co-constructed or contributed to, and which may compromise the research. Many see an admission to altering the research methodology during the fieldwork as a threat to their reputation as "experts." However, in this case, this is a necessary step to take in order to portray adequately the difficulties of doing field research in such a diverse area during highly transitional times.

As Baudrillard metaphorically advocated, the "point is not to write the sociology or psychology of the car, the point is to drive. That way you can learn more about this society than all academia could ever tell you" (1988, p. 54). Overcoming the local initial disinclination toward research proved one of the larger problems I had to deal with. To stay with Baudrillard's metaphor, I needed to get my driving license stamped because this community had no inclination to accommodate new drivers. In addition to this reluctance, there was the prevalent notion that research was an indulgence and that it offered little or no upside for community participation. Hence the need to create added value, of "paying" for information; I would have otherwise been well and truly clamped.

Thus, the main obstacle was coming up with reasons for being in *situ*. In this environment, being a "researcher" was not necessarily conducive to good research. What proved productive was to adopt a role of "interested observer" or, at times, of agreeable "Olympic critic" in order to distinguish myself from the Olympic evangelists that permeated the media and delivered seemingly unbalanced positive narratives of delivery. I needed to provide added value far exceeding being a listening post, an interested party or, heaven forbid, a researcher. While "giving something back," I needed an excuse or a reason for being there; this need raised two important questions. First, Newham as a whole would need to be redefined and appropriate sections of the borough would need to be identified for the study to be representative of the whole. Second, access to these key locations would need to be obtained.

CHAPTER 3

Newham Divide and Document

The promises made by the British Olympic Association's Bidding Committee to the International Olympic Committee (IOC) about the positive effect the Games would have on the host "community" played a determinant role in winning the 2012 Games. The word "community" was never far from the lips of politicians and of those tasked with defining and delivering the Games. "Community" is a political concept, for the term speaks to narratives of power. It is also a contested term in relation to its definition and connotation.

Some scholars have raised concerns about the analytical relevance of the term "community" (Stacey 1969; Seabrook 1984; Hill 1994), for its applicability revolves around a conceptual vagueness. As any cursory examination of contemporary British political and media discourses would reveal, the idea and concept of what constitutes a "community" holds debatable levels of resonance in relation to its myriad uses. "Community" is an overused prefix that has been attached to as diverse concepts as: consultation, care, development, and policing, to name but a few. However, this research follows the argument of sociologists Day and Murdoch in considering that "community," when adequately defined, remains a pertinent term for the study of social space (1993, p. 108). While it would, of course, be folly not to acknowledge potential criticism of this use of the term, I must stress that the use of the prefix "community" in this research relates to the imaginary dimensions of the term as much as to the importance of its structural determinants (Anderson 1983).

In relation to Olympic-delivery Newham, an adequate definition of "community" needed to encapsulate the complexity of life in the borough and the population churn that occurred there. Any generalizations on this population needed to account for difference as a fundamental tenet of any definition of Newham's "community." Crow and Allen (1994) stated that anything claiming to be a "community" study was defined as a means of uncovering ways in which individuals were embedded into sets of personal relationships (p. 177). This definition is pertinent to this analysis in that it seeks to consider the relational aspect of Olympic delivery and the ways in which individuals and groups evolved and interacted. Consequently, the word "community" is used here in relation to place and to social networks and is considered a symbolic construct that illuminates shared characteristics and signifies collective action. Furthermore, it is considered as representational and imposed, both from within and from outside specific groupings.

In this regard, Olympic-delivery Newham was a fragmented "community" that could be considered neither "complete" nor static. The Newham "community" was based around ever-shifting boundaries and compositions. Therefore, a holistic definitive definition of what constituted "Newham," and indeed the "Newham community," remained elusive and ephemeral. This ambiguity was heightened and emphasized by those tasked with Olympic delivery, who—arguably—attempted to create a vision of unity that did not exist, that had indeed ceased to exist since the late 1970s (Hobbs 1988; Fussey, Coaffee, Armstrong, and Hobbs 2011).

Paradoxically, as the Olympic Games drew closer and the media representations of unity became wider and more pronounced, this research uncovered that, in Newham, divisions began to become more prominent as some people felt excluded from specific Olympic locales. This was—arguably—best exemplified by the remarks made by Andrew Altman, the Chair of Olympic Park Legacy Company (OPLC),[1] at a 2009 event held at the London School of Economics. As I have mentioned, at that event, Altman defined the area of East London that was to host much of the Games as *"London's Gash"*—a *"Gash"* that would be healed and reclaimed by the 2012 Olympics. This statement effectively relegated all those living there to the category of *Gash Dwellers* who would need to be dealt with accordingly.

We have seen how the Olympic Games promised to deliver a plethora of benefits to Newham during Olympic delivery and beyond, which, as I have indicated earlier, raises the question, who would experience these modifications most severely? In this chapter, I address this question while considering how best to capture the realities of Olympic delivery. As a result, the discussion divides Newham into three key research zones and draw on the clarity and realism provided by ethnographic examples of everyday life within these zones.

Newham: The Great Divide

Geographically speaking, and building upon the demographics highlighted earlier, the entire borough could not be considered a viable ethnographic lab because, quite simply, it was too large for a lone field researcher to study in its entirety. Regardless of proximity to the venues, all Newham's communities were expected to be impacted by Games delivery to a lesser or greater degree, and all were valuable to this research as a whole.

While it was clear that the lives of all residents would be affected, it seemed logical to assume that those experiencing Olympic delivery in the area surrounding the building site that was the Olympic Park would have a different experience from those living further away. For example, the ExCeL to the south of the borough would host many Olympic events and was expected to undergo a substantial Olympic transition. I devised a triple-fronted approach to field research. I focused on the areas surrounding Newham's two major Olympic venues and facilitated access to key exemplars of the broader community. Thus, for research purposes, I divided Newham into three distinct zones. The first, *Stratfordland* (the area in the vicinity of the Olympic Park), was represented by a housing estate at the boundaries of the Olympic Park. The second, *ExCeLland* (the area in the vicinity of the ExCeL London), was represented by a housing estate at the boundaries of the ExCeL. The third, the *Dispersal Zone*, included the remaining parts of Newham. Research in the *Dispersal Zone* involved working outward from two community bases (Manor Park and Forest Gate, to the northeast of the borough) and treated all uncovered pertinent community groups as representative of its findings.

To accomplish this triple-fronted analysis I was primarily based in four community centers across the three research zones in Newham: *Stratfordland, ExCeLland,* and the *Dispersal Zone.* These centers formed satellite bases from which to conduct community interaction. This methodology led to my involvement in a variety of community-oriented activities, including working with youth clubs and community detachment teams (youth workers that were based on Newham's streets), providing fruit and vegetables to community members who were otherwise unable to get access to them,[2] doing manual labor alongside those completing their Community Service Orders,[3] becoming involved in religious festivals, and so on. These community centers were managed by the Newham's Third Sector and also served inadvertently as research realms for a variety of political discourses to which—crucially—every citizen had potential access and could participate in (Young 1990). These centers proved to be good locations from which to conduct community-orientated research in a highly transitional and diverse locale. Indeed, it was in these three Newham zones that I met a number of *public characters* who resonated with me in a way similar to how the local shopkeepers and community activists did with Jayne Jacobs (1961) during her research. She stated, "A public character is anyone who is in frequent contact with a wide circle of people and who is sufficiently interested to make himself a public character. A public character need have no special talents or wisdom to fulfil his function—although he [sic] often does. He just needs to be present, and there need to be enough of his counterparts. His main qualification is that he is public, that he talks to lots of different people" (Jacobs 1961, p. 68).

Such public characters helped to form my practical wisdom as a researcher. Initially, they were community workers and youth workers but became diversified as the research progressed. Public characters became the gatekeepers to a multitude of research hubs, which were to form a data collection method defined here as *spoking*. This involved cultivating my relationships with these public characters, who held positions in Newham-based community organizations in the borough and indeed in East London. When I tried to map these locations for reflective analysis, these satellite case-studies peppered the borough and the mapping resembled bicycle wheel spokes springing from a single point; hence the term *spoking*. These public characters helped to shape, form, and develop my knowledge. Through their wisdom, they helped to guide the research and facilitated many significant contacts, meetings, and events. They opened doors and helped me to overcome suspicions and transitions.

The Dispersal Zone: A Host Hub

In order to gain an understanding of social practice in Newham and of how it changed during Olympic delivery, I sought a base of research operations that would allow me to penetrate different community levels and regional (East London) and local perspectives of life. A well-connected host hub would—ideally—enable a wide range of networking to be accomplished. The interactions that would follow would contribute to gaining access to the diverse communities and would allow a broader view of the implications of Olympic delivery. The host hub needed to operate on myriad levels to allow this study to contextualize Newham on different levels, including community engagement, participation, local and regional politics and interaction with those who manned the Olympic delivery. The host hub needed to be in Newham and to have long established links to several community groups and organizations; it needed to have a good understanding of the way Newham worked as an urban location and to be actively involved with, and impacted by, Olympic delivery. Such a host hub would provide access to such interplay, allowing my field research to "spoke" out into the borough.

A Newham-based charity, Aston Mansfield (AM), proved to be a perfect fit for these criteria. AM were a long established community hub that focused on facilitating everyday life in the communities that reside in Newham. They were established in 2000 with the purpose of fostering social change for the benefit of local people. They accomplished this by campaigning for social justice, which their General Manager defined as "the quest for fairness and respect that ensures the local people are treated within their expectations of human dignity." AM provided services for education, training, capacity building, and skills development for local people.

AM defined themselves as an organization that "implemented a community development approach" that aimed to solve issues pertinent to the Newham community; they work alongside the community to identify areas of concern and for improvement. To this end, they assist community members in gaining the resources, education, and training that they need to accomplish their goals. AM facilitated community access to decision-makers and helped to create the conditions for the community to resolve their own issues and promote social change, which was particularly pertinent to this research. They also provided learning and meeting venues in community buildings.

Arguably, one of the strongest initial draws to AM as a viable research conduit was its strong links with established groups that were involved during the Olympic bidding and to which I sought to gain access. In addition to providing exceptional links to the broader Newham community, AM were invited to, and often facilitated, Olympic-related meetings or community consultations in Newham during Olympic delivery. AM enabled access to other organizations that interacted with the community throughout the Olympics delivery including, for example, the OPLC, the London Legacy Development Corporation (LLDC), the Newham Youth Providers Partnership (NYPP), Transport for London (TFL), the London Organising Committee for the Olympic Games (LOCOG), and the Olympic Security Directorate (OSD). The findings originated from this host hub—through their vast array of interactions—were utilized to confirm, contribute to, or question the findings from the specific fields of *Stratfordland* and *ExCeLland*. This approach allowed for a greater degree of clarity and an enhanced depth of research, and increased the credibility and generalization of the findings.

Stratfordland

Prior to the bid, Stratford was located at the heart of the *Thames Gateway* development,[4] initiated in 1990 by the *South-East Regional Policy Guidance Plan*. In 1991, a decision was made to create a *Channel Tunnel* rail link between

Paris and central London, via Stratford. This provided an important catalyst for improvements in road and rail infrastructure in the area. By 1995, the *Thames Gateway Task Force* drew up plans for 30,000 new homes and 50,000 new jobs to be established in the areas surrounding the river Thames, which will eventually—by 2021—comprise the *Thames Corridor* (Buck, Gordon, Hall, Harloe, and Kleinman 2002, pp. 84–85). The prospect of East London hosting the 2012 Olympics injected new life into this project and resulted, in 2006, in a government-inspired review of the *Thames Gateway* plan.[5]

The implications of the Olympic vigor injected into these regeneration plans were witnessed throughout Newham. Some of its districts were substantially modified, while others struggled to see any physical Olympic transformation whatsoever. All districts, however, were inundated with Olympic-hosting connotations, leading to the symbolic modification of the borough. *Stratfordland* provided the greatest example of Newham's transformation. This urban locale witnessed the delivery of the Olympic Park, which loomed over the landscape during Olympic delivery asserting most visibly its dominance over the area. First came a walled off building site which was soon replaced by a shiny utopian, self-enclosed Olympic hub. This hub promised to be transformed, after the Games, into an "Olympic City," which would become a large component of the final Olympic regeneration of East London.

An adequate understanding of Olympic delivery needed to recognize that people living in Stratford would experience Olympic hosting differently from those living elsewhere in the borough. In this line, I identified Stratford as a specific research locale—*Stratfordland.*—in which to establish a base for my research. I also needed to establish the criteria by which I would identify my research population, to which I, then, needed to secure access. I decided to engage in exploratory research. Having approached several contacts, particularly in Newham's Third Sector, to whom I explained the research objectives and the intended methodologies, I selected a specific area of West Newham known as the Carpenters Estate as a viable ethnographic option. While several considerations were involved in making this decision, a major role was played by the area's close proximity to the Olympic Park and by its relative local infamy, as residents were moved from their homes for the duration of the Games. The Carpenters Estate had also attracted a plethora of local, national, and international media interest, which continued throughout the period of the Olympics.[6]

The Carpenters of Stratfordland

The area known colloquially as "Carpenters" was located in Stratford at the heart of the Olympic development, in the northeast corner of Newham. It lay some four miles east of the City of London, next to Stratford Regional Station, which would form one of the main entry points to the Olympic Park. Depending on one's perspective, it can be argued either that the Olympic Park and stadium shadowed the estate or that the estate cast a metaphorical shadow over the Games. Indeed the estate was the backdrop to the Games and its poor condition threatened to blot an otherwise unblemished Olympic landscape.

The issues that emerged from research in the Carpenters Estate were representative of a common trend whereby the local authorities passed their responsibilities for social housing on to private housing associations, and property development interests pressured vulnerable communities. Throughout my research, two facts remained constant, which provided insight into the realities of Olympic delivery in this locale. First, Newham Council were committed to decanting the residents of the estate for reasons on which I will expand below, thus displacing many people throughout East London and beyond during this period. Second, as a result of a vast amount of Olympic-related investment in the area and its surroundings, those who remained consistently reinforced the notion that their *habitus* was an ill fit for the evolving *field* in which they had once felt they belonged.

The Carpenters Estate provided an example of a community living through *hysteresis*. The Olympic delivery period witnessed the gradual displacement of the residents living in its tower blocks and the communities's death, which was caused by a thousand cuts related to the birth of Olympic Stratford. Carpenters become emblematic of the poverty and deprivation that the Olympics intended to eradicate from *Stratfordland*. Carpenters's residents were categorized as deprived; they were vilified and perceived as needing to be saved from their social malaise. Let us now turn our attention to a description of this social malaise through a brief history of this estate.

The land that is now the Carpenters Estate was owned in the ninteenth century by a London livery company, the Worshipful Company of Carpenters (WCC). Many of London's factories were located in the vicinity and the workers required housing. The WCC built Victorian terraced houses on their land for this purpose. Therefore, an industrial community was formed, complete with a school and a social club. As with so many industrial areas in East London, World War II brought widespread devastation; factories and docks were ruined by bomb damage. The subsequent decision to move all dock activity some 25 miles downstream to Tilbury caused several decades of stagnation and economic decline. East London was never transformed back into an economic industrial hub and, according to some scholars (Willmott and Young 1957), its sense of community was lost. However, Carpenters remained relatively unscathed until the 1960s, when local authorities throughout

London began to provide cheap, decent homes by building council houses. These social housing projects attempted to alleviate housing issues in deprived and derelict areas, but they failed to address some underlying social issues and their implementation resulted in was a severe polarization (Power 1996). The cumulative effect of such housing policies were spatial and social exclusion and "area-based poverty" (Power 1987, 1996; Power, and Turnstall 1991), something that future policies—such as social mixing—would try to alleviate elsewhere—as we shall see, with debatable success.

In 1969, Newham Council built three 23-story tower blocks and some 700 other units, thus creating what became known as the Carpenters Estate. The Carpenters Estate became well defined and clearly delimited by man-made boundaries. These included a busy road, the London Underground tracks, and what would become the Olympic Park. Margaret Thatcher's policies of the 1980s impacted upon Carpenters with the 1980 introduction of the Right-to-Buy scheme,[7] wherein the more affluent former council residents were able to buy and become freeholders of their homes. In April 1998, residents of the Carpenters Estate collectively took responsibility for managing their homes by creating a Tenant Management Organisation (TMO). A TMO is an organization of residents who employ their own staff to manage services of which the Newham Council has agreed to relinquish the control. These services included repairs and tenancy matters. Basically, the Council remained the landlord while the residents managed themselves. However, for many, living under this new situation was hard to manage and the population of the Carpenters Estate was categorized as amongst the most deprived in England (Office for National Statistics 2007). This fact came as a surprise to some residents. A local informant graphically said, "I'm going to be moved. I've lived on the estate for as long as I can remember, I only found out two weeks ago that I was deprived... It hasn't been a good fortnight" (Interview with Kath, white, English, aged 77, 2008).

At the turn of the 20th Century, the three tower blocks were badly in need of repair. In 2004, the Council decided that the worst of the three—James Riley Point—needed to be demolished and its residents re-housed. In 2007–2008, the Newham Council evaluated a refurbishment program for the other two tower blocks—Lund and Dennison point—and decided that the £50m needed was prohibitive. So also, these blocks would be demolished and the population re-housed. In late November 2011, a Memorandum of Agreement was announced between the Newham Council and University College London (UCL). This MoA stated an intent to clear the site of residents, demolish all the houses, and convert the site into a university campus. However, the decanting of residents had been well underway prior to this announcement, as the tables 3.1 and 3.2 below indicate.

Table 3.1 2005 Carpenters Estate Occupation Levels[8]

Property Category	Secure Tenants	Leaseholders	Freeholders	Total
Estate Wide	514	98	93	705
High Rise	360	74	0	434
Low Rise	106	24	0	13
Houses	48	0	93	141
Total			612	

Table 3.2 2011 Carpenters Estate Occupation Levels[9]

Property Category	Secure Tenants	Leaseholders	Freeholders	Total
Estate Wide	193	65	93	351
High Rise	55	40	0	95
Low Rise	90	25	0	115
Houses	48	0	93	141
Total		258		

The cycle of depreciation and disinvestment in the Carpenters Estate's tower blocks is indicative of how new developments undermine older investments, whereby spending money to maintain high-value land that house low-income tenants becomes difficult to justify when compared to the potential financial windfalls of selling valuable land to developers (Lees, Slater, and Wyly 2008, p. 53). The 2012 London Olympic-delivery period saw the birth of a new skyline surrounding the Carpenters Estate as *Stratfordland* began to evolve at a dizzying pace. The Olympic Park rose from the ashes of faded industry; a plethora of other buildings, flats and offices rapidly began to emerge and dominate the landscape. Stratford's transportation links were enhanced and improved.

As we have seen, the vision for the Carpenters Estate was that it would be erased and replaced by a university campus. According to Sir Robin Wales, such a deal was expected to enhance the prospects of the neighborhood and enrich Newham as a whole. The gradual dispersal—from 2005—of the estate's residents, mostly to alternative dwellings nearby, was justified by the need to embrace the Olympic-related development opportunities. As Sir Robin Wales stated, "people in Carpenters are concerned. I would be too. I completely understand that. But with UCL, we would get an amazing, top university coming to the area. Our vision is for science and hi-tech providing jobs and skills" (Hill 2012).[10] For the residents of the Carpenters Estate, this vision ensured a continuation of the "waiting game" to which they had become used in recent years. During the research, those who remained on Carpenters waited to find out where they would be living in the future, secure in the knowledge that they had no future on Carpenters and strongly suspecting that they had no part to play in *Stratfordland's* Olympic utopia.

Kicked out of Paradise?

The Carpenters Estate was situated at the heart of Newham's Olympic transition; it bordered the Olympic Park and those that lived there were within touching distance of the greatness that was to come. As a result of the decanting of Carpenters, many residents felt that their Olympic gold, in the form of a place in the much-proselytized Olympic City, had been snatched from their fingertips. This regenerative narrative served to reinforce the view that Olympics hosting was oriented " toward a greater level of segregation and separation at the micro-community level, as the Olympic Park attracts residential units that serve the needs of young professionals... This pattern of separation and segregation at the local level has been a feature of regeneration and gentrification schemes in East London over recent years—with stark divisions emerging in the same street between the "gated" and those without." (Imrie, Lees, and Raco 2009, p. 143).

The gated communities would arrive after the end of the Games. During the delivery stage, the Council gradually emptied the estate of tenants. We have seen that the eradication of the Carpenters Estate was planned long before the Olympics, which strengthens the findings of Burbank et al. (2001), who argued that the motivations for a host city to enter the Olympic bidding process are underpinned by "the existence of an established growth regime in the city...(and) a desire to create or change the city's image" (p. 7); a process that, in this instance, could be holistically defined as part of the Newham Master Plan for the widespread regeneration of the borough, some of which was boosted by the 2012 Olympic Games.[11] The following case study encapsulates the realities of the Carpenters regeneration at the time of Olympic delivery.

Sylvie: The Moan that Newham Forgot

As we sat on the sofa in Sylvie's living room in December 2010, she motioned to the TV in the corner. It was covered in dust: "I can dust the room in the morning," she said, "and by the afternoon I can write my name on the top of the TV again with all the crap that gets blown in from the Olympics." Clearly house-proud and conscious of perceptions of others, Sylvie had lived in this flat for 35 years. She had raised her kids and, in her own words, had "seen off" her husband too. She was now being offered a £4,000 moving allowance by the local Council to relocate to "a place of her choosing"; at the time, her choices were limited to much smaller one-bedroom houses in Canning Town or elsewhere in Stratford. She complained that she had been offered the same amount as others who had lived on the estate for considerably less time, suggesting that there was no place for values in the relocation. Sylvie was also aware she would need to downsize, as she was now the only occupant of her family-sized flat.

As we looked out at the emerging Olympic Park, Sylvie commented on what a great "Panasonic view" she had and how she would miss it when she would be gone, believing, quite correctly, that she would not see the Park finished: "Life here has been pretty tough since the Olympics came," she said matter-of-factly. She added, "The new flats over the road block out the sun and it is a lot harder to get to the shops now because they have shut the gateway through the station, making if off-limits for residents. Now it's just for workers. There's 24-hour drilling and alarms going off at the Station (Stratford) every couple of hours; this morning, they went off at 2am and 4am. The other thing is the tannoy announcements that go on late into the night; it would be understandable if they were important but the last one shouted, 'Dave, your tea is ready.'" In full flow, Sylvie turned from the structural to the persecuted, saying, "The site-workers are taking over Stratford. The Poles come over with their women for healthcare and to have babies. You can tell the women: blonde hair, black roots… Sluts. My son is a construction worker and he was bullied on the site by Poles, Croats and fucking Paddies. It didn't stop until he threatened to put someone in the ground. At the end of the day you can build what you like but you can't make a silk purse from a sow's ear, it'll always be fucking Stratford."

Sylvie liked primarily people among whom she had long lived. In a sense, her life had been privileged. "When you grow up somewhere you learn where to go, where to avoid and what's not safe." She said, adding, "That's hard to do again when you're not a kid anymore. We've been spoilt here; we've got shops, the doctors and our clubs right on our doorstep. I might not know everyone to talk to here but I always say hello and am stopping to chat, or to moan, I'm good at moaning. That won't happen in new places."

In Sylvie's world, politicians are evasive. She reported on how such evasiveness created the indecision about her future, which made her avoid spending money on her house. She stated, "Five years ago when Robin Wales came to the estate to talk about the relocation we asked him if we were going to be moved; he didn't answer. He did say how good the Olympics were going to be and how good they'd be for us. But we're not running in the Olympics we're living here. If he'd have said you're moving we wouldn't have liked it but at least we'd know, it's been 7 years now and I still haven't been moved. I needed to decorate 7 years ago but I'm scared to start unless I get moved the next week and waste my money. I don't even recognize the place anymore, it's changed so much in the last year or so, it doesn't feel like home."

Figure 3.1 Carpenters's Residents Memorialized.

Sylvie had lived a solitary life since her grown-up children had flown the nest for the leafier climes of suburban Essex. One might argue that a nostalgic longing for times past had caused Sylvie to become bitter and fatalistic, and that she would see any modification of her neighborhood as further indication that her best years were behind her. Throughout my research, the interactions with Sylvie proved frequently paradoxical. In many exchanges, she demonstrated that she was both open and adaptable to Newham's evolution. She also showed a post-racial outlook which, as her remarks given above indicate, was sometimes accompanied by parochial and intolerant comments resonating with frustration and self-pity more than with outright bigotry. This was most notably evidenced by her intolerance of Eastern Europeans. Eventually, Sylvie and many others like her left the Carpenters. In 2012, a selection of photographs were put up on the side of some of the houses that had been boarded up to prevent squatting and their homes became a temporary reminder of times past.

This display was the culmination of photographer Nicola Pritchard's four years of work on the estate. The aim of the display was to provide insights into the experiences of those who were displaced and to give a human face to the statistics and words that would report the events after the residents had left. For those who remained, life changed markedly in the years leading up to the Games, though for many drastic change had been *the* backdrop to their lives.

Sarah: A Search for Acceptance

"I moved to Carpenters in 2003, from Norwich. I converted to Islam about 15 years ago after meeting my husband. In Norwich a white woman, speaking Arabic and wearing Islamic clothes causes issues, so we moved here. I like how the Olympics have changed the area, it's much nicer to look at now, and it's cleaner. Life here is weird now though, it's become a ghost town. People are going and they are not being replaced. The less people that stay the less people there are to oppose any move or to make sure we can come back after the regeneration [this suggestion was sporadically circulated by many tenants]. CARP[12] keep knocking on my door and pressurizing me to come out and demonstrate against the relocation, but there's no point; it's inevitable. It's like we are on a roller coaster and we can only get off when they say "stop". We have no say. We can scream as much as we like, it makes no difference. I don't see the Olympics as a bad thing but the way they are treating the community is a bad thing. It will take years to sort this community out and to bring people back. They should invest in what's already here."

As these remarks made by Sue in March 2010 indicate, there were sporadic cases of organized resistance against the dispersal of the Carpenters Estate. These groups included the Tower Block Action Group (TBAG), formed in 2003 by the tenants in the estate.[13] People in this group mostly looked back on their demonstrations as a "waste of life," some wishing that they had done something more productive with their time like "read a good book." Following this initial process, a collective was formed in 2011 under the acronym CARP by the leaseholders of the estate. According to one leading member, Joe Alexander, CARP and its leaseholders replaced the tenants that had formed TBAG in "manning the front line against the tyranny of Robin Wales."[14] Both groups were ethnically and culturally diverse, many members were women, and both groups rapidly deteriorated once residents began moving away.

Ultimately, these pockets of resistance failed to attract significant numbers of participants or gain sufficient exposure to resonate significantly during Olympic delivery. Those who did not live on the estate, and even many who did, failed to become involved, to heed the Carpenters residents's call to order. As Bourdieu intimates in *The Weight of the World* (1999), despite their own suffering, those without tangible political power, or the abilities or fora to express their opinions, often comply with the established order and submit themselves to the status quo because they believe the outcome to be a foregone conclusion. Elsewhere in Newham regeneration had already occurred. As we shall now see, these Newham residents experienced the delivery of the Olympic Games in ways dramatically different from those of the Carpenters Estate.

ExCeLland

The Olympic Games were to unfurl in the brand-new Olympic Park, and much media attention was directed to the construction of this Park during Olympic delivery. However, to the south of Newham there was already an Olympic venue—that of the ExCeL—where more medals would be contested than within the Olympic Stadium. The residents that surround this locale were expected to experience Olympic delivery in relation to hosting Olympic events and to all that the preparation for such hosting entails. Consequently, for the purpose of my research, I was looking for an estate in close proximity to ExCeL. One such estate was Britannia Village (from now on, BV), directly opposite the ExCeL London.

The BV was an urban "village" in Newham's Docklands. Its creation resulted from a project begun in the early 1990s,[15] which planned to encapsulate the ideals of the Urban Villages Group (UVG),[16] as summarized by

Aldous (1992, 1995). According to the objectives set down by the UVG, the BV was intended to replace the inner city environment with one that was more sustainable and "positive." Urban villages were intended to restore a sense of place in an otherwise alienating and deprived setting. They offered to address a powerful sociological problem though a new approach to urban planning which arguably could be said to have its origins in the Control Theorists's paradigm of criminological thought (Hirschi 1969; Reckless 1973).

The targets of such policy paradigms often earn what Wacquant has defined as the "disproportionate and disproportionately negative attention of the media, politicians and state managers" (2008, p. 1). These descriptions allow the application of definitions of *"lawless zones"* and *"problem estates"* (Wacquant 2008) to situations that then need to be rectified through policies such as those of the UVG. As demonstrated in BV, the outcomes illustrate many of the basic elements of the Reckless' Containment Theory (Reckless, Dinitz, and Kay 1957; Reckless and Dinitz 1967), which maintains that the dwellers of such *problem estates* can be influenced by social control methods—notably, design is one such method—that can help to assist them in resisting criminality and deviant behavior. Such containments, including an emphasis on family and friend support systems and increased economic opportunities, are thought to help insulate from deviant behavior those who are likely to becoming involved in such behavior by instilling a sense of place ownership, hope, and optimism. Thus BV, built on a former docklands brown-fill site sandwiched between the Royal Docks and the River Thames, was intended to help alleviate deviance and deprivation in the south of Newham through various notions of regeneration, which has significant resonance with the Olympic-related regeneration discourse.

Britannia Village

An urban village has very specific characteristics that include locating 3–5,000 residents into a well-defined urban space (Aldous 1992; 1995). Such villages aim to include a mix of housing tenures, ages, and social groups through a program known as "social balancing" or "mix." Social balancing basically rests on the belief that there is an ideal composition of social and income groups that, when achieved, produces optimum individual and community well-being (Pitt 1977, p. 16). In an attempt to achieve this, the BV comprised 63 housing blocks, which translated to 650 flats. In addition, there were 201 houses and several private parking bays.[17] A solitary road—Wesley Avenue—runs horizontally through the village separating the private and social housing sectors. This road is a literal and symbolic divide that was evident from my first research visit. At the center of the BV, there was a Community Centre that provided facilities for both sides of the local population (privately and socially housed). These facilities included playgroups, after school clubs, and a meeting hall, which formed a community hub in which it was possible to mix with residents from the entire village. Consequently, this Community Centre formed a base for my ethnographic research.

The aim of the BV regeneration was to attract new people to Newham by offering them residence in a gated urban village conveniently located close to the City but without a City price tag. Arguably, the BV was the embodiment of regeneration programs that target mobile, high income, professional groups, or the "creative classes" (Florida 2005). These "creative classes" require high-quality secure environments free from the threat of intrusion and violent crime (Raco 2007, p. 41). However, as the research conducted by Robson and Butler (2004) shows, social mixing policies like those implemented within the BV promised to prove problematic. Robson and Butler (2004) have demonstrated that gentrified London spaces that made inequality manifest experienced greater incidences of crime, particularly robbery and burglary. In fact, the BV social mixing did little to remove the stigma of "*lawless problem estate*" from the socially housed tenants who lived in the areas surrounding the highly securitized, gated private enclaves. This led to an uneasy détente between the two BV communities; a détente saturated with the perception of criminality and occasionally broken by instances of criminality. The ensuing uneasy negotiation of place ownership and identity between BV's two distinct groups evoked a new bipartite regime of sociospatial relegation and exclusionary closure (in the Weberian sense).[18]

Interestingly, this area was not marketed as "Newham" to the newly arrived private tenants; rather, it—ostensibly—formed part of an area called the "Royal Docks." This urban location offered a compelling illustration of what can be referred to as a splintering post-metropolitan landscape; one that, according to Soja (2000), is filled with protected and fortified spaces. The BV's enclosed islands anticipated protection against the real and imagined dangers of daily life on the estate. Soja, borrowing from Foucault, asserted that the post-metropolis was represented as a collection of prison-like cities; an archipelago of "normalized enclosures" and fortified spaces that both voluntarily and involuntarily barricaded individuals and communities into visible and not-so-visible urban islands. The BV's private residences could be seen as such islands, which were overseen by restructured forms of public and private power and authority (Soja 2000, p. 299).

The nature of BV's "urban-village," its restructuring of public and private power, and authority within such diversity, required a move away from traditional categorizations of race, ethnicity, and class (Whyte 1943; Liebow 1967; Anderson 1999; Duneier 1999) toward an adaption of what Nutall (2009) conceptualized as a formative and informative exploration of the entanglement of history, people, and place (Hall 2012) in this particular milieu.[19] The reality of life on the estate indicated that the BV was divided. What follows is a brief exploration of such division, which may provide insights into the likely sociological outcomes for parts of post-Olympic *Stratfordland*, particularly the soon-to-be converted Athlete's Village in the Olympic Park.

Social Control in the Urban Village

I will now consider the outcomes of the application of the premise that to reclaim valuable inner city real estate there is a need first to *civilize* the urban context (see Atkinson and Helms 2007). This conflict was magnified exponentially by the implementation of social mixing in the confined geography of the BV. Two demographic dichotomies were forced to exist within a confined area where a re-negotiation of place was supposed to occur between the socially and the privately housed groups. This approach advocated simplistic solutions to highly complex sociological issues, bringing to mind the neo-liberal assumption that the introduction of greater securitization and wealth would remedy crime and deprivation through trickle-down economic principles (Harvey 2005). However, as we shall see, a change in landscape does not necessarily indicate a wider sociological change. The narrative that urban regeneration is a viable remedy for the underlying causes of urban decay resulted in a complex re-negotiation of place between the communities that lived in the post-regeneration BV landscape. This included people from both sides of the class divide, who were involved in these reclamation policies through choice or circumstance. This estate reflected the argument that regeneration aimed at creating "sustainable communities" was underpinned by safety and security concerns (Raco 2003).

In this urban location, these policies legitimized and privileged the private residents. They also supported the assumption that the re-emergence of urban decay is best symbolized by crime and perceptions of "criminality" that can threaten the philosophy of post-regeneration life and the attendant perception of safety. Consequently, the private residents became fixated upon securing their homes from the "criminal" others, resulting in what Sibley (1995) has described as geographies of exclusion marked by the use of a demonizing rhetoric directed at those assumed to be the likely perpetrators of decay; specifically, the urban poor. This resonates with wider processes, whereby residents of deprived neighborhoods become vilified as undeserving lazy minorities who have been given too much public assistance (Omi and Winant 1994). The highly valuable space they inhabit becomes characterized as misused and abused space (Smith 1996) that needs to be reclaimed.

The bipartite fear of the conceptual *other* that saturated life in the BV was clearly visible to me from the very first research visit right up until the last. The initial guarded discourse that I recorded during the collection of ethnographic data could be viewed as an attempt to manage, legitimize, and rationalize fear to the outsider. For the private residents it was both a generic fear of disorder and a fear of those who were deemed to be the producers of disorder—the, predominantly black, local youths who occupied the streets of the estate.[20] Even within the diversity of twenty-first century Newham, it appeared that "the sight of a young black man evokes an image of someone dangerous, destructive, or deviant" (Monroe and Goldman 1988, p. 27). Those who lived in the social housing were also permeated with fear. For these residents it was generically the fear of vilification and, specifically, a fear of those who were deemed to be the perpetrators of this demonization—the, predominantly white, city workers. The pathology of fear in everyday BV life could be attributed to the socio-political changes resulting in a polarization of the BV class structure that, in turn, had produced a dichotomy of the social and physical structure of the estate. According to Wacquant (2008, p. 25), one of the outcomes of social marginality is precisely a heightened stigmatization in everyday life and discourse which is related to a degradation of place and class. This process was prevalent amongst the socially housed residents.

The notion of *habitus*, as discussed earlier, governed perceptions of urban decay and, indeed, perceptions of everyday life in the BV, be that of the fully functioning citizen, of the vilified product of decay, or of the producer of such decay. Conflict was inevitable in the BV, where two vastly different social groups with vastly different *habitus* were forced to live alongside each other in one small location. As a result, the two communities segregated from each other, and this action linked the fears of the *other* to the fear of conflict. These identity categorizations ensured segregation and differentiating actions that played out in the everyday life of the BV context.

How fear facilitated segregation is exemplified by issues of security. Even from the most cursory walk around the estate, it was obvious that the private residences boasted a plethora of security and surveillance devices, including private security, security cameras, and security gates; clearly, these residents saw it as absolutely necessary to protect themselves from the *others*. This conspired to generate fear and distrust between these two communities, which paradoxically increased the likelihood of inter-community conflict.

Furthermore, as a result of social mixing, perceptions of crime and deprivation became more pertinent to one group than to the other.

The private residents were concerned about crime and about the perception of the fear of crime. They were concerned about the effect that this perception had upon their social status, not to mention its impact on property prices. Consequently, although the fear of conflict and the fear of crime are legitimate in their own right, they are also linked to the broader issue of *habitus*-related anxiety. This can arguably be considered a core component of the post-modern condition, where social significance is evaluated through the prism of social class. Such perceptions are related to the symbolic nature of anxiety, not necessarily to the specific *loci* of such anxiety, which then permeates everyday life through *habitus*.

The contestation of ownership of the BV was an ongoing narrative that extended far beyond this research. The quest for dominance encompassed many levels, including the political, the economic, and the social. The socially housed tended to be longer-term residents who used most frequently the community facilities, such as the community center. The private residents tended to be a more transient community reluctant to engage in the community, which had significant consequences for the estate. As the manager of the community center—which was intended to provide a space available to both community groups—emphasized, "The people who live in the private residences tend to avoid getting involved in the community because they don't stay in the community for very long. They are here for maybe 6 months, or a year and the bank, or whoever it is they work for pays their rent. There is no community "involvement" or "ownership". Once they have finished their contracts they move away. Those who own their homes stay a bit longer but ultimately they move away when they have kids" (Fieldwork notes, May 2012).

The above quote stresses that the private residents were not inclined to engage with the socially housed residents and were not likely to consider socially mixed locations viable, long-term homely places. However, this perception and definition of "reluctance" speaks to more than their lack of will to integrate into the community dynamics; it raises questions regarding the applicability of the definition of what actually constitutes community "involvement" and "ownership" among these two contrasting demographics. Wallman's study, *Eight London Households* (1984), explored how individuals from different ethnicities and classes depended upon social networks to get by in everyday life. She saw these networks as organizations of "time, information, and identity" (1984, p. 29). The notion that time is crucial to the creation of community resonates across much identity-related analyses, such as that offered by Gary Armstrong on football hooligans, where the most essential component was having enough "free time" to participate (1998, p. 169). In this regard, it seems reasonable to assume that the time demands among the privately housed, young, childfree professionals would be vastly different from those among the socially housed single-parent families living in the BV. A good example of this dichotomy was the Friday morning breakfast club held at the community center between 9:00 am and 12:00 pm. The club was intended to provide community integration but was only readily accessible to the unemployed or temporary workers of the estate, bearing testament to the fact that in these estates there were barriers to social cohesion which social mixing alone appeared unable to overcome.

That is not to say that the private residents were not interested in place dominance. They appeared to share a specific set of expectations of order, which would have to be implemented during their occupation of the estate, however transient this might be; indeed, they implemented such expectations through a variety of security related measures. This contributed to conceptualizations of order and identity that were felt on both sides of the divide. The underlying logic of this attitude was succinctly described by Beck (1998, p. 130) as a strongly held belief that "we" must secure our centrality and "they," those who disrupt our homely place, must be pushed out of the center. From such a perspective, "difference" is an attribute of "them"; "they" are not "like us" and therefore they are threatening. This logic questions the entire ethos of sustainable, shared living and social mixing; it also raises problematic issues regarding the underlying principles of Newham's post-Olympic "*legacy.*" If new people are sought to enhance the locale, will their lives be permeated with antagonism directed toward, and received from, those already there? The significance of this, and of the example given below, should not be lost on those tasked with filling the post-Olympic Athlete's Village and the 40,000 other housing units planned on the Olympic Park.

Protection from the Other

A depersonalized observation of the socially housed in the BV would provide much confirmation of the stereotypes that were used as signifiers of urban decay. These people were markedly different from those living in the private residences. This community was ethnically and culturally diverse and had a large proportion of single mothers—some working, most not. Drug use and alcoholism were common, as were accounts of spousal male-on-female abuse. Large extended families were a frequent occurrence; one youth commented that he literally had 80 brothers and sisters, including those from other mothers with whom his father had had children. Education levels were low and unemployment high. Crime levels were comparatively high and in the evenings, groups of youths were a common sight on the streets of the estate. These were signifiers of fear for those who lived in the private houses, and this reality threatened their perceptions of what Bourdieu describes as *doxa*.[21] Bourdieu argued that "one cannot grasp the most profound logic of the social world unless one becomes immersed in the specificity of an empirical reality" (1993a, p. 271); the BV residents had no intention of becoming immersed in an alternative BV life.

While "post-industrial cities have a growing interest in marketing themselves as being built on a foundation of "inclusive" neighborhoods capable of harmoniously supporting a blend of incomes, cultures, age-groups and lifestyles" (Rose 2004, p. 281), this was far from the intended outcomes of social mixing policies aimed at facilitating integration. The exchange between private residents that I cite later exemplifies how they automatically associate the cause of crime to the *other* without recognizing the complex dynamics among the "working classes," whom some of them so abominate. They then demand ever-greater *protection* from the *criminally inclined*, socially housed populace among whom they must walk to get from the train station to the safety of their water-fronted pockets of affluence. This fear was embodied in the multi-layered securitization rituals that are, according to Wacquant, employed as much for their symbolic qualities as for their practical usefulness (Wacquant 2009, pp. xi-xii).

This was best exemplified in the BV by private security measures such as CCTV cameras and gated enclaves, stressing the fact that the realities in this location were somewhat contrary to the social idealism that underpinned social mixing. Private housing was predominantly comprised of gated compounds or privately secured blocks of flats, which, in the small confines of the estate, amplified the sense of segregation. Interestingly, these measures not only kept the *others* out, they also worked to keep the *known* in. In every regard, including design composition, this policy seemed intent on amplifying isolation and muted segregation. It seems ironic that in a globalized age a policy intended to increase social interaction and the breaking-down of social divides the actual outcome appears, in fact, to produce an ever-greater retreat from collective life and an ever-increasing polarization.

The discourse of fear and segregation permeated the social reality of everyday life on the estate. Instances such as opportunistic robberies—usually involving easily spotted items such as mobile phones and laptops—proved problematic in terms of reaction because of the two communities's conflicting *habitus*. The private residents automatically blamed specific members of the socially housed community, but were often unable to do so publicly; so, they became ever more reclusive in the safety of their gated colonies. The main route of fear was the path leading to and from the rail station (the DLR), which cut through the heart of the estate. This was the reality of life grounded in fear; a fear mediated by the perceptions of the response to what was feared. When feared instances frequently become reality in a specific location, this location becomes a symbolic representation of physical and moral decay, of social disorder, as well as a place to avoid. However, this problem becomes increasingly complex when the place to avoid is where one lives and the location cannot be avoided if one is to get to work. As a result, instances of disorder were generally followed by policy measures, such as police sweeps, increases in the numbers of private security guards and in surveillance cameras, which further separated these communities.

Robert Park argued that the fundamental cause of prejudice about people was the insecurity of relations with *strangers* (1967); we fear the *others* simply because they are unknown. During my field research, this view was validated on both sides of the BV social divide. The language used by the private residents to describe criminality (see below) was saturated with the kind of highly emotive vernacular that exemplified the vilification of the *other* and the belief that security was the only way to be safe from such an *unknown* and *unknowable* threat (Wilkins 1991; Stenson 2001). The following extract posted in May 2011 on the on-line Community Forum, which was used almost exclusively by the private residents, reflects this kind of perception. Mark wrote, "Just passing through BV and there has been another mugging. Was walking along Wesley Road opposite Royal Docks Estate agent and heard some screaming. Initial thought was 'it's kids' but stopped to see if I could work out where it was coming from. A young woman ahead of me turned and walked back to me and I asked her is [sic] she too had heard screaming. She said she had, and that she was the woman who was mugged three weeks ago. We had a look around and walked back towards the surgery. At the front of the surgery, we found a young woman (being comforted by another older woman) who had been mugged by two black guys. They grabbed her from behind and made off with her handbag—purse, cards, the lot. They apparently ran back down towards the green, turning left behind the surgery. She called the police who, when I left, were on their way. I went to find the OMNI security guards [private security hired by private residents] but could not find them—just their empty vehicles parked up on the dockside by Eastern Quay. Wandered around a few streets and along the dock, but could not find them (the vans are usually parked there, empty!). Obviously they cannot be everywhere at the same time, but they never seem to be in the right place...which seems to be the area around the surgery and village hall. I really hope the young woman is OK and she gets her property back. Not nice for anything like this to happen to anyone."

The above intimated the expectation of crime on the "route of fear" that linked the private residences to the DLR station. As I have mentioned, this path cut through the heart of the estate and, as such, made the private residents insecure and feel like they needed protection from the socially housed residents, represented by the black muggers in the above citation. The public space that cut through both communities could be considered a *"micro-public"* space (Amin 2002); that is, a social space where individuals regularly come into contact. Amin argued that such spaces were more than spaces of encounter, commenting that they were spaces of participation that required a level of investment to sustain membership. This BV *"micro-public"* space was highly contested because, in accordance with Amin's definition, both communities were investing in it, both used this communal land for their own purposes—either as a space where to meet or as a route to work—and both sought ownership of it. Therefore, this space was inescapably central to BV life, well beyond simple geographical conceptualizations, and was symbolically and literally, a confrontational space that presented inescapable potential for literal and figurative confrontation between members of the two communities.

A private resident's response to the above posting in equal measure validated this perception and vilified the socially housed *other*. In May 2011 Tom wrote, "Gosh, aren't we sitting ducks around here? Given the recession, it does not surprise me that these incidents are becoming more frequent. Mark quite rightly said that the OMNI guys cannot be everywhere at the same time but the fact that there has now been a number of muggings in the past month strongly indicates that OMNI is not doing their job properly. They need to increase their numbers (my ex-flatmate saw these guys being attacked back in April, which proves that they lack manpower or are not an effective deterrent) and that their strategy of keeping the area safe is clearly nor [sic] working. There needs to be an urgent review of the situation. We are sitting ducks."

Travelling from the secured private enclaves to the DLR station required a journey through the heart of the socially housed. For the private residents this journey involved a crossing of boundaries, from the familiar and safe to the unfamiliar and dangerous. Tom's response was indicative of the perceptions of danger. He blamed the failure of the private security measures to protect the private residents from the dangerous *other*. These instances of criminality were seen by the private tenants as pathologies of the lower classes and signifiers of the breakdown of law and order (Banfield 1970). Thus the intimation was that in order to protect the vulnerable "sitting ducks" and increase safety in this "urban village" it was necessary to implement a greater securitization of the private residents. A comment posted by

Waseem, another private resident, on the Community forum in May 2011 further stresses this view. He wrote, "Wasn't there a member of the Royal Docks Neighbourhood Police Team that used to post on here—wonder what happened to him? Once again, I wonder if the CCTV on the green caught the thieving gits at all—I'm starting to question whether it even works."

The exchange given above suggests that affluent groups sought protection through the private security market (Hope 1999, 2001). This was indicative of a shortfall in the private residents's capacity to cope with the demands of 21st Century Newham life, which, according to Hall, is "the capacity to live with difference" (1993, p. 361). What the private residents appear to be seeking is a return to the traditional explicit conceptualizations of race, ethnicity, and class divides, such as those exemplified by many ethnographers (Whyte 1943; Liebow 1967; Anderson 1999; Duneier 1999). The differentiation between these private and socially housed communities in the social dynamics of the estate was apparent. The manager of the BV Community Centre significantly said, "The private residents want to control everything. They want to enforce from afar, they won't engage with the community. We try to put on events to bring them in, to include them, such as a Friday food market and religious meetings, but they do not engage. They just walk through the estate, in groups of two or more as they are advised to do, and quickly get to their homes. They are mostly bankers from the City and use the area as a bolt hole for work, often only five days a week. They have no interest in community engagement. They are temporary residents, for work purposes only, many young people and couples and once they have families, generally, they move away. They see the kids and the community center as a problem for the area and we try to get them to come down and engage with us but they have no interest. We are also suffering because of their political views; we are considered outside the immediate concerns of the Labour Council because the private residents are rich and so vote Conservative. That makes things even more difficult for us to implement things to help the young people of the estate" (Fieldwork notes, July 2012).

With their notions of place ownership, the private residents had, in this instance, formed pockets of intolerance and prejudice that were intrinsically exclusive and inward looking in their perspective on how life should be lived in the estate (Johnstone 2004; Herbert 2005). Their solution to the problems of the BV appeared limited to increasing security measures. When combined with an ever-increasing intolerance of the socially housed *others*, these measures gave rise to "revanchist" actions in controlling the public urban space that links the two communities (Smith 1996, 1998). Many of the socially housed residents suspected that policy makers, politicians, the police and the private residents considered them as objects to be moved or removed, depending on their ability to conform to the expectations and behavioral norms of the privately housed. As Haylett argued (2001, 2003), working-class communities are perceived as problematic in this regard by politicians and policy makers.

In the visions of urban renaissance, "normality' is commonly seen as emphatically middle class in relation to norms and values (Lees 2003; Jones and Wilks-Heeg 2004; Mooney 2004). In the BV, this contributed to a reality of *dualization of the social and physical structure* of the estate, which consigned those socially housed to economic redundancy and social marginality (Sassen 1991; Mollenkopf and Castells 1991; Fainstein, Gordon, and Harloe 1992; Wacquant 2008). They were stigmatized accordingly by those privately housed. In this regard, it seems reasonable to suggest that although place identity is imagined, it is an imaginary embodied in the quotidian context and perceived through the prism of class. In the BV this identity was formed, negotiated, and renegotiated in the houses, streets, communal spaces and, indeed, in the cyber-space. It was clear that in this shared location and in the daily interactions between the communities, identity was enforced, reinforced, challenged, and contested on a daily basis. Both these communities were on the clear quest to fulfil the fundamental human need for belonging, which in this location appeared to be mutually exclusive. With this crucial background, in the chapters that follow we move away from *Stratfordland* and the BV in order to contextualize these areas in the larger 2012 Olympic delivery narrative.

CHAPTER 4

Life in the Shadow of the Olympic Torch

The separation of the ideological and the commercial, in the context of the Olympic Games, has captured the attention of many academics. To paraphrase Bourdieu (1984), if there is no way out of the game that is being played, in this case the commercialization of Olympism, the best option is to understand the game and work out the most appropriate and useful means to achieve a favorable outcome. This view resonates throughout the following IOC statement: "Without the support of the business community, without its technology, expertise, people, services, products, telecommunications, its financing—the Olympic Games could not and cannot happen."[1] This raises the question whether it is a case of the Machiavellian iron fist of global commercialism being covered by the mitigating velvet glove of Olympism, or is it more a case of the nail of Olympism being driven home by the might of the commercial hammer. It would be logical to assume that it is a mixture of both, especially when considering that corporate branding and the attendant capitalistic ideology have become naturalized in Olympics coverage to the extent that the Olympics and commercialism are now synonymous (Slater 1998; Roche 2000; Barney et al. 2002; Scherer, Sam, and Batty 2005).

Some find it difficult to comprehend how Capitalism can fit so readily with Olympism, and vehemently voice their objections to this relationship. These critical views were encapsulated by the French Marxist Jean-Marie Brohm, who argued that, "The primary aim of the organizers of Olympic competitions is not sport for its own sake, but sport for capitalist profit" (1978, p. 117). Brohm's hypothesis of a capitalistic slant to IOC orientation was strengthened exponentially nearly three decades later when in 2005 the IOC were described as "the world's most valuable and important franchise"

(Payne 2005, p. xiv). Other research indicates that those from the commercial sectors are less concerned with Olympism as an ideology than with how, through an association with the IOC, they can use Olympism to build markets, construct brand awareness and create local–globalized consumers and identities (Rowe, McKay, and Miller 1998; Slater 1998; Jackson and Andrews 2005; Silk, Andrews, and Cole 2005; Maguire et al. 2008; Perryman 2012). The Olympics are without doubt a theatre of dreams, which sells a variety of material goods, food, and drink. For many observers, it is hard to find losers in this relationship.

The philosophical nature of the debate regarding the appropriateness of combining the pursuit of corporate commercial interest with Olympism has been addressed by various scholars (Eyquem 1976; Lenk 1979, 1984; MacAloon 1981; Segrave 1988; Maguire et al. 2008). Here, I will not explore such a relationship further; I will instead refer the interested reader to the cited literature. However, it is worth noting that this *modus operandi* has served the IOC and their partners extremely well. There is much evidence to suggest that the commercial underpinning of the Olympics has played a significant role in the global expansion of the Games over the past 30 years, at the same time directly promoting the growth and influence of the IOC (Real 1996; Whitson 1998; Smith and Schaffer 2000; Barney et al. 2002; Ritchie 2002). In this (on-going) pursuit of global significance, the IOC depends upon the media to promote themselves as an organization, their sponsors, their athletes, and the allegory of Olympism.

This is not a new process. As Espy (1979) points out, the origins of the commercialism of the IOC and the Olympic Games began in the 1960s and has expanded ever since. Crucially for my research, these commercial benefits are not limited to the IOC. As Zakus has illustrated (1992, p. 346), the economic benefits are available mostly to the bodies involved in the staging of the Games. In addition to the IOC, these bodies include the Games Organising Committee, the sub-IOC bodies (International Federations, National Olympic Committees, and so on), and other organizations involved with the myriad aspects of Olympic hosting. It seems fair to conclude that the IOC has, in the form of the Olympic Games, a unique, malleable, economically exceptional, globally alluring catalyst of change for hire. It would appear that the benefit of hosting the Games are guaranteed for the IOC, their many official (commercial) partners and whichever other bodies manage to become involved in Olympic hosting.

London's Olympic Bid

Prior to London winning the right to host 2012, the British Olympic Association (BOA)[2] had bid to host the Olympics on two separate occasions.

These bids had promoted the city of Manchester as a potential host for the 1996 and 2000 Games. Following Manchester's second Olympic bid failure, Simon Clegg, the chief executive of the BOA, conceded that as a result of their choice of Manchester they were never really in the race to host the Olympics. He said, "The very clear message was that only when we came back with London would the IOC believe we were serious about wanting to host the Olympics" (cited in Lee 2006, p. 5).

This view was echoed by the Israeli IOC member, Alex Gilady who said, "if you want to be taken seriously, come back with London" (Livingstone 2011, p. 478). So, London was seen to be the only plausible route to attain the ambition of Olympic hosting. In this regard, the Olympic Games must be evaluated in relation to the Games being a facilitator of the hegemonic tools that condense and crystallize "the processes of cultural domination and conflict" through sport (Clarke and Critcher 1985, p. 228). Therefore, the bidding process carried great significance for my research, particularly in relation to how, why and when London committed to the prerequisite time-limited, Games-related urban regeneration.[3]

The various issues involved in the competition for what is arguably the greatest prize in all of sports—that is, the "Olympic legacy"—[4] are often highly contentious affairs; the race for 2012 was no different. The conceptualization of this reward invites us to consider both the sports- and the non-sports-related outcomes that are perceived to be achievable only through Olympic hosting. This widespread conviction has led to the term "legacy" becoming both self-evident and a means to justifying and legitimizing the costs of bidding for and, then, hosting the Olympic Games. Accordingly, "legacy" is often portrayed as a panacea to address the shortfalls—economic, social, political and everything in between—of a host city. In the rest of this chapter, I explore the Olympic bidding milieu and consider the creation of the London 2012 "*legacy*" narrative and its implications in relation to 2012 Olympic outcomes.

Mike Lee, director of Communications and Public Affairs for the 2012 bid, outlined the London 2012 framework for the nuanced bidding campaign. I quote, "It was essentially like an international political campaign. We needed to understand our audiences and develop a global election manifesto. Building domestic support was important but it was just one part of the game. At times, this made us unpopular with the wider group of stakeholders who felt we should have been paying closer attention to their demands. Nevertheless, we were clearly focused on the objective and that was to win in Singapore…We also set about developing key themes that we could reinforce through presentations and communications events. The core elements were regeneration of the East End of London, the diversity of London, the legacy of the Games, use of London's landmark iconic sites, and how much the Olympics could offer British and world sport. Finally, and this was just as vital to our success, we had to get the best use of the star personalities connected to the bid... For us that was always the question we came back to—how can we develop a campaign that will attract votes and give us a chance of winning." (Lee 2006, p. 35).

The focus was to win the bid by any means necessary. To accomplish this objective, whichever themes would resonate most with the IOC delegates were those to be emphasized. East London's Olympics *"legacy"* was simply a means to win votes and influence delegates. On one level, the political processes attached to Olympic bidding can be defined in terms of strategies that favor urban economic development, consumption and the image of the host city (Burbank et al. 2001). In the pursuit of winning, however, the success of the political machinations involved in the bid depended upon appealing to the IOC selectors and ticking their boxes. This was far removed from the concerns of what were arguably the principal stakeholders of the bid; that is, the East London communities where the Games would take place.

The message from the IOC selectors was very clear. Second tier British cities, such as Birmingham or Manchester, were simply not feasible for a UK Olympics. As London's Mayor Ken Livingstone's personal reflections revealed, only a London bid would do. He wrote, "The IOC insist on support of the host city's administration before accepting a bid... Within months of my election [as London's Mayor] the BOA's Craig Reedie and Simon Clegg came to outline their work on possible sites... in the East End it could be the catalyst for twenty years of regeneration... if the BOA would site the Olympics in the Docklands [East London],[5] I would throw everything behind it... and agreed there would be a contribution from [London] council tax payers... a legacy from the games, some continuing benefit from them, was crucial to the IOC and needed a post-2012 commitment of £10 million a year to run the facilities the Games would leave behind. At the key meeting civil servants insisted no government could commit its successor to this so I said I would commit the Mayor's office to support the facilities after the games. Horrified at seeing a decision taken rapidly, a civil servant said, 'You can't do that' but the sports people smiled as I said, 'I think you'll find I just did'" (Livingstone 2011, pp. 478–481).

Ultimately, the financial deal that solidified the 2012 bid was a relatively straightforward affair combining National Lottery (NL) contributions and investment from the London Mayor's office and London taxpayers. Some £1.5 billion would come from the NL and the remaining £900 million from Livingstone, through the London Development Agency (LDA),[6] the Mayor's regeneration body, and an increase in Londoners' council taxes.

This financial package symbolically and literally united the New Labour government, both locally and nationally, behind the 2012 Olympic bid and identified specific East London locales and their communities. The consequences of this held the potential to alter the lives of many East London citizens and to impact directly on policy decisions. The outcome of all this will undoubtedly be frequently returned to in the political realm; a process in which the notion of accountability will probably be missing.

One key credential of any successful bid is its ability to generate significant public support for the venture; for Olympic bidding to gain traction, evidence of such support needs to be supplied. At the outset of London's Olympic hosting crusade, David Stubbs was employed as London 2012 Head of Environment in order to assess the practicalities of the London 2012 bid. In 2005, Stubbs stated that to be a credible candidate, public support was critical and London had to "engage with the community so that they felt part of the process."[7] Stubbs went on to explain that his "advisory group"—made up of representatives from NGOs, public authorities, academia, and business—"did a lot of work with the voluntary groups to get them involved in the process. By the end, they were really championing the whole thing" (cited in Kinver 2005).[8]

But was this really the case? The case study given in the following section indicates a London 2012 delivery reality seen from the perspective of the community representatives who were included in the bidding process. It illustrates how during the bidding phase the local communities were portrayed as being "behind the Games." The unified front claimed by Stubbs was the product of an interaction with selected members and groups; then portrayed as indicative of community attitudes.

Backing the Bid?

The London 2012 Bidding Committee approached The East London Citizens Organisation (TELCO) to seek their contribution to the bidding process. TELCO (formed in 1996) encompasses an alliance of active citizens and community leaders that promotes democratically selected causes intended to benefit the local community. TELCO were a social movement that acted on behalf of East London's citizens in the negotiations with the Olympic delivery team.

TELCO felt that their support for the 2012 bid should be conditional upon the Bidding Committee's offering certain guarantees to the benefit of the East London population. These guarantees included employment opportunities, affordable housing, greater sporting provisions, and better educational opportunities. An agreement was put in place to publicize the rewards for public demonstrations of support for Olympic hosting. This became known as the "*Ethical Olympic Charter*," consisting of six key points:

   i. Affordable homes to be built for local people and managed through a Community Land Trust, where the value of the land is removed from the property price—making homes more affordable.
  ii. Olympic development monies to be set aside to improve local schools and health services.
 iii. University of East London to be the main higher education beneficiary of the sports legacy, with a view to becoming a sporting center of excellence.
  iv. At least £2m to be set aside immediately (upon winning the bid to coincide with the first building phase) for the construction of an academy in Leyton to train local people in employable trades.
   v. That at least 30% of construction jobs be set aside for local people, which would require the implementation of a 30% local labour clause with the contractors responsible for construction.
  vi. The Lower Lea Valley to be designated a "living wage" zone with jobs in the defined boundary guaranteed to pay a "living wage" (set at £6.70 per hour in 2004).

The proposed benefits were agreed upon between the TELCO and the Olympic bidding team. As a result, Lord Coe stated that the Games were now "eminently more winnable" (Lydall 2004, p. 12). This agreement was solidified through a public signing in 2005. Signing on behalf of the Olympic Bidding Team were its Chair, Lord Sebastian Coe, the incumbent Mayor Ken Livingstone and John Biggs, Deputy Chair of the LDA.

This act of unifying the community through a written agreement between Olympic deliverers and TELCO was meant to address the expectations of the local population. This was an agreement that encouraged hope, promise, and expectation. The assurances evidenced by the signatories of the "*Ethical Olympic Charter*" instilled a sense of ownership of place, and of the resources therein, during Olympic delivery and beyond; they instilled a sense of entitlement among the communities represented by TELCO, which were generally fragmented entities in the varied post-industrial, transitory, impoverished, and deprived Newham. The members of the communities whose everyday lives would be the most severely affected by 2012 Olympic delivery were assured that they would benefit commensurately.

As Foreign Secretary Jack Straw reminded Parliament the day after London was announced as the 2012 Olympic host, the London bid was premised upon "a special Olympic vision. That vision of an Olympic Games that would not only be a celebration of sport but a force for regeneration. The Games will transform one of the poorest and most deprived areas of London. They will create thousands of jobs and homes. They will offer new opportunities for business in the immediate area and throughout London... One of the things that made the bid successful is the way in which it reaches out to all young people in two important respects: it will encourage many more to get fit and to be involved in sport and, whatever their physical prowess, to offer their services as volunteers for the Olympic cause" (Hansard, House of Commons, July 6, 2005).

It seems evident that the 2012 bid was disseminated as a panacea to make East London healthy, literally, socially, and economically. The Games were to be a special-purpose vehicle for these outcomes, which reached far beyond the sporting domain and whose success depended on how this ideal Olympic "*legacy*" narrative resonated throughout Britain and beyond.

An Ethical Olympics?

While "Olympic *legacy*" had been the buzzword of the 2012 Games, some local communities felt strongly that the much-anticipated Olympic delivery benefits would not help local communities. These groups attempted to raise community concerns by creating a dialogue with the Olympic deliverers; their aim was to challenge the hegemony of Olympic delivery and make the process more accountable to the public. The complex interplay involved in these processes is explored in the following case study that returns to the *Ethical Olympic* charter.

Following the successful bid, TELCO's priority was to solidify the *Ethical Olympic* charter with the relevant parties; notably the Mayoral Office, the LDA responsible for upholding the Mayoral pledges, and the newly formed Olympic Delivery Authority (ODA).[9] Theoretically, the local government should be accountable for anything occurring within its designated boundaries, yet the pressure to see the 2012 Olympics up and running necessitated the transfer of control to the ODA, which was accountable only to the central government. This ensured that the ODA had relative freedom from local authority planning controls and regulations. Meanwhile, while the LDA maintained a rapport with TELCO concerning the *Ethical Olympic* charter, the "living wage" and proposed construction of academies now fell outside the LDA mandate, making it imperative that a dialogue between TELCO and the ODA be established.

However, the ODA would not meet with TELCO and refused even to acknowledge them. As the ODA had not been in existence when the agreement was signed, they claimed that TELCO's "*Ethical Olympics*" was not their concern. Consequently, in an attempt to achieve ODA recognition, TELCO organized a collective action and picketed the hotels providing the high-power breakfast meetings favored by David Higgins (the ODA chief executive).

This nuisance tactic attracted some local and national media attention for TELCO and eventually led to a series of meetings with Higgins.

Community Consultation: The Discursive Battlefield

These meetings provided TELCO with the chance to question the ODA on behalf of the community through negotiation. Their inclusion in the talks was given value because of the investment required to get a seat at the table. In this context, some TELCO members became concerned that, should they dispute matters too strongly, they might jeopardize a relationship they had worked hard to forge and would then have to start again from scratch. The consultation meetings formed a symbolic battlefield where language, and its mastery, was the weapon of choice. As with other weapons, the impact of language and organized discourse depends on the skills and experience of the users, as the following excerpt from my field notes of June 2008 illustrates, the Olympic deliverers were in possession of machine guns, while the community representatives wielded peashooters:

> After a short walk from the underground station, I arrived at the TELCO offices to meet the team who were finally ready to hold the ODA to account regarding the lack of Olympic-delivery opportunities for local people. I was representing Aston Mansfield and was eagerly anticipating meeting the other democratically chosen TELCO representatives who were my equivalents form various other community groups. The small ensemble whom I met was drawn from a pool of members who were available for this 1 pm meeting, held on a Tuesday afternoon in London's Docklands.
>
> As is TELCO custom, the team personified diversity and this was arguably their primary strength. This band of brothers [and sisters] about to march off into discursive battle included school children, religious leaders, teachers, retirees, housewives, students and two full-time members of the TELCO team. As they spoke, I began to get a sinking feeling. Although diversity and inclusion was commendable and fully in accord with the spirit of TELCO's democracy, I couldn't help worrying about this group's varying levels of discursive competence, as they marched towards the underground station. Thus commenced their journey towards the luxurious ODA conference rooms located at the top of one of the shiny Canary Wharf skyscrapers.
>
> I was still unsure exactly what our objectives in this meeting were to be but, reassuringly, they were to stop for coffee and a strategy discussion before they entered the scheduled meeting. I hoped that one of these bright young persons would provide me with an amazing scheme outlining what they wanted to discover, exactly how they would discover it and what they

wanted the ODA to do next. As they sat in a café over cups of tea and coffee, the excitement was palpable. They would get answers to why local people weren't getting jobs on the construction sites; they would find out how the ODA were enforcing the London living wage and they would get them to commit to a series of progress-report meetings in the near future.

Caffeinated and confident they arrived, striding across the marbled floor. After being searched by security they were directed to some leather sofas to wait. They sat and waited; the ticking of the expensive clock on the wall was matched by the footsteps of the unending hordes of suits who eyed them suspiciously as if they were something altogether foreign. Half an hour ticked by. Confidence was eroding. Agitation and nervousness was kicking in and, for most, the caffeine had been passed into the bathrooms by the time they were eventually collected and taken to the top floor in the well-polished, mirrored lifts that only operated with a confident swipe of an ID card.

David Higgins and his PA led them into the conference room, apologising for the wait, and proceeded to spend the next ten minutes expounding platitudes and outlining the fantastic progress made so far on the Olympic site. Then, after 15 minutes of foreplay, the moment, their opportunity to ask their questions, arrived; this was their chance to really put the ODA on the spot and get their much-valued answers. It started promisingly. Higgins made rapid notes in his leather-bound notebook. Optimistic glances were exchanged, until it became clear that the two religious leaders on the team were not singing from the same hymn sheet. They disagreed on the level of importance of the two crucial points of the meeting—namely, wages and the hiring of local people—and began to interrupt each other.

The ODA resolutely maintained that 95 per cent of the Olympic work-force was earning over and above the average wage and that guidelines were in place to hire local residents—proof of residence would be required from those seeking work on the Olympic site. This was challenged by raising the point that, because tenure of residency was not stipulated, those described as 'local residents' might only have been living in the area for 24 hours before being offered employment. Therefore, it was argued, the guidelines must surely only be a means of placating local people rather than actually improving their employment prospects. No immediate answer was forthcoming from the ODA. Silence momentarily prevailed, until one of the religious leaders took the opportunity to break the silence and change the course of the conversation to her own personal agenda. Thus the issue was left unresolved, with Higgins saying, somewhat relieved, 'we can only do so much.'

After this, the meeting petered out and all members of the TELCO team were presented with glossy ODA packs that illustrated Olympic progress. Promises were made to look into the points raised and to email the results in due course. Once diaries had been checked, a follow-up meeting would be arranged at some point in the future. With that, all went back in the lift. The sinking feeling in the stomachs of the group may well have been the result of plummeting towards earth in the light-speed lift, or of the inescapable feeling that they had just been run rings round by the ODA and had achieved little. I would witness this feeling becoming commonplace throughout Olympic delivery and most evidently during the community's consultations with the Olympic deliverers.

Participation in consultation, a field in which community groups attempted to challenge the hegemonic order of Olympic delivery, was only possible if the participants had the resources, the time and the abilities to gain access to dialogue. Once access had been negotiated, the community groups were far less likely than the Olympic deliverers to possess the sort of social capital necessary for achieving the desired outcomes. Anyone aspiring to succeed in this kind of political field needed the right social capital, the right contacts, the requisite amount of cultural capital and a feel for the game of political discourse. This need for social and cultural capital generally ensured that those who controlled the balance during community consultations sat on the side of the Olympic deliverers at the negotiating table.

Community Representative Recruitment

It is relatively straightforward to see the strengths of the Olympic deliverers and the apparent weaknesses of the local communities in the contestations that took place during Olympic delivery. In order to consider the value and validity of the local communities' attempts to challenge the perceived disparity, we need to look at how these groups were formed. As Brown argues (2007, p. 213), to motivate communities to become active, it is important for community organizers to deliver the message that they are "not in the business to serve you. It is your group. You, the members, are responsible." This philosophy is vital to establish a sense of collective ownership and of personal responsibility for the group's advancement.

TELCO promoted this philosophy by giving group members the opportunity to be integrated in all aspects of the movement. However, as Kleidman and Rochon (1997) demonstrate, difficulties often arise in such situations, for the balance between presenting a professional structure and still remain inclusive to all (and incorporating well-intentioned but less able volunteers) can be problematic. This difficulty became significant in another of TELCO's Olympic-related meetings. My fieldwork notes of July 2008 read,

I have gradually found that the TELCO representatives often had little or no negotiating experience. Many were often unable to comprehend the nuances of the wider political debate—something well mastered by those they met, such as Labour Whip and GLA member, John Biggs. After one meeting in July 2008 on TELCO "home turf" (their Whitechapel HQ), Biggs commented that he had been shocked at the 'easy ride' he'd been given; he had expected a group of Londoners intent on social change to be more fervent or aggressive. Yet, in the post-meeting TELCO discussion, which involved all TELCO delegates, the debate focused on the meeting's 'good points,' ignoring the fact that they had failed to gain the additional information which Biggs, in his parting comments, had hinted that he was willing to divulge.

TELCO were typical of most of the community groups with which I interacted during my research, in that they were represented by individuals who lacked experience in political discussion, debate, and nuance, did not have the contacts or the resources to compete and did not have the necessary information (obtainable through research) to challenge the dominant narratives. Consequently, the field of community consultation was dominated by a perpetual interplay between the powerful and the powerless, whereby the "communities" were dominated because of their lack of the right sort of capital to compete in these games. In this regard, the Olympic deliverers controlled the facts, the official discourse, and the legitimate language.

Symbolic Power

TELCO's Olympic delivery role was very anticlimactic and did little to achieve their goals, which led to different interpretations as to the success of the endeavor. Srinivasa (2006, p. 30) highlights how, in the information flow of any system, information can become distorted and how this generates various alternative versions of an event. This provides one theoretical explanation as to how TELCO members formulated different interpretations of the same meetings and formed diverging agendas for future progress.

Additionally, the organized protest demonstrations that provided TELCO with the opportunity for dialogue with the Olympic deliverers were considered a victory for this community organization. This ensured that a value was placed on achieving a seat at the negotiating table. On the other hand, the ODA pursued a strategy of carefully limiting community dialogue and community inclusion. Such a strategy generated a sense of value for those occupying seats at the discussion table, for it was translated into a sense that these selected groups, in this case TELCO, were special and facilitated a sense of gratitude from those who were included. My fieldwork notes of July 2008 provide an example. They read,

> after the ODA meeting with Higgins, segments of TELCO considered the need for more social action—namely, public protest; others, however, favoured further committee-room discourse. Many TELCO members were unable to challenge critically the distorted information they were offered from the ODA, which further emphasised the need for better planning, reflective group meetings, and good leadership. Matthew Bolton, one of two full-time Community Organisers employed by TELCO for over five years, defended TELCO by arguing that anyone selected to speak at a meeting was already an expert in their field, by virtue of their experience, and that TELCO included many who knew a lot about a little; an attitude that, he felt, stands up well to those who know a little about a lot. Furthermore, he argued that prior to every meeting all members were as well briefed as possible, that at the end of every meeting a period of reflective learning takes place and that these learning experiences are then, ideally, taken back to their individual groups. This, he contended, increases the individual and collective skill-sets and subsequently strengthens TELCO.

It proved prudent for the ODA to give the community groups the impression that they were an entity willing to compromise and negotiate. This kept malcontents at the negotiating table and dissuaded them from protesting on the streets. The insidious nature of Olympic delivery was exemplified by the fact that those groups that publicly challenged the authority and legitimacy of 2012 Olympic delivery and gathered sufficient support were rewarded with a dialogue. To follow Poulantzas (1973), Olympic deliverers—as hegemonic structures—had the dual function of representing the general interest of the people/nation, while maintaining dominance over how this "interest" was defined and pursued. Olympic deliverers kept control and strengthened their position by conceding some pre-determined acceptable ground, thereby placating opponents with the illusion of progress, and maintaining their hegemony.

Olympic hegemony consists in the dominant representations and practices of those in power who maintain the "dominant story lines" to consolidate their standing (Agnew 1998, p. 6). The ODA disseminated this perception by ceding a modicum of symbolic power to TELCO in view of future meetings between the two groups. For TELCO, this indicated legitimacy and progress, but it had very little impact on the meetings. TELCO had cultivated a system to control the flow of information during meetings in order to maximize their opportunities with organizations such as the ODA, which were notoriously smooth operators. This was achieved by requesting at the outset of a meeting that a pre-determined TELCO member should chair them. TELCO's paid Community

Organisers would brief the chair on the points to be raised, on the ideal duration of the debate and on who would present the issues to be discussed. The chair was intended to control the progression toward a predetermined set of objectives by ensuring that progress was made on each point in a timely fashion.

As Srinivasa (2006) states, the effective use of such information crucially depends on the selective release, or indeed the withholding, of information. While, theoretically, the chairing of meetings was a sound proposal, in Olympic delivery reality, it proved flawed because this stratagem is only as successful as the choice of chair. For example, at one TELCO/ODA meeting that was intended to produce updates on the Ethical Olympics, a 16-year-old schoolboy was selected to chair the interplay. In my fieldwork notes of July 2008, I recorded what followed. They read,

> During this hour-long discussion, the ODA regularly talked over the unconfident chair, who looked completely out of his depth when confronted by two wily veterans of boardroom interplay. The ODA delegates never deviated from a carefully choreographed script and were clearly intent on delaying events and limiting the information that we (TELCO) required. When pushed, they reverted to their script or to the stock answer of not having at hand the necessary information to answer the questions asked; most notably, this information related to construction employment figures. This might, of course, have been true, although the problem could have been easily avoided through better pre-meeting planning and communication between TELCO and the ODA. It was clear from the brief analysis that TELCO should have requested the information prior to this meeting in order to ensure a more informative discourse. The lack of forethought and the consequent absence of the data prevented any real progress at the meeting. TELCO were reassured that the data would be available later, via e-mail, from the department that had those figures. Even though they came to the meeting short of the facts and figures necessary for TELCO to argue against any lack of substantial progress regarding their campaign, the ODA representatives did produce another 'Site Update" leaflet, which again demonstrated the "excellent Olympic progress' that they were making.

A post-consultation TELCO meeting emphasized the symbolic power of the Olympic deliverers; a kind of power that, according to Bourdieu, "can be exercised only with the complicity of those who do not want to know that they are subject to it" (1991, p. 164). Bourdieu argues that symbolic power is similar to gravity in that, although it is clearly restrictive and limiting, it is not regarded as oppressive; it simply is. Similarly, Bourdieu believed that individuals comply with domination not through agreement but because no practical alternative course of action is available that is considered likely to produce a different outcome. On this topic in *Masculine Domination*[10] he writes, "By what might be called the paradox of doxa—the fact that the order of the world as we find it, with its one-way streets and its no entry signs, whether literal or figurative, its obligations and its penalties, is broadly respected; that there are not more transgressions and subversions...still more surprisingly, that the established order, with its relations of domination...ultimately perpetuates itself so easily" (Bourdieu 2001, p. 1).

Strength in Numbers

As the examples given above indicate, the dichotomy of power between community groups and Olympic deliverers proved problematic for tangible results to come from a discursive interplay between the two groups. That is not to say that community groups do not wield substantive power in certain situations. However, it appeared that this power was most effectively wielded through the use of ambush tactics. The example below, taken from my fieldwork notes of June 2008, indicates this:

> TELCO's intermittent strength was evident at an Olympic legacy public meeting held in Newham in 2006, when members adopted what they called a "pincer movement" strategy. This involved members spreading themselves around the room and barracking, from various locations, any speaker who avoided answering a question. This strategy gave the illusion that a wide and articulate audience was present, and increased the pressure on the speaker. This tactic unsettled the authorities present. A TELCO member asked Lord Coe 'who would pay the council tax for the Olympic Stadium and the new facilities after the Games finish?' Coe avoided giving a direct answer and was barracked by the dispersed members. Ultimately, he conceded to the pressure in the room and stated that the University of East London (UEL) would pay the council tax—at which point (according to TELCO members in the audience) the UEL representative 'nearly fell off her chair,' insisting that such an imposition would bankrupt the institution.

In attempting to challenge the hegemonic structure of Olympic delivery, community groups such as TELCO were competing against the organizations backed by a national "*Olympic identity.*" These major organizations enjoyed a multitude of resources and a vastly superior accumulation of capital and were able to both dominate the consultation outcomes and easily navigate their way past community concerns. As Bourdieu advocates, in such contexts the dominated groups are often unaware of their complicity with the domineering discourse of such interactions.

As exemplified by the ODA, the Olympic delivery governance structures were characterized less by democratic properties and more by hegemonic objectives. As Swyngedouw, Moulaert, and Rodrigues (2002, p. 34) stated, such organizations are particularly skilled in giving the impression that their actions are democratic and legitimate when decisions are actually made well in advance with little or no possibility of reversal. The consequence of this philosophy is that all community consultation events, such as the TELCO/ODA interactions, were token gestures aimed at maintaining the façade of democratic process; one in which the community had no real possibility of influencing any decision that would be made.

This on-going consultation process was a peculiar abstraction to observe, particularly in relation to the intended community outcomes and motivations for participation. Basically, it was obvious that when a position of representation and dialogue was secured and consultations occurred it was extremely difficult, if not impossible, to affect change. However, as Sherry Arnstein wrote regarding such participation in the decision-making process, "Citizen participation is a categorical term for citizen power" (1969, p. 216; see also Dowding, Dunleavy, King, and Margetts 1995). It is thus significant to explore the validity of Olympic delivery community inclusion, and what it represents, regardless of the likelihood of affecting change. To

Figure 4.1 Burns, Hambleton, and Hoggett's Ladder (1994, p.16)

Citizen Control

12. Independent control
11. Entrusted control

Citizen Participation

10. Delegated control
9. Partnership
8. Limited decentralized decision making
7. Effective advisory boards
6. Genuine consultation
5. High-quality information

Citizen Non-Participation

4. Customer care
3. Poor information
2. Cynical consultation
1. Civic hype

analyze TELCO's participation in Olympic delivery discourse is to consider their power. In this regard Burns, Hambleton, and Hoggett's 12-rung ladder of citizen empowerment can be applied (1994, p. 161).

The evidence discussed in this section could, in accordance with Burns et al.'s classification guide,[11] be classified as a "citizen non-participation" that speaks to a lack of citizen power during Olympic delivery. The examples given provide an indication of the many community consultation events that I attended during the course of this research, all pointing toward the same conclusion—that Olympic delivery consultation events were tokenistic tick-box exercises or "cynical consultations" that delivered "poor information." The "outsiders" who were given access were only permitted to represent a specific perspective, that of the "community." Furthermore, they were only authorized to discuss specific issues in relation to specific concerns. This effectively restricted the role of their representatives to little more than information givers/gatherers, with little or no legitimate power. Regardless of the actualities of consultation, the fact that they existed provided Olympic deliverers with an illusion of equity, which they were able to trade off when challenged on the lack of community inclusion and which provided them with proof that the views and perspectives of marginalized groups were represented during Olympic delivery. One has to conclude that TELCO were emblematic of a larger community who became dispossessed and silenced during Olympic delivery.

These processes are indicative of Gramsci's postulation that power relations need to be sustained by more than brute force and economic domination, that power must be constantly re-made by securing common consent (cited in Rowe 2004). The uneven negotiation process demonstrated by TELCO's pursuit of an "Ethical Olympics" was evocative of the strategy of providing subordinate and subaltern groups with sporadic tactical "victories" that illustrate "progress" but do not provide any significant challenge to hegemonic structures.

Unsurprisingly, TELCO drifted away from their pursuit of an ethical Olympics to focus on other democratically selected concerns, such as their *"CitySafe"* campaign.[12] As we shall see in later chapters, other groups sporadically emerged in their stead, pursuing entry into a consultation process for a myriad other causes. The futility of these consultations contributed to the impression that the dominated communities were unable to compete with the Olympic deliverers. TELCO were not a mass movement. They could not claim to speak for all Newham residents and it could not be said that all residents were in support of or were even aware of their *"Ethical Olympics"* campaign. We now turn our attention to the consequences of Olympic delivery for Newham residents, starting with Olympic-related employment.

CHAPTER 5

Employment and Capital Gains

In this chapter, I look at Newham's employment realities, perceptions, and possibilities and consider how these were affected by Olympic delivery. In particular, I shall explore the practicalities and assumptions that underpinned the notion that Olympic delivery would provide a large number of employment opportunities for local people. I shall then consider Newham's ability to benefit from the employment opportunities that were created by the Olympics, offering an evaluation as to whether these should have ever been considered as beneficial for or accessible to the majority of Newham residents. Ultimately, this chapter examines the impact that localized perceptions of a lack of Olympic delivery employment opportunities for "local people" had upon the "*legacy*" narrative and the overall perceptions of the 2012 Olympic Games. Let me start with an overview of Newham's employment demographics.

Newham's Olympic Employment

Statistics published in the 2011 Aston Manfield (AM) report[1] showed that Newham was not seeing the expected widespread Olympic delivery benefits. The report indicated that in 2008–09 Newham's employment rate was the lowest in London at just 56.2%, significantly below the average London rate of 62.7%. The report commented that "over recent years this gap widened with employment rates for women and ethnic minorities being particularly low, for women 46% (compared to the London average of 62%) and ethnic minorities 49% (compared to 59% across London)." These statistics indicated that Newham's Olympic delivery employment boon was not narrowing the gap with other boroughs; instead, the gap was increasing.

This AM document demonstrated that levels of what in political circles is referred to as "economic inactivity" were higher in Newham than anywhere else in the country. The categorization of those not in paid employment included the sick, the disabled, caregivers, students, and retirees. Of these 57,000 Newham residents, less than one in five were recorded as "wanting to work." The report illustrated that Newham had far more manual, poorly paid workers than anywhere else in the country and far fewer workers in management or professional occupations. During 2009–10 the employment rates increased in both Newham and London (Newham's employment rate was 59.5%). However, in this period the negative difference between Newham and the rest of London grew from 6.5% in 2008–09 to 8.6% in 2009–10 (the London average for this period standing at 68.1%). This picture did not meet the Olympic expectations. This should not have been the case. As the Borough Council explained, "The London 2012 Games represent a once-in-a-lifetime opportunity for us to raise the profile of the borough, improve our transport networks and inspire people to participate in sport and healthy lifestyles. They will speed up the regeneration of Newham, East London... providing hundreds of jobs and business opportunities before, during and after 2012. To ensure that we take full advantage of this opportunity, we have set six objectives [which included the maximisation of]... the Games delivery process to develop a thriving economic legacy—*where all people share in the growing prosperity*" (Newham London website, accessed in 2009, emphasis in original[2]).

The difference between the much promoted employment opportunities and the statistics produced during the Olympic delivery period indicated that employment opportunities were either not reaching local people at the expected level or were not in fact those that the local communities had been promised. The fact that local people were not gaining employment prompted the Mayor of Newham, Sir Robin Wales to launch a scathing attack on the residents of the borough at a conference organized by the Commission for Racial Equality during a debate regarding London 2012 and its benefits for ethnic minorities. His comments, printed in a national newspaper,[3] described Newham residents as follows. They

- Were too idle to get jobs on 2012 projects.
- Struggled to get out of bed before 11 a.m.
- Were used to being unemployed.
- Had the sole aspiration in life to be given a council house.
- Were lazy and the outcome of their laziness was the hiring of Eastern Europeans to fill the employment void.

Responses to the above comments reverberated around Newham's Third Sector organizations. Robin Wales was dismissed as a heavy drinker and as a man prone to outlandishly foolish comments that he would later seek to retract. Throughout Newham's Third Sector, the comment was made that he "was as much of an arsehole as we thought he was." It was also accepted that there were few, if any, possibilities to get rid of him as a mayor because he was publically elected—the only possibility was for him to stand down or be defeated at an election. Somewhat perversely, however, there was also a commonly held begrudging deference to him as an incredibly astute politician who would prove very difficult to defeat on any issue. One such issue concerned hard-working incomers to Newham.

Eastern People but Not East-Enders

The perception that "Eastern Europeans" were filling the Newham employment void and taking the indigenous communities' jobs highlights the preposterousness of attitudes around race and ethnicity in Newham. Here, vast majorities are immigrants or the sons and daughters of immigrants, and the only difference among the many groups that form Newham's diverse cultural mosaic lies in the length of stay. Sir Robin's comments did, however, resonate with some members of the white working class whom I met during my field research. The following excerpt is from a conversation with Maureen, a "decanted" member of the Carpenters Estate, aged 75, white Irish, and a life-long resident of Stratford. Maureen is now living in Forrest Gate some two miles away. Her remarks indicate the complexities of having what might best be considered aging white working class values in contemporary Newham. She said, "I don't hate foreigners; there's just too many of them. Where I live (Carpenters), I'm the foreigner. Even Ava moans about it and she's Iranian. You can't go to Stratford now and hear English, and going to the doctor's (on Carpenters Estate, which had its own surgery) is like going to Bangladesh. Those I don't like are the Eastern Europeans, even the Indians moan about them. Everyone knows that if there are jobs going over there (points to the Olympic Park in construction) the English need not apply" (Private interview, November 2009).

The Olympic Park was the largest construction site in Europe during the Olympic delivery years and, as such, it attracted many immigrant workers seeking employment. The examples of politicians' declarations, community members' remarks, and media articles that are analyzed here provide easy-to-follow narratives that blame both local people and foreigners for these construction jobs not being filled by Newham's residents. What follows explores why this was the case and considers the reality of Olympic construction employment through the use of case studies. The analysis begins with the story of two Eastern Russian immigrants who came to Newham specifically to take advantage of Olympic employment and thus formed a small part of this vilified group of economic occupiers.

Maria and Yosh: Coming in from the Cold

I draw on my fieldwork notes of September 2011 on Maria and Yosh. They were both 28 years old and came from a small town near Siberia. They had many tales of the bleak, cold landscape that they called home and welcomed the opportunity to work in the relative warmth and luxury of Newham. Back home, Yosh was an "odd-job" man and Maria was a schoolteacher. Between them they earned very little in Russia and struggled to make ends meet. They lived in a small house with Maria's parents and their four-year-old daughter. In 2009, they decided to move to Newham and try to save enough money to return home and buy a house of their own. They left their daughter with her grandparents and came to the UK to seek a better future by becoming part of Newham's Olympic gold rush. Upon arrival they rented a small room in a shared house; in this room they washed, cooked, ate, and slept. The house was a three-bedroom, one bathroom terrace that they shared with 9 other Russian men who were seeking construction work on the Olympic site too.

Yosh, like the other men in the house, found work through a Russian contact he had been told to meet in a local pub and began manual unskilled minimum-wage labor on the site almost immediately. The men worked long hours. The work was hard. Life in the house was noisy as most nights were alcohol fueled, as it is likely to be when nine young men live together. However, the couple was generally happy with their lot.

Maria, despite being a qualified teacher, sought work in Newham in any employment area she could. She, like Yosh, did not speak much English, so communication—and employment—was difficult. Eventually, she stumbled into a Kurdish café where the owners also did not speak much English, which was the only thing they had in common. Somehow, through a laborious exchange in pidgin English, Maria got her message across that she was looking for work and, to her delight, was offered a job serving all-day breakfasts. Now, also for Maria, Newham life entailed working long hours for low pay.

As the novelty wore off and reality began to set in, the transition into Newham life began to take its toll on Maria and Yosh. While Maria gradually learnt to speak Turkish to communicate with her employers and co-workers, she continued to speak very little English, Yosh likewise. So, they had problems understanding life outside their particular diaspora. Language and cultural barriers became minimized, however, as they became more and more inclined to stick to their own. A more pressing issue was the cost of living. Although they were living in squalid and over-crowded conditions, they found the cost of rent prohibitively high, and the savings they expected to make were not materializing. Therefore, after a year away from their daughter, they decided to return to Maria's parents' house in Eastern Russia. Maria returned to a £15 per month teaching position, Yosh sought manual work. Their dream of building a house out of Olympic gold failed to reach fruition.

Local and national newspapers perpetuated the view that people like Maria and Yosh were taking Olympic employment away from more deserving local people. This view was disseminated through headlines such as:

- 579,000 East Europeans register for work (*The Telegraph*, February 28, 2007)
- Influx of 10,000 foreign workers for Olympic jobs (London Evening Standard, March 4, 2009)
- Polish plumbers return: Number of migrant workers from East Europe hits new high (*The Daily Mail*, November 18, 2010)

Figure 5.1 The Froud Community Center.

We have seen, however, that it was not plain sailing for those who did move from Eastern Europe. My fieldwork notes of May 2012 bring this point graphically home. In 2009, I noted, two filthy, smelly, disheveled Eastern Europeans were found sleeping in the doorway of AM Froud Community Centre. It was AM policy to offer such rough sleepers a cup of tea and some food but never any money and to request them to move away from the center's entry point. The two men graciously accepted such charity and went on their way. This ritual continued for some days as a relationship began to develop between the two men and an AM's British cleaner; through these daily slow and stilted morning exchanges in Pidgin English, a level of trust and understanding grew among them.

It transpired that the two men, Stan and Evgeny, had moved from Russia seeking Olympic-related employment but, once here, found things incredibly difficult. They had not found the construction work that they were expecting and had ran out of money very quickly. They could not afford to return to Russia and soon they had to resort to sleeping on the streets. To make sleeping rough a little more bearable, they turned first to alcohol and then to drugs. Both were now addicted to heroin, a habit they funded through acquisitive crime; notably shoplifting and stealing items from parked cars.

Despite concern expressed by other members of AM staff, about the wisdom of helping obvious strangers and drug dealers, the AM cleaner offered these two men the opportunity to get their lives back on track and invited them to sleep in her home in Manor Park. This was a very strict arrangement, whereby the men were only permitted to stay in the house while she was present, generally between 10:00 pm and 5:00 am—when she left for work in the morning. This regime suited Evgeny, who remained. Stan, however, went back to the streets after a few weeks and was not heard from again. Evgeny even managed to abstain from drugs and enrolled in ESOL (English for speakers of other languages) classes.[4] He became clean (literally and figuratively) and in mid-2012 was in search of gainful employment.

Contracts for Olympic delivery construction were awarded to construction companies through competitive tender. Project completion was extremely time-sensitive and a considerable amount of employment came about through sub-contracting. Olympic deliverers could not easily regulate such "subbing-out," nor could others who sought to monitor the demographics of those hired to work. Hiring in this milieu was, to a large extent, conducted through word of mouth. The proportion of employment opportunities going to local workers was always questionable. Jobs went to men who knew men who were hiring. Some of these only employed foreign-born professional labor. Though not widely followed, this practice was calculated, for those employed were used to poor wages and long hours in their native countries. A more significant issue was matching local skills to the specialist requirements of the construction period. There was simply insufficient time to redress the balance between the skill requirements of the construction companies and the existing skills of the Newham workforce. The following case material illustrates this point.

The Immigrant Job Thieves

Newham's Albanian population provides an example of Eastern Europeans who could be classed as representative of those who were vilified during the Olympic delivery period, despite the vast majority having been Newham residents long before the Games, most having arrived in the early 1990s.[5] Having been in Newham for the previous decade, some Albanian residents formed an organization known as the *Shpresa* program. This was a user-led organization that promoted the participation of Albanian-speaking residents in the wider community. Shpresa was established in Newham in 2001 to fulfil a self-diagnosed community need to facilitate opportunities for Albanians in many aspects of everyday life, including employment and socialization opportunities. They aimed to provide advice, help, and support to their members and, since 2005, have been a registered charity receiving numerous awards, including in 2006 the nationally recognized Queen's Award for Volunteering. Shpresa support some 500 people per week and are funded through a combination of membership fees and government grants.

An interview held in October 2011 with Luljeta, a 37-year-old white female Albanian who was a founding member of Shpresa, illustrates aspects of the Albanian diaspora in Newham and gives, in a sense, the Albanian perspective on Olympic-related employment. Luljeta said,

> Albanian culture is very family-oriented and traditional in its values. The men are seen as the providers; they work and women raise the children. However, in the UK such cultural mores are different. The men have had a difficult time in adjusting and have had great difficulty in finding work and are often turned away from any jobs they apply for without the courtesy of a response, even from jobs shelf-stacking in Asda. You cannot get a job in Asda unless you can complete an on-line application form, which is something that the men do not understand; they go into the shops and are turned away and are told to find a computer rather than talk about even the most lowly positions. Traditional Albanian roles have begun to invert because the women are inclined to begin at the bottom and often volunteer to work for free until paid opportunities become available,

which has often led to paid employment. However, the men perceive volunteering as beneath them and would not consider working for free. This has resulted in many men feeling worthless and spending time together mourning the lack of opportunities in local cafes, when they feel they should be working. Also, the men are not very open to study as they feel it goes against their traditional values; studying is considered by many as childlike. As an organisation we aim to guide our members into work. The more successful members of our community are those who have started their own businesses such as cafes and restaurants or car washes. However, all this changed when London was bidding for the Olympics. We were promised many opportunities for employment by (Sir) Robin Wales if we won the Games. We were invited to community meetings between us, the Mayor of Newham and the Olympic people and were told that there would be free training for the unemployed that would lead to jobs in construction and not just the menial work but skilled positions too. London obviously got the Games and because of the meetings we really pushed the education in our community and encouraged the males to participate in training programmes. Many did and became trained in various fields. However, once the men became qualified they could not find work anywhere. Sub-contractors that we wouldn't even know how to contact to apply for work did a lot of the construction work and hardly any positions were advertised openly. It was a closed shop. Worse than that though, the jobs that were openly advertised were the menial positions and when our members applied for these jobs they were turned down because they were thought to be over-qualified as a result of attending the training courses! This caused incredible stress between our members and us as an organisation, and has ensured that the men feel even more outsiders than previously. They now feel more suspicious of the institutions and their traditional views have been validated that education is worthless and will lead nowhere. We attended a community meeting with the Mayor of Newham recently and I challenged him on this point, he flat out lied and said that he had made no such assurances and refused to take any other questions on the matter.

That Newham residents of various backgrounds and origins could be transformed from unskilled into skilled workers in time to take advantage of Olympic employment proposals proved to be an illusion. Those outside the community seemed to take into account the needs of the Newham communities, but what they promised had little plausibility in relation to these communities' abilities and aspirations. Meanwhile, the trend that blamed foreigners for taking "indigenous" (local) people's jobs in Newham continued.

On March 7, 2009, the ever-reliable *Daily Mail* commented, "(Indian construction site workers)... earn 55 times more than the daily £1 pittance paid to unskilled labourers back in their own country—India. Although they only wield shovels and dig trenches, Amit, Gurpreet and Randeep think they have struck gold. They have the jobs that local—and better-qualified—men like Scott, Robert, and Glen can only dream about. Yet those three Britons... like thousands of jobless in the area, they don't stand much of a chance."

The shortcomings of this kind of reporting will not be fully explored here. However, I will note that the underlying premise—that local people were not benefitting from Olympic construction jobs—was being raised with consistent regularity. One might well assume that Scott, Robert, and Glen did not in fact dream of digging ditches in the Olympic Park; they were qualified and experienced bricklayers, carpenters, and builders. To put it simply, while the Olympic employment opportunities were proving far from ideal from a variety of perspectives, there were Olympic volunteerism opportunities for Newham to depend upon.

Volunteerism: Something for Nothing?

The Olympic volunteering scheme was advertised as one way to help increasing the skills and employability of local people. In 2010, when applications for Olympic volunteering closed, LOCOG had received a staggering 240,000 applications for the 70,000 posts as Games Maker.[6] However, Olympic volunteerism is arguably less about the learning of the volunteers, or about integrating local people into the Olympic experience, than about unpaid labor where participation is its own reward. According to MacAloon, "The most important category of emergent actors in the Olympics is unquestionably the volunteers, tens of thousands of whom are now required to stage any Olympics at all (Moragas, Belen and Pulig 2000). Though commentators, whose only source of information about Olympic Games are media texts, typically fail to realize it, growth in the numbers, training and dedication of the volunteers has been the chief means of absorbing the 'spectacular' growth of the Olympic Games and of their burden on the host city... they are (with the Police) the most important category of actors in determining whether the tone for a vast public navigating the hurdles of passage among event venues will be good-natured and convivial or stressful and antagonistic... Their chief reward... is the very festival experience that they themselves do so much to create" (2006, pp. 22–23).

This 2012 Olympic volunteering resonated with Durkheim's theoretical perspective as outlined in his *The Division of Labour and Society* (1964). In this line, the success of Olympic delivery would depend on a division of labor where each person fulfils different but inter-related roles. Drawing on the assumption that the by-product of the division of labor is solidarity, the net result of all of these inter-locking components is idealistically believed to facilitate integration. This does not appear to fit well with much of contemporary society. According to the Department for Culture, Media, and Sport, "Community volunteering, arts centres and sports clubs all provide activities for young people to make new friends, learn new skills and bolster self-confidence. Getting young people engaged in community activities benefits us all, regardless of age. 2012 will generate a host of these kinds of opportunities. We want to use the London Games to inspire more young people to get involved, to reap these benefits, and to engage more with the communities in which they live. Our plans... [are to create] an active generation through an unprecedented range of volunteering opportunities for everyone around the UK, including young people before, during and after the 2012 Games. We will need around 70,000 volunteers during the Games-time, and Pre-Volunteering Programmes across the UK will give people with no qualifications the necessary skills to volunteer in 2012 and help them towards a volunteer placement, job or further training" (DCMS, 2007, p. 13).[7]

As the following ethnographic excerpts indicate, for the majority of Newham residents the notion of volunteering was a fantasy. The belief that even if they applied they would not be chosen was based on their *habitus*. They refused to contemplate applying for the positions and making themselves vulnerable to what they believed to be a likely rejection. Questioned on this, informants gave the following explanations for not applying to volunteer:

- "All the volunteering jobs are going to old white people." (Charles, 21)
- "What's the point in that, we don't get paid, and it don't lead to no job?" (Herc, 24)
- "I don't know anyone that is doing that." (Vanessa, 19)

For the unemployed Newham residents who gave the above views voluntary Olympic employment opportunities appeared more conducive to a sense of alienation, castigation, or vilification than to anything resembling integration. It seemed obvious to them that the average Tesco shelf-stacker did not come to feel satisfied and fulfilled by their minimum wage employment thanks to an increased awareness that they were a necessary component of a functioning society. So, why should an Olympic volunteer work for free? Interestingly, this division of labor theory did have resonance among Newham's working population throughout Olympic volunteerism. The following example is indicative.

Celina: The Public Face of Newham

Celina, a 55-years-old white British Newham resident volunteered to participate in Olympic delivery through the Olympic volunteering initiative. Working as a community development worker and a cycling teacher in Newham, Celina was a capable, skilled, and qualified professional careerist who volunteered to work as coach driver during the Games. As I interviewed her in May 2012, she said that she applied in order "to play a part in the world event that would occur only once during my lifetime." Money did not matter when the opportunity to be involved in London 2012 and to show the world how great a place London is presented itself.

In contrast, when spoken with in June 2012, the chair of the Newham Youth Providers Partnership (NYPP),[8] argued that he "could not name a single young person that I know in Newham that is an Olympic volunteer."

These examples indicate a clear dichotomy between those with the disposition to invest in the *Olympic identity* and those without. For the former, Olympic volunteerism and the notion that "everybody has a role to play" toward the success of the Games has a productive role to play; for the latter, the concept of working for free is ludicrous. Such reactions are indicative of the *habitus* of these groups.

Capital Gains and Taxing Situations

The application of Bourdieu's theory helps to understand and explain the relationship between Newham's residents and their inability to take advantage of the Olympic opportunities, including both employment and volunteering. The contexts—discourses, institutions, values, rules and regulations—that produced and transformed the attitudes and practices of these communities could be seen as *cultural fields*, which Bourdieu defines as fluid and dynamic rather than static; made up not simply of institutions and rules but also of the interactions between institutions, rules, and practices. A *cultural field* can be defined as a series of institutions, rules, rituals, conventions, categories, designations, appointments, and titles that constitute a formal hierarchy of power. This produces certain discourses and activities and helps to legitimize them by virtue of real or perceived hegemonic authority. Alternative discourses and conflicting activities occur within *cultural fields* when groups or individuals attempt to determine what constitutes *capital* within that *field*, what that capital represents and how it is to be distributed. As Harker, Mahar, and Wilkes state, "The definition of capital is very wide for Bourdieu and includes material things (which can have symbolic value), as well as untouchable but culturally significant attributes such as prestige, status and authority (referred to as symbolic capital), along with cultural capital (defined as culturally valued taste and consumption patterns)... For Bourdieu, capital acts as a social relation within a system of exchange, and the term is extended to all goods, material and symbolic, without distinction, that present themselves as rare and worthy of being sought after in a particular social formation" (1990, p. 1).

Newham's cultural capital was a contested fluid concept the perceived importance of which varied accordingly, much to the apparent frustration of Sir Robin Wales. Resonating with Bourdieu's argument that "the subjective hope of profit tends to be adjusted to the objective probability of profit" (2000, p. 216), here those with the least amount of capital tend to be less ambitious and more satisfied with their lot. As it is illustrated by the case study below, this inevitably leads to a reproduction of symbolic dominance between those who are able to take advantage of opportunities and those who are not.

Anthony: A Carrot or a Stick?

On a sunny morning in ExCeLland, a community worker, two young unemployed men who lived on the estate and I met at the BV Community Centre. This morning we were to transport soil for the Community Centre's garden from a location half a mile away. This involved numerous journeys back and forth pushing wheelbarrows, it was hard work for no pay but the two young black unemployed men did this job happily and with gusto. One, Anthony, aged 21, had left school at 15 with no qualifications and had been unemployed ever since (Fieldwork notes, June 2012).

Anthony was part of a growing group of young men whom the government refers to as NEET; this is the acronym for young people Not in Employment, Education, or Training. According to research published in 2009 by the *Learning and Skills Network*,[9] in recent years NEET have risen by almost 2% annually. The findings for the second quarter of 2009 indicated that, compared to the previous year, 24,000 more 16–24-year-olds were NEET. In August 2009, the total figure stood at 950,000.[10] It was concluded that this "research shows that disengagement at this age is disastrous in personal terms; causes problems in the community in the form of nuisance and crime; leads to long-term costs in increased criminality, welfare, dependency, housing and a wide range of social and economic factors... combating this growing problem, which is likely to be exacerbated by the recession, requires thorough research into disengagement in a local area to tease out the particular demands of the locality... the effects of the recession, however, may be dramatically changing the landscape and how we see the issue" (Hodgson, Spours, and Stone 2009).

Anthony lived at home with his mother and three sisters. They were Courtney, a bright, outgoing, vocal 18-year-old studying sociology at Newham College; 24-year-old Flower who was a dancer; and Britney, aged 15. Their father had died of a heart attack on Christmas day when Anthony was 9. Ever-present at the community center, Anthony seemed to enjoy the social gatherings, although his motivation for attendance seemed as much to look out for his sisters as to be there for his own enjoyment. He was difficult to engage with at first; reluctant to speak and hesitant to offer his opinions. Football was the topic that broke the ice. What follows is drawn from the various conversations that were facilitated by our shared passion for football.

Anthony was trying to get a community football team going. He spoke with passion about this dream of playing in a league, but this passion was tempered by an undercurrent of skepticism and by a pre-emptive sense of failure; that he would not be able to get enough players, investment, and opportunities to realize his aim. This attitude was emblematic of his overall perception of life. He would love to achieve things, he had dreams but he did not feel he had the skills, abilities or opportunities to turn them into a reality. Basically, he steeled himself for disappointment because his experiences had taught him that life would let him down at every turn. Thus he had removed himself from the wider society and, secure in his microenvironment, was reluctant to reengage.

Anthony refused to sign on to collect state benefits. This raised an interesting issue in the overall structure of society and of NEETs. Anthony explains his refusal with the stigma attached to signing on and with the hopelessness and futility of hanging around job centers and attending the compulsory interviews that the office would send claimants to. Consequently, he opted out. Sarah, a local resident and sociology lecturer at a nearby University, argued for another perspective to explain opting out. She felt that Anthony, and many others like him, did not want to sign on because they did not want to be recorded on official records; they preferred a life of anonymity from the state. This, she feels, is the result of consistent instances of abuse of authority by the police and other officials, which has fostered a distrust of officialdom.

Like many other local young men, Anthony could recount many stories of police racism and persecution. Such stories included physical violence, victimization, threats, and personal vendettas. Every young man on the estate that I came into contact with had variations of the same story to tell, which resulted in both fear and distrust of the police. As community center manager Fred stated with reference to a Police Community Support Officer who had worked in BV for a while until he "cracked" and began racially abusing some of the young men: "It takes a long time to build relationships but only a matter of seconds to destroy them. We thought he (the PCSO) was a good guy but we were wrong."

For those who work, earn, and pay taxes, Anthony's rejection of many of society's norms constitutes incontrovertible proof that he lacks the necessary attributes to be a contributing member of society. He and most like him form part of a sub-culture from which they must be protected by any means necessary. He, they would say, lacks the aspirations, goals, and desires of a person who achieves employment, self-worth, and functionality. The residents of BV who live on the other side of Wesley Avenue from Anthony and his cohosts do not allow themselves to dwell upon subjunctive conditionals; they refuse to believe that if Anthony had not opted out of society someone else would have. They find it difficult to accept that Anthony is a product of the same society that they themselves inhabit and influence.

Through their inaction, Anthony and his peers support this sense of opting out. Through the vilification and castigation of Anthony, and others like him, his critics are perpetuating the very cycle that creates what they fear and want to be protected from—a violent, criminally intent, hopeless underclass. They believe that Anthony operates within a different set of norms and values to that which they do because they would never allow themselves to be in a position where they would not be prepared to do whatever it takes to get themselves off the bottom rung of society—let alone opt out. Refusing to claim benefits and to engage with employment opportunities is not straightforward "laziness." Of course, it does not help that Anthony has trouble explaining exactly why he opts out, shrugging the questions off amid monosyllabic responses, occasionally saying "I dunno" or "no point." This creates further misconceptions and misunderstandings.

Fred, the BV Community Centre manager, suggests that lack of educational opportunity is a major factor in this opting out. The primary school in the BV, whose pupil numbers have increased by nearly 30% in the last five years,[11] is considered to be a great school compared to others close by. According to Fred, it is when children leave this school and have to move away from the estate to further their education that "issues" begin as these young people fail: "most of them leave with no qualifications to speak of and get involved with gangs." Fred is attempting to facilitate further education opportunities for the BV's children, so they can get a better education locally and avoid the potential pitfalls easily observable among people such as Anthony. Others articulate better Fred's point. For example, according to Schiller, "The children of the poor undeniably drop out of school earlier than other children... Schools, in lower-income areas are notoriously ill equipped to transmit interest, enjoyment, or ability... Middle-class school experience is both more pleasant and more profitable... Given these inequalities in opportunity, it might be equally valid to conclude that the poor value education more highly than the non-poor because of the greater sacrifices they make to get as far as they do" (Schiller 2004, p.143).

Regardless of the reasoning behind opting out, which could conceivably become the object of a research project in itself, a key issue to consider is how social class divisions and prejudice create the predictable beliefs, actions, thoughts, and behaviors on both sides of the street that mark life in the BV. Bourdieu's forays into psychoanalysis might well go some way to explaining the life perspectives of Anthony and many others like him; particularly that "the realistic, even resigned or fatalistic, dispositions which lead members of the dominated classes to put up with objective conditions that would be judged intolerable or revolting by agents otherwise disposed... help to reproduce the conditions of oppression" (2000, p. 217).

Combined with this quote from Bourdieu, the fieldwork notes reported above suggest a bleak picture of the presumed benefits of Olympic delivery; a perspective quite different, that is, from that established through no direct experience of the context. The easy-to-follow pro-Olympic rhetoric was that Newham was a borough economically and socially "lacking" and the Olympic Games were regenerating the area and were simultaneously providing endless opportunities. The implication was that local people would automatically take advantage of these opportunities and that Newham's Olympic *legacy* would benefit all. However, as it has emerged, the reality is more complex. This complexity will be further explored in what follows.

We Have Work...

The injection of Olympic-related employment opportunities into this deprived borough was delivered with the expectation that local people would grab them with both hands. We have seen that these expectations were built on weak premises. The question then becomes: were there studies done with the aim of matching the likely Olympic employment opportunities with the unemployed local population? The answer to this question is yes, there were. For example, in January 2006, the LDA and the Learning and Skills Council conducted a major "Skills study for the London 2012 Games."[12] This study was aimed at identifying the range of skills that the local community lacked in relation to the employment opportunities linked to the Games and, then, address the shortcomings by designing a curriculum that would deliver the necessary skills. This initiative was promoted as a way to ensure that local citizens were given the opportunity to compete with migrant workers for employment opportunities during the

construction period. Incidentally, this research began over six months after London had been awarded the Games; it did not take much effort to realize that, at that point in time, the recruiting process for construction was already well underway.

Despite this, David Hughes, the LSC regional director for London, enthused, "For London to host a successful Olympic and Paralympic Games the LSC has an important leadership role in delivering the training and skills to the employers who will build the infrastructure and deal with the competitors and visitors."[13] In effect, this injection of employment opportunities into Newham communities required local people to participate in a sociological game of stick or twist, where they were expected to forget their past experience of the education system and be willing to gamble their *habitus* for *capital*. This was based on the expectation that local people would believe that such training would improve their standing in the ever-changing *field* of Olympic-delivery Newham.

In line with Bourdieu, those willing to take this gamble were largely doomed to failure, as exemplified by the case of Shrpresa given earlier. Bourdieu argues that, "although lower class migrant families may strive to get their children educated, the habitus of the children will, in advance, disqualify them from success, both in the sense that the children will signal, in everything they do and say, their unsuitability for higher education, and as a corollary, the children will themselves recognise this, and more or less expect failure"... those "who talk of equality of opportunity forget that social games... are not 'fair games.' Without being, strictly speaking, rigged, the competition resembles a handicap race that has lasted for generations"(2000, pp. 214–215, cited in Webb, Schirato, and Danaher 2002, p. 24).

Many Newham residents, such as Anthony, refused to participate in such schemes, saying that they were futile. These attitudes underscored Sir Robin's venomous anger and frustration; a manifestation of what Bourdieu would recognize as *symbolic violence*, which he defines as "the violence which is exercised upon a social agent with his or her complicity" (Bourdieu and Wacquant 1992, p.167). In other words, agents are subjected to forms of violence (treated as inferior, denied resources, and limited in their social mobility and aspirations) but they do not perceive it that way; rather, to them their situation seems to be the natural order of things. In 2008, an unattributed *Daily Mail* newspaper article reported Sir Robin's comments regarding Newham residents' inability to take advantage of Olympic employment; it quoted him saying, "Olympic employers would simply look elsewhere for the new workers they needed. They won't get the jobs because they aren't ready for them. They haven't got the skills, haven't got the training and they can't afford to lose the benefits. I have people who aspire to a council house. There are also people who won't come in for work even at 11 o'clock. If we can inspire people through the Olympics we can change this, but at the moment they are not ready for jobs." To back up his argument, Sir Robin pointed out that 400,000 jobs had already been created in the area in recent years, but the jobless total had dropped by only 40,000. The reason, he said, was that employers had recruited outside the existing population, often hiring eastern Europeans who had the attitude and skills that firms wanted. Although the problems were spread across different ethnic groups, the worst levels of unemployment and lack of skills in Newham, which has a 60 % ethnic minority population, were among white residents. David Higgins, the head of the Olympic Delivery Authority, who was sitting alongside Sir Robin as he issued his warning, insisted that every effort would be made to ensure that local residents were employed as much as possible.[14]

Olympic delivery employment practices and discourses contained a political and segregational logic. Publically, officials such as Newham Mayor Sir Robin vented their frustrations that those who lived in his borough were not taking advantage of the opportunities presented to them. However, in reality many lacked the *habitus* to understand the *doxa* required to benefit from Olympic opportunities during the short time-frame in which they were made available. This resonates with Fussey et al.'s consideration that the benefits of regional and economic *legacy* can often be seen to exacerbate social disadvantage and inequality (2011, p. 18). At best, it could be argued that Newham's politicians held the false hope that many of the local residents would be able to exploit these employment opportunities despite being "unemployable" or not "inclined to work" before the Games came to town. However, it could also be argued that for Sir Robin, and others like him, the real frustration was not so much that Newham's residents were unable to grasp these opportunities but rather that these people were living in Newham in the first place. The situation experienced throughout this research indicated that many of those who lived in Newham felt segregated and excluded from Olympic delivery benefit and from the regenerated Olympic locales. The following chapter explores this sense of segregation, looking in particular at the 2012 Olympic security milieu.

CHAPTER 6

The Rings of Exclusion

In the previous chapters, I have argued that an *Olympic identity* resonated throughout Britain. Its athletic-inspired inclusivity gave strength to the hegemonic practice of securing consent through an Olympic-themed provision of "bread and circuses" (Eisinger 2000) that allowed distraction from the realities of Olympic delivery and, more generally, of everyday life. The inclusive narrative that hosting the Olympic Games intimated the Olympics would boost the national economy, provide local and national Olympic legacies, and deliver a once-in-a-lifetime sporting "Mega-Event" for all to invest in, consume, and enjoy. It was assumed that these positive Olympic outcomes, not to mention the spectacle of the Games themselves, required a significant securitization of the areas where the events would be held. This assumption forms the basis of this chapter. I explore the policing concerns that were of particular relevance to Newham during Olympic delivery and offer an analysis of organized resistance to the Olympic security processes. The analysis begins with an overview of some 2012 Olympic-related security issues.

Securing London 2012

Giulianotti and Klauser have noted that "In recent times, sport Mega-Events have grown into major global spectacles that possess huge economic, political and social significance...One issue which has become central to the planning and implementation of sport Mega-Events is security...the budget for London 2012 stands at a projected US$1.7 billion. Such expenditures are realised through the mobilisation of more security personnel, such as the 60,000 additional police officers to be drafted in for London 2012...As security at sport Mega-Events has grown exponentially in recent times, so the diverse effects of these processes on the host cities and nations become increasingly complex and problematic" (2011, pp. 3157–3168).

The 2012 narrative of Olympic securitization revolved around the notion that if the many security measures were not implemented to the required levels, there would be no Games, no inclusive identity, and no Olympic benefit. These assertions drew on fear of any perceptible threat to the Games, which included everything from acts of terrorism to more innocuous hazards, such as the unauthorized use of the Olympic rings. The penalties for the slightest oversight were predicted to be harsh.

Some obeyed the Olympic deliverers.

Many didn't.

Irrespective of perceptions of what constituted a "threat" to the success of the Games, the securitization narrative segregated the local communities during Olympic delivery. It prevented their access to specific locales by instilling the belief that the Games were not for them; they were for "the tourists." As we shall see, the Olympic deliverers issued a clear warning through a variety of media, the bulk of which was that the entire Games period would be a time of huge aggravation for the local communities, and

Figure 6.1 Café Lympic

Figure 6.2 Ringing in the Customers

if they had any sense they would modify or suspend their everyday lives for the duration of the Olympic Games.

This message of expectant disruption also resonated on a deeper level, through symbolic exclusion. This deprived, diverse populace was excluded through an Olympic securitization that exacerbated the gaps between their *habitus* and the evolving Olympic delivery *field*. These messages and the attendant prohibitions of access encouraged the local communities to abandon hope of inclusion and Olympic benefit. Many Newham residents had experienced this kind of exclusion throughout their lives; why should things change now? As Bourdieu would put it, such considerations may well be "a result of the hysteresis effect necessarily implicated in the logic of the constitution of habitus, practices are always liable to incur negative sanctions when the environment with which they are actually confronted is too distant from that in which they are objectively fitted." (Bourdieu 1977, p. 78)

This situation brought significant segregational issues to the fore and emphasized the differentiation between those who held the *habitus* necessary to accumulate (the various forms of) Olympic delivery capital and those who did not. With reference to the above quote, the previous chapter explored *hysteresis* in relation to employment; this section explores another, less tangible manifestation of Olympic delivery *hysteresis*—namely, security-related exclusion. This is perhaps best exemplified by the description of *Stratfordland*'s Olympic Park as an "*Island Site*" (Fussey et al. 2011, p. 3), which emphasizes the dislocation of the Olympic space from the rest of Newham.

Securitization involved modifying the landscape to prohibit access of some local people, both literally and symbolically. Bourdieu would suggest that in the contest for discursive power a battle for position between social groups could be observed, where all struggle to impose their own representations of the world but where the élite impose and institutionalize definitions (Bourdieu and Wacquant 1992). The Olympic deliverers and the community held exchanges on the community impact of the Games, which are worth exploring.

Narratives of Exclusion

Olympic delivery was fixated upon one date and one event—the Opening Ceremony scheduled for July 27, 2012. This was to be the culmination of all the years of blood, sweat, and toil behind the 2012 Olympic project. The powerful *Olympic identity* grew in stature and resonance as this date approached and began to dominate the media and British public consciousness accordingly. This created a trajectory of Olympic fervor that gradually escalated throughout the land as the Games approached.

The 2012 London Olympics would not be primarily celebrated in the newly built Olympic Park but, rather, on the couches of the world's living rooms. The *Olympic identity* would allow armchair Olympians to be fleetingly elevated from their unremarkable existence to transitory significance by a sense of vicarious association with great exemplars of physical prowess who competed in the world's premier sporting events, where the results of individual competition did not matter as long as Britain won something and everybody had a jolly time.

For those inebriated by the "*Olympic identity*" spirit but unable to get their hands on one of the rarest commodities in London during 2012—a ticket to the Games—there would be the option of consuming the Games at local bars and restaurants or even at one of the many big screens, where consumption could be shared with the likeminded. This might be understandable for those who lived in Cardiff, Manchester, and Glasgow, but slightly less so for those who lived in the immediate vicinity of the Newham Olympic venues. For many those locales were traditionally part of their everyday lives. During Games time, however, they were told both implicitly and explicitly to keep away, unless they were officially ticketed guests.

As I have illustrated, the 2012 Olympic Games did not exist in a vacuum. However, this research shows that significant attempts were made for them to do exactly that—exist, that is, in a vacuum. Toward such an end, the local communities had been managed, minimized, and marginalized by the Olympic deliverers through a well-orchestrated campaign that attempted to convince them that the 2012 Games should be consumed in Newham in the same way as they were consumed in Glasgow, namely, at home or in a specific public venue. That choice was theirs, but either way it was emphasized that they must stay away from Olympic venues and locales unless they had paid for a ticket. This policy of exclusion led to the introduction of a new Newham *doxa*; one that did not resonate with the local communities' *habitus*, the exploration of which forms the basis for the discussion that follows.

Transport for (Some) London(ers)

As I have mentioned earlier, the Olympics carry security challenges. Addressing a large number of logistical issues included planning strategies to deal with vast volumes of visitors. An independent 2011 report conducted by Oxford Economics estimated that the number of visitors staying in London for the 2012 Games would exceed 450,000. In addition to these, the report estimated that there would be 5.5 million daytime visitors to the Capital over the duration of the Games (O'Ceallaigh 2011). These vast—if perhaps overestimated—numbers presented significant security challenges; particularly, in relation to the notion that 2012 would be a public transport Games—making use, that is, of a public transport system on which vast swathes of Newham residents relied for their everyday lives.

Concerns about visitor numbers revolved around the potential to cause disturbance, disruption, offence, or upheaval. In turn, visitors needed to be protected from part of the native Newham population. The rules for governing this influx followed a narrative of exclusion best exemplified by the creation of transport restrictions that would cover the entire Olympic Games period. The ODA predicted that 78% of the spectators would travel to and from the Olympic Park by rail.[1] More generally, the London 2012 transport strategy was for 100% of the spectators to travel to the Games by public transport, walking, or cycling. It was widely believed that the public transport system would struggle to cope with the combination of Olympic influx and regular passengers. How Newham would cope caused much community consternation. A Community Support worker typically said (June 2011), "There is no information given to us in the local community about how we will be affected during the Olympics. They [Olympic deliverers] are controlling the information because they fear organised resistance once we know how badly we are going to be affected."

The above quote exemplifies community concerns about the imposition of securitization. The local people with whom I spoke voiced their concerns regarding the impending disruption and the policing and security implications of the Games, which, they feared, would disproportionately affect the local population. This view was strengthened by the conceptual vagueness of "community consultations" and interactions with the Olympic deliverers. In January 2012, a Third Sector Community Representative significantly remarked, "I've been to a huge amount of different forums and heard the same things at all of them; everyone is concerned. For example, at a recent meeting with health professionals—not at the Janet and John level, I'm talking 'Director level'—the worry was how they were going to be able to fulfil their health obligations to the local people during the Olympics."

These excerpts indicate the feelings that permeated much of the community. An atmosphere of fear and concern was fostered by not knowing what was to come. These concerns grew when, weeks before the beginning of the 2012 Games, official information on the expected community impact of the Olympics eventually began to filter through to the local community.

A Community under Siege

The following case study drawn from my fieldwork notes of April 2012 illustrates a community consultation event that was meant to address the impact of the London 2012 Games on transport. This meeting, called by the LOCOG and facilitated by the Newham Voluntary Sector Consortium (NVSC),[2] was an invitation-only event that took place at Stratford Town Hall between 9:30 am and 12:00 pm on April 26, 2012.

In a ground floor room of Stratford Town Hall, the tables were arranged in a U-shape and were oriented toward a large projector screen. In front of this screen sat representatives from LOCOG, TFL, and the London borough of Newham, ready to inform the audience of their vision of the likely transport impact that the 2012 Games would have upon local people. The invited audience included 35 members of Newham's Third Sector and representatives from the NVSC, Stratfordland, ExCeLland, and the Dispersal Zone.

Upon arrival, each member of the audience was presented with an information pack containing maps of impending road closures, parking restrictions, and other traffic management implementations. The package also contained a pamphlet describing how travel in Newham would be affected during the Games period and a flyer indicating how individuals could plan to adjust their schedules in order to avoid the impending influx—which was known as the "Get Ahead of the Games" strategy.

All documents illustrated the belief that mass disruption was pending but there were clear policies and strategies in place to counteract impediments to daily life. The initial opening and browsing of the documents led to much muttering and searching of the maps to consider how each representative's community group would be affected. This muttering was cut short by the LOCOG representative—who chaired the meeting—who, as was the standard procedure at Olympic meetings, began by describing the fantastic progress that was being made toward the Games delivery. The representative went through some general security measures that were considered to be crucial to the successful delivery of the Olympics and touched upon the higher levels of policing, and the police muster point located at Wanstead flats. However, to avoid any direct questioning from the audience on these points, the representative reminded the audience that this meeting was about transport and handed the presentation over to the TFL representative.

The TFL representative explained transport regulations and provided some information on the maps, pointing out where specific restrictions would take place, which roads were to be closed, where right hand turns would be outlawed and so on. Despite the most visible agitated response from the audience, she continued talking in a depersonalized fashion about the need of "free flowing traffic for successful Games." As questions and comments began to be voiced, she reminded the audience that there would be plenty of time to answer all questions at the end and attempted to carry on regardless. The tension grew. One member visibly fidgeted in his chair, reminiscent of an infant school pupil with his hand in the air waiting patiently for the teacher to ask him what his question was. This atmosphere lasted for a few more moments until the TFL representative began discussing the alterations to a nearby junction, described as a significant pinch-point for traffic that needed to be dealt with. The modification of this busy junction would entail various restrictions that would allow the road system "to work for the Olympic family" (including VIPs and officials) as they would reduce background traffic by 30%.

At this point, the fidgeting man exploded, shouting, "Background traffic? You mean me!" This comment started an unabashed free-for-all, with comments being fired at the TFL representative around the theme that during the Olympics "the community" were considered to be second class citizens and all the traffic strategies were intended to restrict their movement and exclude them from their everyday lives. The TFL representative made her excuses and left to jeers of "watch out for background traffic on your way home."

The LBN representative took over from TFL to illustrate other restrictions that painted an equally bleak picture for the local community. This speaker covered such issues as the need for all cars in Newham to join a database and obtain a permit to be in the borough; failure to do so would result in a heavy fine or in the vehicle being towed away. The LBN representative also explained that local businesses needed to change their delivery times and warned that the LBN would be recruiting vast numbers of Traffic Enforcement officers who would enforce such regulations. The impression was of a zero-tolerance highly securitized Olympic Newham, where the community needed to either adjust or suffer accordingly.

Away from this meeting, the warning to local people to "Get Ahead of the Games" was broadcast through various means. This advice was displayed on billboards, on public transport and through the media. Essentially, such information warned local people that any journeys made during the Olympic period would (very likely) be horrendous. These public transport warnings were replicated across London's roads, disseminating messages of impending traffic chaos.

The measures implemented to control traffic included changing signal timings to manage traffic lights, bus diversions, suspensions of parking in key areas and road closures. One specific modification was that the 35 miles of major roads around the Olympic Park would include "Games Lanes" that would be accessible only to VIPs and to the coaches used to transport athletes, Games officials, and media people.

Olympic road lanes and the Olympic Road Network (ORN) became a reality on many busy roads in and around East London over the two months prior to the Opening Ceremony. Combined with various Olympic-related road closures and parking restrictions, these innovations were widely expected to disrupt and restrict movement in a local situation of habitually heavy traffic. Information on the penalties that would be imposed on those breaking such restrictions was widely publicized in newspapers and Olympic-related literature. Other measures included restricting foot traffic; borough-wide dispersal zones would permit people to be ordered out of the Olympic areas for a specific period of time, usually 24 hours.[3] All these measures enforced the message that local people were best off avoiding Olympic locales and leaving them to those who were in possession of Olympic tickets.

The dialogue between Olympic deliverers and community groups addressed this exclusory narrative at various forums and events. The message of the Olympic deliverers was that the borough would be under a heightened securitization and all rules had to be respected, or stiff consequences would follow. These Olympic modifications, both literal and symbolic, altered the applicability of pre-Olympic symbolic and economic capital to the evolving urban landscape and redrew barriers of inclusion and exclusion accordingly. Newham's communities felt as if they were required to adopt the role of passive recipients of services who depended on the benevolence of Olympic delivery for intangible benefits that they had yet to receive. The cost was their exclusion (literal or symbolic) from Olympic benefit, which generated insecurity and fear in some sections of the community.

The Management of Fear

The following statement encapsulates the feelings caused by the Olympic-security measures broadcast through the media. The statement was given by a 28-years-old local woman whom I interviewed immediately after the meeting described above. She said, "It feels like being in a community under siege; the vast numbers of security guards and police and the army that are being brought in to our community worries us tremendously. The levels of security will be oppressive during the Olympics and the clear message is that we should stay away. I don't know anyone with tickets to see anything; it isn't for us. Everyone is living in fear of what it's going to be like here during the Olympics; all we hear is about security, about cars going to be towed away or roads closed. We hear that there are going to be so many people coming to see the Olympics that we won't be able to do anything. I think it would just be better if we all went on holiday while it's on, I think that's what they want us to do."

As Wacquant warned (1993), in all advanced countries whenever the police (and in this case security guards and the army) are considered as an alien force by the population they are supposed to protect they will find it extremely difficult, if not impossible, to fulfil any other role than a repressive one. This point was exemplified throughout this study, as many local people felt that the securitization of the Olympic Games was something that was being done *to* them, also indicating that the Games were not *for* them at all. Simply put, they felt that the Olympic Games and the attendant benefits were not something that they would be able to access.

An understated problem was that the *gradual* dissemination of information into the community regarding the expected Olympic impact, and securitization was delivered by pleasant but ill-informed volunteers who staffed the display stalls at various community events. These events combined drip-feeding limited bits of information with child-oriented entertainment, including balloons, face painting, and coloring sessions.

Initially, community skeptics suspected that the security measures were not being clearly defined and described because they would cause outrage and would lead to organized resistance; that is, if the community had sufficient time to mobilize. These perceptions were left to fester until the turn of year 2011, when security and traffic regulation information gradually began to be released by people with the "know-how" at events such as the LOCOG meeting described earlier. This information did much to support the feeling of fear among local people that Newham would be placed under intense securitization and flooded with police, security personnel, and all the other practical ramifications of securitization. The message to the community was that disruption was on its way and that they should avoid specific zones at all costs. This message of fear and apprehension suggested that the 2012 Olympiad could go one of two ways for local communities:

- The local community could carry on as normal and be disproportionately affected by the securitization and suffer commensurately
- The local community could abandon all hope of inclusion in the Olympic experience and plan to modify their lives accordingly

For some, the twin outcomes of Olympic delivery *hysteresis*—literal and symbolic—perpetuated fear and led to withdrawal from the Olympic experience. For others, they resulted in loss of position and power, following the enforced revaluation of symbolic capital and sources of legitimacy.

What follows explores the links between the objective nature of the changes brought by the implementation of Olympic delivery security (and discourse) and the implications of local people's responses to these changes. I seek to offer an understanding of the nature and consequences of the changes, as they were experienced both individually and on the larger social environmental level. I begin with an overview of Olympic securitization and of its role in 2012 delivery. Examples of security implications and interactions between the deliverers and the community will help to highlight the possession of symbolic capital in these interactions. Then, I consider how the specter of these Olympics securitization measures had a negative impact on some of Newham's community groups, facilitating organized action and leading many local people to feel detached from the entire Olympic process.

CHAPTER 7

Securitization: The Olympic Lockdown?

The 2012 Olympic Games were to open with a grand ceremony that would showcase London to a global audience. The cost was estimated at £41 million. As British prime minister David Cameron stated in 2012 after doubling the budget for the event, the Opening Ceremony is "a great advertisement and if you think of the millions of pounds we are spending, it's probably worth between two and five billion of free publicity for the country."[1]

This announcement might be best assessed in relation to what Toohey and Taylor define as "terrorist capital" (2008). The Olympic Games are widely considered an appealing target for a variety of terrorist attacks, a view justified by previous Olympic hosts having fallen victim to terrorism. Prominent examples include the kidnapping and execution of Israeli athletes by Black September during the 1972 Munich Games (Aston 1983; Reeve 2001; Toohey and Veal 2007) and the Centennial bombing at the 1996 Atlanta Games (Atkinson and Young 2008). These incidents, among others, have influenced the securitization of the Olympic Games (Fussey et al. 2011). Any Olympic host must accept a myriad potential dangers and security concerns, which are intrinsically linked to Olympic hosting. Talking to the Press Association in 2012, Lord Sebastian Coe, the LOCOG chairman, emphasized this point as he succinctly stated, "everything we do at an Olympic Games is underpinned by security."[2] Hosting the Olympics exponentially multiplies all security concerns; not only does the host have its own "domestic problems to deal with, it also must deal with all the problems of all nations of the world" (Oquirrh Institute Report 2003, p. 36).

"Terrorism" is arguably the most infamous of these hosting concerns, because the Games are perceived as soft targets, where a successful terror attack would guarantee vast media exposure (Coaffee 2009). However, "Mega-Event" exploitation is not limited to terrorism and security concerns cover a variety of potential occurrences. These obviously include severe lawlessness, such as acts that cause mass casualties (Toohey and Taylor 2008), but also the quasi-illegal, such as ambush marketing campaigns, as witnessed at the Beijing 2008 Games (Preuss et al. 2008), or more innocuous, such as the 9,000 arrests at the Atlanta Olympics for the "crime" of being homeless (COHRE 2007, p. 197) and much more besides. The unifying factor for these concerns is the manpower and resources required to deal with them, all of which come under the same prefix—"Security."

There has been much contemporary research conducted in the field of "Mega-Event" security and surveillance (Boyle and Haggerty 2009; Giulianotti 2011; Cornelissen 2011; Schimmel 2011; Coaffee et al. 2011; Eick 2011; Samatas 2011). There has also been much research on the sociological impact of "Mega-Event" securitization, including concerns such as the threat to civil rights and freedom of the press, the criminalization of homelessness, and forced evictions (Boykoff 2011; Lenskyj 2000, 2002 and 2008; Shaw 2008). However, no attention has been paid to the implications of these measures in the everyday lives of those living in the Olympic securitization shadow. Let us focus on this issue.

Securing the Mega-Event Host Community

Olympic security policies are unique and they do not resonate with traditional community perceptions and methods of controlling space. As Olympic security expert Peter Ryan (2002) emphasized during his keynote address to an Olympic Security Review Conference,[3] Olympic security planners must consider scenarios that would seem "bizarre and outlandish to non-security experts" and that would obviously include those that lived and worked in the areas that were to be affected by such measures. This inimitable security paradigm proved problematic for London's urban Olympic Games in that it required the imposition of Olympic security on a complex urban population who would be trying to get on with their lives.

Hosting the London Olympics was the largest peacetime security program in the country, which would involve all the cities that the Olympics would visit. Wars, noted Ryan, are "planned and executed in less time and with less people" (2002, p. 24). There can be no argument that securing and policing the 2012 Olympic Games was a tremendously complex undertaking. Things were further complicated by numerous security issues, not least of which was the murder of 52 people in the Islamist terror attack on the London transport system on July 7, 2005, the day after the Games were won.

The inquest for these bombings revealed that London was "woefully unprepared for a terrorist attack on 2012 Olympics" (Rayner 2011). This conclusion firmly placed security threats in the realm of reality during the Olympic securitization process. Another highly visible example of a security threat were the August 2011 "English Riots" on the streets of North London. These riots spread throughout parts of the Capital, including areas in the vicinity of the Olympic Park, and to other English cities, which raised additional concerns regarding Olympic security (Hill 2011). Many believed that these riots were caused by the shooting of a young black man by the police,[4] while others saw them as a sign of "Broken Britain."[5] Either way, these riots carried significant consequences for the securitization of the 2012 Olympics.

Problematically for the 2012 Games, this civil unrest occurred on a day where 200 delegates from countries participating in the Games gathered in London for the briefings on the logistics of various Olympic venues. The 2011 riots provoked global concern; several nations publicly raised questions on the safety measures and the adequacy of security in a London situation marked by significant Olympic securitization—with China (Foster 2011) and America (Hopkins and Norton-Taylor 2011) being particularly outspoken on the security of the impending Games. Hopkins and Norton-Taylor reported on how "The US raised repeated concerns about security at the London Olympics and is preparing to send up to 1,000 of its agents, including 500 from the FBI, to provide protection for America's contestants and diplomats...American officials have expressed deep unease that the UK has had to restrict the scope of anti-terrorism 'stop and search' powers...after conceding it [LOCOG] had underestimated the number of security guards needed...Originally it had thought 10,000 guards would be enough, but after a review over the summer it now believes it will need up to 21,000...but the organising committee does not have the money to pay G4S [the private security firm contracted to find and train security guards] to make up the shortfall, and does not believe the firm has enough time to do so, forcing ministers to turn to the Ministry of Defence for help. The MoD has offered 3,000 soldiers and another 2,000 in reserve" (Hopkins and Norton-Taylor 2011).[6] This prompted an IOC spokesman to emphasize in a national newspaper that "security at the Olympic Games was a top priority for the IOC."[7] This statement was stressed by the estimated 60,000 police officers from around the UK who were to be drafted into London to help policing the Games and the Capital for the duration of the Olympic Games (Giulianotti and Klausner 2011); this was in addition to 10,000 private venue security guards, a figure raised to 40,000 in 2011.

The ever-increasing number of security personnel needed to safeguard the Games and to convey an image of safety was clearly proving logistically problematic for the 2012 Olympic deliverers. An additional logistical concern was the need to house such personnel and to provide adequate bases for operation within range of the Olympic venues in order to utilize these forces effectively. The impact of this combination on the community provides the setting for the following case study.

Wanstead Flats: Is the Land Ours?

Wanstead Flats is part of East London's Epping Forest. Epping Forest is a taxpayer-funded amenity protected by the Epping Forest Act of 1878.[8] The City of London Corporation (CLC) governs this land on behalf of the public. To ensure the land is safeguarded for community use, the 1878 Act stipulates that Epping Forest must be kept unenclosed and the land cannot be built upon. Problematically, most of this area (1.35 square kilometers) is flat, open grassland in the direct vicinity of the Olympic Park, which makes the land extremely valuable and useful real estate.

The Metropolitan Police Service (MPS) intended to use sections of this grassland as a muster point for briefing thousands of officers during the Olympic Games. So, Home Office officials drafted an amendment to the 1878 Epping Forest Act enabling the temporary use of the site for the implementation of a security-related infrastructure. The Security and Counter-Terrorism Minister, Baroness Neville-Jones, stated that "London 2012 poses a unique policing challenge and this temporary amendment will help to deliver a safe and secure Olympic and Paralympic Games."[9] This statement reinforced both the narrative of fear and the need to take ownership of community land in order to ensure that the Olympic Games, and all that they would bring, would take place.

This change in usage proved to be a contentious issue. The MPS described Wanstead Flats as the only site "fit for purpose." The CLC, who were ultimately responsible for the forest on behalf of the public, promised to demand guarantees to be put in place over the appropriate restoration of the site and appropriate compensation, conditional on the community at large being appropriately consulted. Ultimately, an agreement was reached that allowed the MPS to utilize the area for a rental cost of £170,000.[10] However, not all were happy with this arrangement. A "Save Wanstead Flats" (SWF) campaign opposed the agreement.[11] From June 2010, SWF activists campaigned to fight plans that would allow the MPS to base its Olympics operational center on the land. In order to facilitate the agreement, the Home Office needed to amend the Act of Parliament that, as I have mentioned, has protected Wanstead Flats from enclosure and development for well over a century. An amendment of the Epping Forest Act was passed with little debate by Parliament. SWF opposed this turn of events on four levels. First, they felt there was inadequate community consultation. Second, they objected in principle to the alteration of the Epping Forest Act and to the potential ramifications of allowing the Act to be altered. Third, they campaigned for greater transparency regarding the selection of Wanstead Flats and the characteristics of the other areas that were considered but ruled out. Finally, they felt that the compensation figure that had been agreed between CLC and the MPS was totally inadequate.

On this fourth point, one local resident summarized their case concisely during a SWF campaign meeting held in an AM-owned building—Durning Hall in Forrest Gate. This resident made his case by comparing the rent for the operational base to what the CLC charged Newham Council for holding their annual fireworks display on the same site. I quote: "Newham Council are charged £5,000 for 2 hours access to the site. That's £2,500 an hour. Ninety days is 2,160 hours, I think you can reasonably argue the police operation will be 24/7, so 2,160 x £2,500 is £5,400,000... The paltry £170,000 equates to £78 pounds per hour." This disproportion, as it was perceived by SWF, was even more iniquitous when considered in relation to a statement that appeared in the CLC's Epping Forest. It read: "Currently, it costs the City of London £4.4 million per year to run Epping Forest including income generated. Carefully targeted reductions in service are being made totalling £457,000, which will sadly result in reductions in funding for tree work, ride maintenance, equipment, and machinery, together with less improvement work on the Forest's farmed estate. Safety will remain paramount."

The SWF campaigners continued to argue that because the consultation carried out by the Home Office was, in their opinion, "insufficient" it denied local people their democratic right to challenge the decision, which should, therefore, be overturned. Ultimately, their stand petered out as interest waned and a sense of futility prevailed for, as the Games approached, the muster point began to be built. However, conflict between the police and Newham's communities was not limited to the development of muster points on public land. Racism was one far more fundamental issue pertaining to perceptions of policing and to community concerns about the vastly increased number of police officers and security personnel that were about to police Newham's streets.

Policing a Complex Society: Institutional Racism?

One of the most infamous moments in the contemporary history of London occurred in 1993, when Stephen Lawrence, a black British teenager, was fatally stabbed in a South-East London racist attack. During the initial investigation into this murder, five suspects were arrested but not convicted. This led to a 1998 public inquiry that examined the MPS and their murder investigation. The results, published in a 1999 inquiry report, labelled the MPS as "institutionally racist" (for an excellent review of the Stephen Lawrence literature, see Rollock 2009).[12]

This 1999 finding came as no great surprise to some in East London's communities. One example of a pre-Lawrence response to institutional racism, discrimination, and injustice was the creation of the Newham Monitoring Project (NMP). The NMP was formed by campaigners in 1980 as a direct response to another racist murder that the police were considered to have failed to deal with adequately. In this instance, it was the murder of teenager Akhtar Ali Baig in Newham. As an organization, the NMP "believe that racism remains rooted in the very fabric of British society, as shown by recent anti-terrorism legislation and stop and search powers, disproportionately affecting working class black communities." (NMP Manifesto)[13]

Disturbingly, a report on the community perceptions of the instigating factors of the riots led to headlines such as that published by the regional on-line newspaper and information source *London24: London for Londoners*, which read: "London riots: Police stop and search blamed for tension that sparked Tottenham riots" (Youle 2011). For the report this policing tactic was at the root of the tense relationship between the police and the community which caused the escalation of the London rioting. Although the report does identify a number of alternative causes, the quoted headline is supposed to encapsulate the public's perception of what caused both the riots and their rapid escalation. During my research, this perception was reiterated in innumerable accounts by white and non-white residents. The following excerpt from an interview held in June 2012 with a 19-year-old black man from *ExCeLland* provides a good example. He reported, "I had just got home from work [and was] in my uniform. I was just hanging around with my family outside the house and they [the police] threw me on the ground, put a gun to my head and started kicking me. That's when they went too far, there was no need for that. One police tried to get me on my own and hit me with a cosh, that's when I started shouting [to get other people's attention] and he put his cosh away. The police are always offering to fight us one-on-one but we always say 'take your vest off' that's how we know if they're serious. We've got them on tape [mobile phone video recording] doing [assaulting] a friend. We always tape them now but what can we do? We can't go to the police, the only option is the media, they're the ones that can do something. The police label you and take your picture."

One example of the media using such recordings to raise awareness of this kind of incidents unraveled in March 2012, just months before the Games and the securitization began in earnest. The day after the 2011 riots, a 21-year-old black man from Newham was arrested and placed in a police van. What follows is a report of this incident based upon his mobile-phone recording. "Scotland Yard is facing a racism scandal after a black man used his mobile phone to record police officers subjecting him to a tirade of abuse in which he was told: 'The problem with you is you will always be a nigger'...he was made to feel 'like an animal' by the police. He has also accused one officer of kneeling on his chest and strangling him. In the recording, a police officer can be heard admitting he strangled the man because he was a 'cunt'...another officer...subjects the man to a succession of racist insults and adds: 'You'll always have black skin. Don't hide behind your colour'" (Lewis 2012).

I found that, as a consequence of such instances, local people were generally very distrusting of policing and security. Furthermore, because Olympic policing and securitization would vastly increase the numbers of police in the borough, a fear of escalating persecutions formed a significant part of the *habitus* of many non-white Newham residents. This fear can be encapsulated in the following example, which illustrates how the controversial policing tactic known as "stop and search" and its application contribute to fostering fear.

Stop and Search: The Implications of Section 60

During an interview conducted in May 2012, a community worker (white, female, 35) said to me, "With the Olympics around the corner the whole of Newham has been made into a control zone. This is particularly to do with limiting parking and traffic, but it has implications for the dispersal orders and the powers to move people out of the area. Our expectations are that community members, particularly young people, will continue to be targeted by the police and the security forces because of the heightened state of alert created by the Olympics. This is where the stop and search techniques will be used. Stop and search is a very aggressive and intimidating form of policing that is conducted by a group of police officers, often against the individual. It often leaves the recipient angry, frustrated and resentful when they have done nothing more than walking down a street. This does the police no favours with local perceptions of police tactics or their opinions regarding public service or racial stereotyping."

Stop and search is a policing technique intended to be used as a preventive measure to reduce crime and increase safety.[14] In 1984, this new legislation empowered the police with the right to stop members of the public and search them for a variety of reasons. More precisely, Section 60 of the Criminal Justice and Public Order Act of 1994 states that police have "the right to search people in a defined area at a specific time when they believe, with good reason, that; there is the possibility of serious violence; or that a person is carrying a dangerous object or offensive weapon; or that an incident involving serious violence has taken place and a dangerous instrument or offensive weapon used in the incident is being carried in the locality."

There are two justifications for stop and search, both based on "suspicion." In the generic use, a police officer must have a good reason to conduct a stop and search and before doing so, s/he is required to inform the person of this reason. According to the MPS website,[15] being stopped does not mean that one is under arrest or has done something wrong. In some cases, people are simply "stopped as part of a wide-ranging effort to catch criminals in a targeted public place." Furthermore, the website lists other *legitimate* reasons for being stopped and searched. They are:

- If the police think that an individual is carrying a weapon, drugs or stolen property
- If there has been serious violence or disorder in the vicinity
- If the police are looking for a suspect who fits your description
- As part of anti-terrorism efforts

The MPS claim that this tactic has the support of the public. In 2012, Commander Tony Eastaugh stated that "stop and search is an important policing tactic and a deterrent to crime. We know from public attitude surveys that communities support us when it is used fairly and professionally."[16] However, in response to public allegations involving the perceived racial profiling of "Stop and Search," the Independent Police Complaints Commission (IPCC) stated that searches that yield no arrests were "antagonistic and highly intrusive" (Townsend 2012). Indeed, a study conducted by the London School of Economics and the Open Society Justice Initiative revealed that "a black person was 29.7 times more likely to be stopped and searched than a white person." The findings, based on government statistics, represent "the worst international record of discrimination involving stop and search" (ibid). In an area of hyper-ethno-diversity, such as Newham, "Stop and Search" becomes increasingly problematic. When such a tactic became magnified by the ever-increasing fears linked to Olympic securitization and the associated threat of terrorism, the number of people who were stopped and searched increased exponentially.

The overriding perception that Section 60 has racial connotations is perhaps best emphasized by the following excerpt from my interview of October 2011 with a founder (female, 33) of the Albanian migrant community organization Shpresa. Her remarks somewhat absent-mindedly provided an unbiased perspective on this key aspect of "Stop and Search" tactics. She said, "We, as an organisation are invited to lots of community events to talk about the policing of the area. Stop and search doesn't really affect us because we are white. Although, the blacks and Asians do have a lot of issues with it."

Olympic Neighborhood Policing

It was beyond debate that the Games brought additional concerns regarding the drafting of police and security from outside of the MPS. These concerns were highlighted in a personal interview I had in March 2012 with the Chair of the NYPP, a white male in his mid-fifties and to some extent a quintessential middle-Englander. He said, "There is a London way of policing and there is significant community anxiety concerning bringing in police officers from outside of the Metropolitan area that do not understand how to police within Newham. This is a unique community because of its composition and demographics. The local policing style reflects this uniqueness. For example, the local police know you don't shake a Muslim woman by the hand and you take your shoes off when entering someone's home. Little things like that make all the difference. It's a London attitude, it's basically how you walk and talk. People unfamiliar with the culture simply act differently and will not know the particular dynamics of interaction within this community which is vastly different from anywhere else. Unfamiliarity and ignorance breed tension. This anxiety will, I feel, be increased by the vast numbers of police officers that will be working in this area that are not from within the Met [MPS]. The concern is that heavy handed policing will occur as a consequence of simple miscommunication, difference, or unfamiliarity. The community concern is that this will disproportionately affect young people from ethnic minorities, which will raise levels of discontent. This will provide a flashpoint. We are worried about the consequences for young people and, indeed, the whole community."

De facto, the implementation of security measures during Olympic delivery engendered a highly visible occupying force made of a massive additional number of police, security people, and British troops. Security narratives also took non-human shape. This was most visible literally and through media reports, such as those on the deployment of high-velocity anti-aircraft missiles in residential areas. Some of these missiles were deployed on top of council tower blocks; some missile-bearing aircrafts were deployed along the river Thames. Both focused on Newham's airspace. Residents of the Fred Wigg tower block in the London borough of Waltham Forrest, who had to endure living underneath such weaponry, sought what ultimately turned out to be a futile judicial review regarding the legality of the Ministry of Defence's (MOD) decision to place missiles in a residential area. Reporters described the residents' shock, anxiety, and worry regarding the prospect of missiles being stationed on the buildings where they lived and the fact that they were under a misapprehension about the nature of the equipment to be deployed and the risks brought about by such deployment (Norton-Taylor 2012).

In relation to this research, the lawfulness and appropriateness of the positioning of these missiles are of secondary importance. What interests us is the belief that they were necessary in the first place. To refer back to Ryan (2002), such actions not only seemed "bizarre and outlandish" to the local communities; they seemed to be downright troubling. Various organizations engaged in initiatives intended to offset what they believed would be the considerable negative implications of such actions for local people, including possible police persecution, particularly of the local youth, restriction of movement and living in fear of the consequences of their homes becoming temporary missile silos.

An example of these initiatives was an NYPP information pack first distributed to Newham's youth workers who, in turn, disseminated it among Newham's youth. This information was to be relayed primarily to the local non-white and/or non-British youths, whom they believed would be disproportionately affected by Olympic security and policing. The pack contained information for young people explaining how they could expect their routines to be affected and a "Safe Passage Card" bearing dates and destinations of "appointments" at youth centers. The NYPP believed that as a result of Olympic securitization, local young people were inevitably going to be stopped and searched more frequently; this card was meant to provide them with what was hoped to be acceptable reasons for walking on Newham's streets during Games time.

Another example of reaction to the impending Olympic securitization was the Newham Monitoring Project's (NMP) "Community Legal Observer" initiative.[17] NMP recruited some 150 local people from various backgrounds and trained them to function as "Community Legal Observers" (CLOs). Teams of CLOs would monitor the police during the Games. They were to document the impact that the police would have during the Games and question the legality of certain policing tactics. The CLOs were trained over a series of events led by NMP staff at their offices, near Upton Park. The volunteers were taught how to document and record Olympics policing and how to report to a centralized control room manned by NMP staff at their home base. This was intended to produce a "real time" picture of Olympics securitization. The CLOs would also disseminate throughout the community "Bust Cards"[18] detailing one's rights when stopped and confronted by the police.

Clearly, Newham's securitization was the cause for much consternation amongst local people. Arguably, they had good reason for this apprehension. In 2006, Her Majesty's Inspectorate of Constabulary (HMIC), who have the statutory responsibility for the inspection of Police forces, identified Newham as "failing," in policing terms, in regard to "the fact that every category of Newham's performance sits within the bottom quartile of its MSBCU (Most Similar Basic Command Unit) group, recent declines in performance in all categories except one (robbery reduction) and its under-performance over the past three years, indicates a pressing need to review and significantly improve upon many fundamental BCU processes" (HMIC 2006, p. 1).

This chapter has shown that the security measures attached to 2012 Olympic delivery, which were widely publicized as pre-requisite for Games, were in fact seen by many local people as aimed at restricting movement, prohibiting access, and relegating quotidian Newham life firmly into an inconsequential category for the duration of the Games. The discussion has also indicated that little attention was given to the political and social implications of Olympic delivery, which is emblematic of the politics of "bread and circuses" and of building a city for a visiting class (Eisinger 2000). Looking at key examples of Olympic-related security outcomes, we have seen that the Olympic Games not only brought a "Mega-Event" circus to Newham, they also brought connotations of place ownership intimating that the borough belonged to a demographic that was entirely different from the people who lived there. This desirable demographic was specifically being sought to visit Newham for the Games and then, through an Olympic-themed dissemination of a particular set of norms and values that ill-fitted pre-Olympic Newham, to populate this locale after the Games. The next chapter will consider the implications of this process.

CHAPTER 8

Big Game Hunting: Baiting the Hooks

As the previous chapters have illustrated, Olympic delivery was a meticulous construction that had a divisive impact upon some sections of the Newham community. Olympic delivery outcomes were underpinned by the widespread belief, portrayed by politicians and Olympic deliverers in the media and at community-consultation events, that all delivery measures were necessary preconditions to successful Olympic Games. One widely touted aspect of Olympic *legacy* was the inevitability of East London's regeneration. This regeneration—never actually defined—ran parallel to the delivery of the Olympic Games and is explored here in relation to the physical and symbolic implications of urban modification. What follows is an analysis of the outcomes of Newham's Olympic-related gentrification.

A Brave New World: Newham's Urban Safari

Olympic-delivery Newham was a place of transition. The Olympic Games were used as a catalyst to make the borough more appealing to live, shop, and work in, with a view to attracting a new wave of residents. This process, which has been illustrated in earlier chapters, fits with neighborhood modification models that can be categorized as gentrification. In a review of gentrification literature Slater, Curran, and Lees argued that this phenomenon related to all aspects of the "production of space for—and consumption by—a more affluent and very different incoming population" (2004, p. 1145). Gentrification is deeply rooted in the social dynamics and economic trends of an area and its signifiers and effects are heavily influenced by the nature of economic restructuring and by the goals of those charged with urban regeneration (van Weesep 1984, p. 80). The study of gentrification has addressed topics, such as policing strategies and the role of retail (Zukin 1995; Smith 2002; Atkinson 2003; Atkinson and Bridge 2005), which are worth considering in the Newham context.

Drawing on my research, I contend that the primary Olympic outcome in Newham can be seen to be a redressing of the "Rent Gap"[1] in a deprived but potentially valuable location that lay within easy commute distance from *The City*. The Olympic healing of the "London's Gash" ensured that during Olympic delivery and beyond, the area would yield higher returns from its land in the form of rents and property values. As result, it has, and will continue to attract new residents to the area.

This was intended to help alleviate the many social problems that marked this borough as one of the most deprived in Britain, which rested on the assumption that benefits, particularly in terms of housing, would "trickle down" to the lower and working classes. However, a significant body of research indicates that often these anticipated benefits are completely captured by the middle and upper classes (Holcomb and Beauregard 1981, p. 3). In line with Holcomb and Beauregard (1981), the outcomes of some pre-*legacy* independent urbanites' adventurous forays in Newham did indeed point to the folly of such assumptions, which we have seen exemplified most notably in the form of the BV (of *ExCeLland*). There, regeneration did not appear to result in a "trickling-down" of benefits to the lower or working classes; instead, it appeared to facilitate the social exclusion of disadvantaged groups at the hands of incoming affluent people who were increasingly uncomfortable in their new surroundings. In this locale the rhythms of post-gentrification life resonated to the beat of inequality, disparity, division, and distrust. Paradoxes of poverty and affluence uncomfortably coexisted in the same urban location, as a direct result of a social mixing that facilitated incredible and inescapable contrasts. For example, on one side of Wesley Avenue (the road that separated the estate's private and social housing) sat a two bedroom flat for sale for £425,000;[2] on the other side, an ecstatic young black girl aged 18, crouched on the kerb-side, proudly told me how she had managed to get a job for the duration of the Games, serving food at the Olympic Park for £8.25. She stated that this wage was more than double what she could get for the day-to-day job of delivering fastfood. Furthermore, a little way down the street was a 4-bedroom flat for rent at £555 per week;[3] the view from the bedroom window was of a small, dilapidated one-bedroom flat on the opposite side of the road. This one bedroom flat housed 15 recent migrants seeking work from Nigeria.

In Bourdieu's "species of capital" model (1986), *economic capital* is considered to be the most efficient form of *capital* because it can be easily converted into appropriate forms of *cultural* or *symbolic capital* (Calhoun et al. 1993, p. 5). Quite obviously, the private residents maintained economic dominance in the BV, where *economic capital* was converted through its literal and symbolic representations. These representations allowed access to specific social groupings, which involved access to a degree of *social capital*. In this regard, *social capital* refers to the sum of actual and potential resources that are mobilized through one's networks, which emphasizes the relational aspect of this form of *capital*. It appears that the BV, once an inclusive borough, may well become populated with a variety of securitized gated communities that segregate themselves from the conceptual *others*; that is, those lacking the *capital* to succeed in the reordered areas of Newham. If we take the BV as indicative of life in a post-Olympic gentrified Newham, it becomes clearer how this process is altering the fabric of the borough. This needs attention.

Newham's Urban Emperors and Stepford Wives

Moving away from predictions of future outcomes and applying the lessons learned from BV to the wider context of Newham's Olympic delivery, it appeared that Games-related modification introduced a proliferation of indicators of change that demanded access to (or at least familiarity with) a certain level of *economic capital*. These indicators included the Westfield Stratford City shopping mall and the Olympic Village,[4] long advertised as a post-Olympic living space, both of which may be considered exemplars of gentrification. They were symbolic and physical creations that generated and validated specific norms and values of *social capital*; they attracted only those with the requisite *habitus*, who were predisposed to feel comfortable with such capital and to succeed. This process was understood as a core aspect of middle-classes' cultural reproduction that is established and maintained through the ownership of *economic capital* (Allan 1989; Butler and Robson 2001; Willmott 1987).

Newham's Olympic-themed renewal is considered a means to attract people who are well endowed with *economic capital*. Such groups have been described as transnational élites (Friedmann and Wolff 1982), stateless persons (Wallerstein 1993), cosmopolites (Hannerz 1992), or "rich ignorant pricks who look down on everyone who's not like them" (James, 17, black, Newham resident, private interview 2012). Often written about as postplace *flaneurs*, such residents believe they live in a world of culture (King 1993, p. 152) and seek to occupy new and emerging "trendy" places that satiate and validate their pursuit of a "trendy" living. One model of this demographic was outlined in the work of the human geographer Brian Berry

(1985), who listed the following common denominators that often indicated inclusion into such classifications, which he referred to as an *Urban Gentry*:

- *Childless Households*
- *Unmarried Adults*
- *Higher Education Levels*

Newham's Olympic-related reordering aspirations resonated with the notion that young, usually professional, middle-class people have, since the late 1970s, been more inclined than the previous generations to postpone marriage and children and explore independent urban living (Lipton 1976; Smith 1979). Arguably, in this regard Newham's Olympic-related regeneration was emblematic of the regeneration of other post-industrial settings, where white-collar service sector workers and the associated culture of consumption have guided urban developments (Ley 1996). This process was perhaps best exemplified by the Westfield Stratford City shopping center, which included specific kinds of designer shops, high-end restaurants, and a casino. Amongst others social cues, the injection of such a model in the area, informed expectations of inclusion and exclusion in modified Newham that were increasingly based upon class and wealth. Interestingly, Westfield Stratford City was awarded planning permission two years before London was awarded the Olympic Games but, as with so many other examples, has become inseparable from the 2012 Games; it has indeed become synonymous with the Olympic *legacy*-related narrative. Therefore, Westfield Stratford City has become a key signifier of Olympic-related regeneration discourse and in doing so has become a key center of activity that must be analyzed as part and parcel of the reproduction and transformation of the Olympic delivery schema (Harvey 1989, p. 355). What follows addresses the Westfield milieu in greater detail looking at what this shopping mall represents in the Newham context.

Westfield Stratford City: The Shiny House on the Hill?

When it opened, Westfield Stratford City was the largest urban shopping center in the European Union. Boasting 300 stores, restaurants, and entertainment facilities, the mall was positioned next to Olympic Park. For Newham's mayor, Sir Robin Wales, Westfield's opening represented much more than the inauguration of a shiny new shopping complex. As he stated at the grand opening in September 2011, "Westfield represents more than just bricks, mortar, fabulous shops and restaurants. It has been instrumental in helping us transform the lives of our residents by providing them with employment and jobs that they can turn into fulfilling and rewarding careers... Shoppers, tourists and visitors will also bring economic benefits to Newham and will leave a lasting legacy long after the Olympics has rolled out of town." (Sir Robin Wales, 2011)[5]

In this study, I have documented various instances of Sir Robin Wales's public announcements. It is crucial to bear in mind that Sir Robin, like many others examined in this study, was engaged in a specific role-related highly political interplay and in all that that entailed. Accordingly, his actions may have had the goals of appealing to voters and of stressing his personal satisfaction for creating jobs in his borough. The statistics he quotes may provide "a kind of continuous justification for existing" (Bourdieu 2000, p. 240), a validation of his mayoralty.

At the community events in which I participated, the evaluations of Westfield were marked by reiterated claims that its malls could offer employment opportunities for local people. Westfield's own official statistics indicated that this shopping complex created 25,000 construction jobs while it was being built and 18,000 permanent jobs once it opened; 10,000 of these jobs were in retail.[6] According to Workplace, a Newham job brokerage scheme set up in 2007 to help local people into employment, 1,050 Newham residents gained work in Westfield in 2011.[7] These figures did not differentiate between full and part-time or temporary positions. In other words, they indicated best-case scenarios of employment ratios of approximately 1/18, if one optimistically assumed that all Newham residents were employed on permanent contracts—1,050 new jobs do not seem quite so impressive when considered in this light.

However, I would argue that Westfield's primary impact should not be measured in terms of employment figures, but rather in relation to the levels of *hysteresis* that it created in the Newham's communities during Olympic delivery. This shopping complex offered an opportunity to contextualize the reordering of Newham's local communities, playing a role in the physical and symbolic segregation of Newham. It was emblematic of what happened in Newham throughout Olympic delivery and synthesized the intended outcomes of Olympic regeneration—to attract more desirable, that is bourgeois, residents to post-Olympic Newham. This is exemplified by the following case study.

Craig: A Branded Life

When I conducted my research, Craig was a 29 year-old; he is white and English. He was the subject of an article in a London newspaper, which presented him as an ideal Westfield customer.

Craig lived with his wife Clair and their three-year-old son in Upminster, Essex. In a private interview we had in July 2012, that is after the newspaper article was published, Craig explained that they had chosen to live there because it provided them with access to the space and seclusion of Essex, as well as to good school networks. Moreover, it allowed easy commuting to The City where Craig worked as an IT support team leader for a large American Bank. Craig felt that his opinions of the 2012 Games were representative of the views of many people "like him"; that is, young affluent, educated family men. The Olympics would, according to Craig, have a significant impact upon "local areas," including Newham, which, when considered without the beneficial Olympic lens, were described as a "bit rough" and "not the sort of place I'd want to go to." This perception began to change during Olympic delivery. As Craig said, "Now they've got Westfield. It's changed a lot of people's minds about the area. Now we do go there for dinner and the casino after work on a Friday, instead of going to Liverpool Street or another of the usual places." Moreover, "Me and the missus [sic] go there at the weekend to do a bit of shopping and have a day out, it's really nice. It's a bit more convenient than going into central [London] and a bit more up to date than Bluewater [an Essex shopping Mall]." When pressed on whether he would venture away from Westfield to explore the surrounding areas, Craig replied with an emphatic "no" and laughed, "Why would I want to do that?" before adding "I do go to Upton Park a bit [West Ham United's home ground located in Newham] to watch the football but I'm a Man U [Manchester United] fan so I don't go often, that's enough for me there's nothing else." Craig's final perspective in relation to attracting young families to move to the area post-Games was telling: "I wouldn't want to live there, Essex is an easy commute to London and it's such a nicer area to live in, I will keep going to Westfield and I will go and watch the Olympics, but I like it where we are [living in Essex]." Craig's perspective bears considerable weight to the prospects of Newham's post-Olympic legacy.

The above remarks indicated that perceptions of "Newham" were beginning to evolve during Olympic delivery as a result of a Westfield-inspired regeneration of the borough. Arguably, Westfield was indicative of a broader change of perceptions of Newham that might expand to include larger swathes of the borough in the post-Olympic years. However, during Olympic delivery, the rest of Newham was not quite so amenable to accomplishing the aim of keeping Hugo Boss-loving Craig and his like comfortable and content. Consequently, access to Westfield and the Olympic Park had to be carefully choreographed to enable this demographic to avoid the areas that might be deemed to be "a bit rough." The physical segregation that enabled people like Craig to differentiate between Olympic Newham and traditional

Newham took the shape of what could best be termed "corporate kettling."[8] Such corporate kettling both restricted and guided the movement of affluent Newham visitors directing them toward the key landmarks of consumption that lay between public transport entry and exit points, namely Westfield itself and the Olympic Park. Interestingly, it was predicted that 70% of Olympic visitors would pass through Westfield's doors.[9] Considering that the Olympic planners estimated that 10 million people would visit during the Games, this means that 7 million would be subject to this "corporate kettling" during the Olympic Games alone.

It was thus ensured that people could easily enter and leave the area without setting foot in "old" Newham. Plenty of private parking spaces were provided in the bowels of the shopping complex.[10] Moreover, the entry and exit points of *Stratfordland's* public rail hub were redesigned to encourage public transport travelers to emerge within the confines of Westfield, as opposed to entering *Stratfordland* itself. However, in case one did inadvertently use the traditional entry/exit point, the old *Stratfordland* was masked from view by the creation of a visual and symbolic concealment that suggested there was nothing worth seeing in that direction. Let us now examine the measures employed to mark "old" Newham as a no-go area and some of their implications.

Fences and Walls: Concealing Ugly Newham

Newham was home to much that could not be considered beautiful and needed to be masked from Olympic sight. In *Stratfordland,* there was a particularly dated shopping center that was shielded by a purpose-built 250m-titanium sculpture named "The Shoal" because of its likeness to a shoal of fish.

In 2009 Newham council held a competition[11] to "solve the problem" of masking the 1970s shopping center that would blot the Olympic landscape. This "public realm intervention" competition was won by Egret West, a London-based architecture, urban design, and landscape Studio. According to the designers, this "beautification" was intended to "turn a negative into a positive." Newham Mayor Sir Robin Wales commented that Newham was undergoing unprecedented transformation and the Shoal was a significant part of the £13.5m public realm project to "improve" Stratford for residents and businesses, and to offer a unique visitor experience.[12]

Those looking in from outside were not the only ones who appreciated this transformation. There were local residents who also appreciated the "improvements." Narratives of gentrification that vilify areas and damage culture have been overwhelmingly criticized (Atkinson 2003). However, in

126 • Living with London's Olympics

Figure 8.1 The Shoal.

the Olympic delivery Newham context, especially when considering the lack of a holistic identity in the borough, it was not surprising to find some local positive views on these outcomes. Indeed, as exemplified by the following case study, such positive views became increasingly more apparent as the Games approached.

Jasmine: A Pro-Olympic Local?

At the time of my research, Jasmine was 38. She is a white Austrian Muslim who had moved to Newham in 2003. She was married and had five children. In an interview that we held in February 2012, she claimed to be pro-Olympic. "I like what is happening in the area," she said, "they have invested lots in the shop fronts and on fixing the pavements. It is making the area more attractive. I try to keep informed with what is going on in the community but I have never been consulted and never had any chance to have a say in how I would like the Olympics to change this area but they have done a nice job so far." For Jasmine the only real concern about the 2012 Games and the concomitant regeneration was its implications for local traffic levels, "It used to take me 15 minutes to get to work, now it takes 40 minutes on a good day. That is going to be a nightmare during the Olympics; I think I'm going to have to take time off, all the road closures and them digging up the roads is really causing problems, it's been like that for ages now."

However, while for some, like Jasmine, Westfield and the social setting it represented were welcome modifications to the Newham landscape, for others they reinforced a sense of fear and of exclusion from all things "Olympic." Olympic-related regeneration modified large swathes of the Newham landscape, most notably in *Stratfordland*, at the same time delivering a symbolic reordering of the location that became increasingly manifest as the Games approached. What follows demonstrates that although individuals were not *physically* restrained, Olympic delivery reordering ensured that some considered Newham's regenerated locales *foreign*, no-go areas that were not for them.

Tasha: An Un-stereotypical Stereotype

Tasha is a black Dutch-born Newham resident who, at the time of my research, had lived in the borough for 15 years. After enduring 14 years of abuse, she had recently divorced her Nigerian husband on grounds of domestic violence. She recounted stories of being kicked down the stairs while pregnant and other similar kinds of abuse with the detachment of someone discussing what they had watched on television.

Tasha had three children. The eldest, an 11-year-old boy, was into "gangsta rap" music and "hung around on the streets" with his peers. Tasha reported a discussion she had had with him telling him that he needed to change his attitude because, like it or not, he was a fit for the negative Newham male stereotype. She stated that all the kids that were brought up in her area (*ExCeLland*) fitted that stereotype, "coming as they did from single parent families that were either on benefits or in low-paid work." Tasha believed that "there was no hope for most of the kids who grew up that way." She did not feel that any of the Olympic delivery outcomes would filter down to them; rather, it would be the rich who would benefit. When asked whether she had been to Westfield she said, laughing, "How could I take three kids there when I knew I couldn't buy them anything? It was my daughter's birthday last month and she wanted an iPod touchscreen. At Westfield they cost £150 but I got one locally for a lot less [implying that she had not bought it in a shop], Westfield's isn't for people like us. I mean, look at us."

This account builds upon the securitization issues addressed earlier by providing insights into the unsettled nature of life during Olympic delivery, when society was under constant renegotiation. Perceptions of such uncertainty became manifest through blasé attitudes to life, the Olympics, and the "*legacy.*" Unsurprisingly, these tactics alienated the communities that were intended to be hidden from the Olympic visitors, kept away from Olympic locales, or otherwise vilified. An exceedingly common thread linking the perceptions of those who lived in *Stratfordland*, in *ExCeLland* and indeed throughout Newham was that *Stratfordland* had taken on a new resonance. For some long-term Newham residents this meant that the area was no longer accessible; they felt they did not fit there, therefore had little desire to adapt, and avoided *Stratfordland* and other regenerated areas. On many levels, they felt excluded from this newly created, reordered Newham space.

This situation speaks to notions of heightened social inequality and inadequacy as they were exemplified by Olympic delivery. It brings to mind the work of urban sociologist Mike Davis on Los Angeles (1990), where he commented that the dispossessed often become trapped in new forms of spatial apartheid, whereby they are confined in their own areas and become the objects of remote surveillance and repressive controls. Davis' perspective resonated with Suttles' (1972) idea that in a city, individuals collectively assign a "cognitive map" or a classification of people and places based on an historical and social ranking of space. This correlation between the worth of the individual and the accessibility of place (see also Sampson 2009) suggests a correspondence between Tasha's perception that Westfield is inaccessible to her and her version of accessible Newham, which in turn is perceived as inaccessible by those who feel comfortable in Westfield. The wider consequences of issue of cognitive accessibility became evident as Tasha described her concerns, as a parent, over her relationship with her son.

We have seen that Tasha had realized that her son would inevitably be stereotyped as a black "hoodie" who was a gang member and listened to gangsta music. Having realized that the boy came from what many would call a broken home with a history of violence, she had warned him that this perception would limit him in life. On the one hand, Tasha reasoned that, if acted upon, such a worry might make him withdrawn and liable to stay at home and have no friends, as all his friends were, in her opinion "the same." She also worried that if that happened he would become a "victim" because he would be different, not conforming to the masculine codes of the street. On the other hand, Tasha's main concern was that if her son continued on his present path he would likely become involved with gangs and would get in trouble with the police. It was a Catch 22 situation and she knew it.

When, in a conversation we had in March 2012, I asked her to describe how such concerns affected her life and that of others like her; she gave many examples of what could be called the prisons of—Newham—parenthood. These prisons of parenthood consisted of single parent families where the children witnessed domestic violence, which, according to numerous local people to whom I spoke during my field research, was emblematic of Newham life at the lowest end. These parents had little social structure in their lives and were unable to afford the childcare or access the advice that would enable them to enter meaningful paid employment. This "trap" ensured that they either brought up their children and were there for them, or worked, letting them fend for themselves. In the areas, there were visible instances of both.

When asked whether she intended to seek Olympic-related employment, Tasha stated that because the only Olympic jobs that were available for people like her were temporary contracts that would end after the Olympic Games, coming off benefits for such opportunities was not an intelligent move. She added that it was difficult to get her state benefits started because of the various complexities of the processes. She dreaded having to go through this again. She stated that the benefits did not begin until a month after signing on, which effectively would mean that she would have no income for a month.

Tasha's view on the shortsighted "benefits" of temporary Olympic employment was indicative of the research conducted by Marrs (2003), who explored the validity of such short-term employment as a beneficial outcome of Olympic hosting. The views illustrated above are those of one Newham resident and clearly do not speak for all. However, they are indicative of a demographic who represented a lifestyle in sharp contrast with that typical of Newham's urban renewal, as it would be obvious even from the most cursory comparison between areas like Westfield and the average Newham high street.

Viva Las Newham: An Adult's Playground?

The differentiation between the old and the new in terms of shopping illustrated that the most fundamental components of everyday life in Newham were deeply laden with meaning in this particular place at this particular time. The photograph above illustrates the high-end retail outlets that proliferated in Westfield; it shows the Aspers Casino dominating the skyline behind John Lewis—a high-end department store, to the left of Waitrose, another high-end grocery store. The Aspers Casino catered for well-heeled clientele who sought to gamble after eating and drinking in one of the many restaurants or bars in the mall. The photographs below illustrate the contrast with the typical Newham high street and the traditional Newham population.

This fundamental dichotomy illustrated the juxtaposition in everyday life during Olympic delivery. A particularly good indicator of this dichotomy was to be found in the contrast between Aspers Casino and the proliferation of betting shops in Newham.[13]

130 • Living with London's Olympics

Figure 8.2 Viva Las Newham...

In spite of this continuing dichotomy, Newham was undoubtedly changing and new affluent residents were attracted to the area as a result of regeneration both before and during Olympic delivery. As exemplified by the BV, these residents brought with them affluence, attitudes, and expectations that did not necessarily sit easily within "old" Newham. For example, this new wave of residents had particular demands for shopping, entertainment, security, and transportation links. As it is exemplified by the following case study, these demands often became manifest through a reluctance to engage in Newham life outside of their comfort zones and through a differentiation from the perceptible *others*.

Blair, Vicky, and the Patter of Tiny Feet...Leaving Newham

When I spoke to him in July 2012, Blair, a 27-year-old white Scotsman, was married to Vic a white 26-year-old East Londoner. Blair worked as a

Figure 8.3 Electric Avenue.

Figure 8.4 Eating Out.

lawyer for a Fleet Street Law firm; Vic worked across London as a freelance decorator. In 2009, they were looking to buy their first property and move from their rented accommodation in Vauxhall, in the London borough of Lambeth. Their preference was to stay in Vauxhall but they eventually moved to a two-bedroom flat in ExCeLland because they "got more for their money and it was just as quick to get to work from there." Blair recollected that when they decided to move to ExCeLland many friends questioned why they would move to a location that had a reputation for being "unsafe" and "full of foreigners." Vic's family were particularly opposed to the whole idea because she had been brought up in East Ham until she was 10 when her family chose to move from Essex because the East Ham area was "getting run down and full of immigrants." They thought it was ironic that the family had moved away from East London for Vic's benefit only to see her move back of her own accord some years later. However, undeterred, the young couple bought their flat and moved in in late July 2009.

The couple's perceptions of living in the area were informed by their intention of using their flat as a hub from which to travel outside their local environs. They realized that, other than staying in their flat, they rarely spent time in ExCeLland. During a private interview, they commented that on their way home from the DLR station they walked past "one road that had on one side nice homes and on the other the run-down homes that 'were council'." The couple were quick to articulate that they would "hate to live there and have to look out their windows at homes that people didn't take care of; the people living there are just Chavy[14] basically." Their life in ExCeLland was one of seclusion and isolation from the local community, with Blair saying that the only interaction they had beyond their gated flat was when attending the local gym. Those who shared their block of flats were "people like us, young professionals from outside the local area." The couple liked to socialize, and when they did, they would select specific areas where they felt comfortable, such as "Canary Wharf, central London, and the O2 [in the borough of Greenwich across the Thames from Newham]." However, this young couple's view of the area changed in 2011, when Vic became pregnant and they began to re-evaluate their home and their locale.

In mid-July 2012, while searching for a "child-appropriate" property, Blair commented that the Olympics had changed Newham for the better. He said that he wished the Games had occurred sooner and that he and Vic had had the opportunity to enjoy Westfield more when they were childfree. For him, Newham had become "more attractive" as a result of the Olympic regeneration. He reasoned, "I like Westfield because it's convenient and gives the area a bit more prestige, Stratford is not just a shit-hole anymore. All the talk about various Olympic legacies are not necessarily going to help the area but one thing that will definitely benefit all is the improved transport links." However, these modifications had not, in his opinion, fixed the fundamental problems of the area from the perspective of young families. He wanted a "cleaner and safer area" to bring up his daughter, where

English was the predominant language to be heard and where the schools were much better (that is, not prone to gang violence and bullying). It is for these shortcomings that the couple had decided that Newham was not a place where they wanted to bring up their daughter and planned to move. This time, they wanted to move further east—to Essex. Blair added that the Olympic-related modifications of Newham, although "nice," did not "take precedence over fundamental parenting considerations. Suburban life is much more appealing." In this regard, Vic's life had now truly come full circle, as they repeated the flight of her parents from East London to Essex for the sake of their child.

The findings discussed here are indicative of Berry's (1985) "*residential choice theory*," which presumes that couples and families evaluate prospective locales in relation to a number of key criteria such as the quality and price of housing and the services available locally. This theory suggests that the arrival of children originates a reevaluation of these criteria; couples with children inevitably prioritize safety and education to a higher degree than those without children. This reevaluation often results in moving from recently gentrified areas to locales with more established and more highly regarded education systems (Berry 1985). Research suggests that a school's proximity to social disadvantage has a direct correlation to lower school performance involving barriers to the children's improvement (Woods and Levacic 2002; Levacic and Woods 2002; Clark, Dyson and Millward 1999). In fact, Blair and Vic were unwilling to risk their child's education for the other benefits of Newham life.

Blair's remarks are suggestive of Berry's (1985) argument that childlessness is a particularly important factor in relation to the continued occupancy of post-gentrified areas, which tend to have low-quality schools. As confirmed by the comments of the community center manager of the BV, once people who move in gentrified areas settle and have children they tend to move away from these areas in search of better schools. This insight meets the findings of Robson and Butler (2001), whose gentrification-related research in the inner London borough of Lambeth demonstrated that middle-class families with children left the area when the children were at or around secondary-school age. They could not find a single child from a middle-class family in a Lambeth secondary school, due to the perceived poor standards of education. In short, building a city as an entertainment venue is a very different undertaking from building a city to accommodate residential interests (Eisinger 2000, p. 317).

Gentrification permeated Olympic delivery discourse via the interchangeable epithets of renewal, revitalization, and regeneration (Wyly and Hammel 2005, p. 36). The outcomes were primarily oriented toward the *Urban*

Gentry (Berry 1985) or indeed the *Creative Classes* (Florida 2002), rather than toward the needs of Newham's pre-Olympic populace. In accordance with Florida's argument (2002), this chapter has indicated that Newham's regeneration will continue to be oriented toward the "creative class" rather than the "conservative middle classes," such as Blair and Vic or Craig and his "missus," who have young families and prefer life in the suburbs (Florida 2002; Ley 1980, 1994 and 1996). This "creative class" includes, among others, young childless couples, gays, bohemians, academics, scientists, artists, entrepreneurs, and students, who are seen as fundamental to economic growth in the regenerated contemporary city (Lees, Slater, and Wyly 2008, p. xix). Perhaps most crucially for Newham, Florida's hypothesis rests upon the divisive model that this "creative class" seeks diversity to validate its choice; however, their introduction dilutes the very diversity and creativity that attracted them to the location in the first place by raising the cost of living and pushing the, oft economically impoverished, perpetrators of diversity elsewhere (Cole 1987; Ley 2003). Therefore, the fate of Newham's long-term regeneration and its transformation into a place where people and families truly want to "live, work and stay" may well depend upon the widespread improvement of its state schools, which would truly be an Olympic "*legacy*" for all.

CHAPTER 9

Going for the Gold: The All-Consuming 2012 Ethos

The issues raised in the previous chapters did not resonate greatly on a national scale. Arguably, this was due to the allure of the Olympic Games and the role of Olympic *legacy* diverting attention away from the oft-mundane nature of everyday life. This chapter considers the process and implication of living through Olympic delivery in relation to geographical location and first-hand experience. To paraphrase public relations expert Philip Lesly (1974), London 2012 spoke to the urges, interests, and desires of contemporary Britain, and was attuned to the mental and emotional bent of the British society. There are significant complexities in this debate that need attention and so do the contested narratives that mark this context.

As we have seen, there is significant evidence to support the applicability of hegemonic theory to this milieu. However, the voices of those from the ground level, which often go unrepresented in social analysis, raise doubts on such applicability. In order to address this problematic we must differentiate between these people and the wider perspective of an Olympic delivery that was practiced in absentia of first-hand experience, in the local context.

An Olympic Identity?

The presentation and pageantry associated with the Olympics has been described as fiercely nationalistic (MacNeill 1996; Hargreaves 2000; Billings and Eastman 2002; Wensing and Bruce 2003). This interpretation has led to research into the nationalist undercurrents of Olympic reporting and broadcasting (Hoberman 2004; Barnard, Butler, Golding, and Maguire

2006; Elder, Pratt, and Ellis 2006). That the Games are portrayed as representations of nationalistic imagery and promotion is true to an extent. However, my findings suggests that the London 2012 Games transcended traditional, segregating nationalistic overtones and created a temporary, powerfully inclusive hybrid form of identity that was both *universalist* and *politically quietist*.

The 2012 *Olympic identity* was delivered through carefully choreographed narratives that created and perpetuated a specific perception of the London Games. Accepting that all identities are based on division, be it race, class or any of the other myriad segregating factors, and that every identity is a political rather than a natural collective, here I would argue that identity is generally based upon violence; literal, discursive or symbolic. The less literal forms of this violence ensure that identity can be created and bolstered through rhetorical narratives that establish baselines for inclusion and exclusion. While a football World Cup could be said to be based strictly upon nationality, as a general rule the 2012 *Olympic identity* does not fit in this traditional model of segregational identity formation.

This is the result of two key factors. Firstly, very few people who embraced the 2012 *Olympic identity* were invested in the sporting contests that took place during the Games. This minimized the importance of the competitive outcomes and ensured that each event was merely a small facet of a much larger, diverse whole. This meant that investment in the experience and the *Olympic identity* far exceeded the outcome of the events, which minimized the importance of nationalistic contests. Secondly, as a result of this lack of personal investment in the sporting outcomes, the *Olympic identity* was not segregational. This second factor is supported by the altruistic image of Olympism; true or imagined, Olympism is built on the impression of amateurism, fair play, and ethical competition, where taking part is more important that winning.

During Olympic delivery, this idea of an inclusive identity was promoted on a regular basis through the British media. This discourse was bolstered by figures of authority, such as politicians and Olympic delivery officials, who contributed to the construction of an "official" history and a holistic national image of the 2012 Games. The beneficial outcomes of Olympic hosting were inferred to be natural, inevitable, and virtually unquestionable. Furthermore, easily understandable expressions, such as *legacy*,were created which seamlessly associated the Games with positive outcomes, thus lending legitimacy to the association between the Games and the benefits that they would bring. These expressions were repeated so often that they entered the vocabulary of the British public. As theorized by Lesly (1974), this kind of inclusive process has the greatest power to sway opinion; it is incredibly powerful in relation to identity formation and the management of subjectivity. When a concept is continually repeated, individuals tend to take its premise for granted. It becomes part of life and taken for granted as knowledge.

Shaping the Olympic Narrative

The race to host the 2012 Olympic Games was a contest in which success depended on differentiating between social, political, and cultural characteristics. The bidding involved a contest of cities and nations, where the narrative was based on the notion that the Olympic Games are a national—indeed a nationalistic—event. This national perspective ensured that the outcome of the bidding contest depended upon a sociologically created "image of the nation state" (Billig 1995, p. 53). Moreover, the use of the nation-state as the pre-eminent constituent of Olympic bidding supports the views of those scholars who see nationality as the fundamental differentiator between peoples; for example, in this line Calhoun stated that nationality acts as a "trump card in the game of identity" (1997, p. 46). Interestingly, during the Olympic bidding Britain's *trump* card was the ethnic diversity of its East London identity.

Such diversity formed a significant component of the bidding campaign, as the following excerpt from Sebastian Coe's 2005 Singapore speech to the IOC indicates. He said, "London's vision is to reach young people all around the world. To connect them with the inspirational power of the Games. So they are inspired to choose sport. I'm delighted we have with us today representatives of the next generation. Here on stage, Amber Charles, an emerging Basketball player: Amber delivered our Candidate File to Lausanne last year. And in the audience, 30 of her contemporaries, aged from 12 to 18. Why are so many here, taking the place of businessmen and politicians? It's because we're serious about inspiring young people. Each of them comes from East London, from the communities who will be touched most directly by our Games: And thanks to London's multi-cultural mix of 200 nations, they also represent the youth of the world. Their families have come from every continent. They practice every religion and every faith. What unites them is London. Their love of sport. And their heartfelt dream of bringing the Olympic Games to our city" (Lord Sebastian Coe 2005).[1]

The results of this contest were broadcast throughout the globe, offering a multitude of water-cooler moments for the days, weeks, months, and indeed years to come. Interestingly, in the immediate aftermath, on June 6, 2005, Prime Minister Tony Blair attempted to distance the bid from a London-centric rhetoric, saying that the award of the Games marked a "momentous day for Britain."[2] The idea was to lend a multi-dimensional identity to the Olympics, which, depending upon the context would shift ownership toward or away from the "local," that is London, at the same time promoting London as the coolest city on Earth.

Following the award of the 2012 Games to London, Lord Sebastian Coe argued that the Games offered "the most fantastic opportunity to do everything we've ever dreamed of in British sport... We have a chance over seven years and way beyond that to change the face of British sport."[3] It was, therefore, of paramount importance to demonstrate how the nation could expect to both benefit from the Games and enable all to have a stake in them. Several documents were produced which outlined such an ideology. For example, the DCMS government document: *Before, during and after: Making the most of the London 2012 Games*,[4] published in 2008, described the expected outcomes of Olympic hosting and placed "sporting outcomes" as the number one priority. This action plan drew on a strategy document published in June 2007, titled *Our Promise for 2012*, and was intended to re-emphasize the previously indicated national Olympic benefits. To avoid repetition, here I will focus on the 2008 outcomes. These were:

1. To make the UK a leading sporting nation
2. To transform the heart of East London
3. To inspire a generation of young people
4. To make the Olympic Park a blueprint for sustainable living
5. To demonstrate that the UK is a creative, inclusive, and welcoming place to live in, to visit, and for business.

This DCMS document stated that in relation to sport the "Headline Ambitions" were to "inspire young people through sport," to get "at least two million more people in England [it is interesting that they used the word England and not Britain], to be more active by 2012," and to "aim for fourth in the Olympic medal table" (p. 6). Furthermore, the DCMS were "determined that the evidence that emerges from the London 2012 Games will be of a significant and sustained increase in participation—across all communities in the United Kingdom [now shifting perspective back to Britain], including ethnic minorities, men, and women, and young and old."

Unfortunately, the premise to these benefits was that the Olympic Games would have a significant bearing on inspiring young people to take up sport (DCMS 2008, p. 19). This premise is highly debatable, especially when considering research conducted in 2003 by Sport England (the government agency responsible for community sport) which indicated that ordinary people watching "models of perfection" performing on an élite stage were actually put off participating (2003, p.5). Furthermore, in a 2002 strategy document titled *Game-Plan: A Strategy for Delivering Government's Sport and Physical Activity Objectives* the UK government itself concluded that hosting an Olympics would not inspire people to take up sport. "depending on the scale of the subsidy, it would seem that hosting events is not an effective, value for money method of achieving...a sustained increase in mass participation" (DCMS/Strategy Unit 2002, p.75). However, shortly after this report, the Government released the *Legacy Master-Plan Framework*, which directly contradicted the earlier *Game Plan* professing that hosting the 2012 Olympics would result in the UK becoming a leading sporting nation and would encourage its population to participate in sport. As Harold Wilson once memorably stated—a week is a long time in politics.

Sport England was responsible for a target of one million people who were to be involved in sport and the Department of Health was tasked to co-ordinate health-related activities to engage another million. Unsurprisingly, these objectives were never achieved, despite the UK Department of Health inventively cataloging pursuits such as "gardening" as "activity" to help boost participation figures. An evaluation of the actual increase in participation during Olympic delivery is muddied by the fact that there was shared accountability for the figure. However, in March 2011, Olympic Secretary Jeremy Hunt, blaming the previous UK Government, quietly but officially scrapped the target.

The "second target [the department of health's million people] had been quietly dropped [without registering in the press] shortly after the coalition government came to power [in 2010]. The first target, towards which the sports have made only glacial progress, nominally remains in place for now but it is understood that it too will shortly be dropped in favour of a 'more meaningful' national measure."[5] The official figures released by Sport England in December 2011, only eight months from the start of the Olympics, did not come as a surprise. These figures indicated that only "111,000 more people... [participated] in sport since 2007, just 11 per cent of the target they have been pursuing for the last four years."[6]

Interestingly, this apparent failure seemed to do little to temper Olympic fervor, which would suggest that the outcomes of governmental targets had little bearing in terms of *Olympic identity* or Olympic enthusiasm. One reason is that Olympic *legacy* is incredibly pluralistic and, accordingly, there are myriad diversions for Olympic scrutiny to follow. One frequently relied-upon justification was the potential "boost" that the Olympic Games would give to the ailing national economy through Games-related tourism (Stevenson 1997; Chalip and Costa 2005). Headlines such as "Games: A £2bn UK tourism boost"[7] proliferated in the media. For example, citing the VisitBritain campaign, an article in the *Daily Mail* reported that the 2012 London Olympic Games was "worth more than £2billion in tourism revenue for the country."

These articles intimated that the responsibility for Britain attaining such an economic boost from hosting the Olympics lay outside the remit of the Olympic deliverers. It was, instead, the responsibility of the British tourism industry to capitalize on the impending opportunities. However, as the European Tour Operators Association (ETOA)[8] stated in its *Olympic Report* (2006), estimates of the profits associated with the audiences that would attend the Games were exaggerated. Moreover, it was also pointed out that these tourists displace normal tourists, rather than adding to their numbers. The ETOA stated that because of their nature and spending habits, Olympic tourists are less financially beneficial than regular tourists would be, and went as far as to suggest that hosting the Olympic Games is actually bad for the tourist industry of a nation.[9]

Such a dichotomy between the *facts* offered by those who have on-the-ground experience and the proliferation of *beliefs* peddled by Olympic *apparatchiks* is crucial to the epistemology of Olympic benefit and *legacy*. The foregoing sheds light on the fact that Olympic euphoria is not about *truth*, it is about *faith*; it is not about sporting outcome, it is about the spectacle of the event and all that it brings. Consequently, there must be aspects that facilitate this peculiar Olympic-related identity formulation; that which supersedes sport and transcends nationality—but what precisely are they?

Nailing down the Olympic ID

One answer to the question of what constitutes *Olympic identity* that particularly resonated throughout this research lay in the human psyche and in the innate, fundamental need for what we can call "belonging." There appears to be a kind of safety and reassurance in identifying oneself as "pro-Olympic," which is rarely apparent in other aspects of identity-formation. Being "pro-Olympic" expresses more than not being "anti-Olympic" and, as we shall see, it can become manifest in several different ways. Indeed, being "pro-Olympic" appears to be an additional identity that one can assimilate into one's existing self-perception without fear of contradicting most other facets of the self.[10]

In the contemporary context, the inclusivity of Olympic-related identity satiated a fundamental social hunger, encouraging a sense of national unification. Rather than being segregational, this *Olympic identity* was made accessible to all. Unlike Olympic tickets, it did not require ownership of a VISA card and was inclusive of creed, color, age, gender, sexual orientation, and race. As such, it was not "embedded within (segregating) notions of nation-state, citizenship, and national society" (Urry 2000, p. 6) but into—largely—accessible notions of time, place, and being.

The Olympic spirit (for want of a better term) can be argued to epitomize bland political correctness in the realm of identity, which is perhaps its most significant and endearing quality. All that is requested is not to object too strongly to the Games, even better if one participates and engages in the events. In the interests of brevity, here I use the expression *Olympic identity* to refer to this inclusive, highly accessible identity affirmation.

Olympic identity needed to be something instinctive; something easy to engage with, universally accessible, and instantly comprehensive. The attendant re-imagination of Great Britain could not be exclusive of other imaginations of identity, at any level. This was probably best exemplified by the easy coexistence of *Olympic identity* and the highly nationalistic fervor created by the Queen's Diamond Jubilee celebrations that occurred in June 2012. The two events proved to be extremely compatible. The malleability of *Olympic identity* allowed the individual to take ownership—or maybe possession—without making sacrifices in terms of other forms of identity. This malleability was bolstered by the positive portrayal of the Olympic implications, which was widely reported by the media. Arguably, for many British citizens this deeply resonated in the banality of everyday life and facilitated its widespread appeal.

Interestingly, demonstrations of *Olympic identity* were not a prerequisite for belonging. However, opportunities for such demonstrations, both individual and collective, permeated the local and the national during Olympic delivery. When combined with the short time frame allowed for the Games (17 days of Olympic Games plus an additional 12 of Paralympic Games), this optionality of participation in identity affirmation ensured that the numerous signifiers of *Olympic identity* were extremely unthreatening. These safe reminders permeated the communal and private spaces of everyday life through signs, conversations, in the newspapers or on television, gently informing people on what to think, what to do and how to behave. This *innocuous* Olympic invasion into Britain's daily routines facilitated a subconscious engagement with Olympic delivery, which was complemented by spectacular, but safe, releases of identity-affirming belonging.

From the outset of, and throughout, London's Olympic delivery, the articulation, and re-articulation of *Olympic identity* was grounded through daily demonstrations of inclusive ownership peppered with the use of the empowering word "we," which was used to signify the sense of belonging associated with the concept that there is an "us"—the members, that is, of the 2012 Olympic collective, an *Olympic family*. As I have observed earlier with reference to the DCMS report, this narrative was prevalent through the more public articulations of Olympic delivery made by local and national politicians and the media. For example, according to Sir Robin Wales, "There will be massive regeneration but what we are already seeing is the extent to which sport can really impact on people's lives" (Sir Robin Wales, mayor of the London Borough of Newham, cited in Muir, 2005).[11] The foreign secretary, Jack Straw, declared, "Today we can celebrate. From tomorrow, we start to realise the Olympic vision in our bid...before the summer recess, the Government will introduce a Bill to set the statutory framework that we need to ensure the delivery of a successful Games" (6/7/2005).[12] Finally, the *London Metro* published a telling report titled, "London 2012: How we won the Olympic bid."[13]

Much of the time, such representations are consumed unconsciously. As Billig (1995) pointed out, these messages are reproduced in the assumption that the "us" and the "we" referred to require no qualification and will be uncritically accepted by consumers. In the Olympic delivery scenario this intimated belonging appears to be a self-fulfilling prophecy of sorts in which the "we" (those residing in Britain) are assumed to be part of the imagined community; that is, part of the "us" who are experiencing Olympic delivery together. This constitutes a major part of the *Olympic identity*. At both national and local levels, the *Olympic identity* seemed to inhabit a space that was separate from reality. The conceptualization of *legacy* and *Olympic identity* often seemed to disguise some crude strategies for engineering consensus; this included labelling Olympic delivery realities as necessary precursors to the event, any scrutiny being offset by a simplistic *legacy* argument. As Durkheim noted, to "illustrate an idea is not to prove it" (1964, p. 155), a point apparently lost on those who readily consumed the *Olympic identity*.

This "pro-Olympic" identity would require people either to opt out, visibly and demonstrably, of supporting the Games, or be presumed to be Olympic advocates. This reality was evident from the outset. For example, during the bidding phase the document, *London's Response to the questionnaire for cities applying to become Candidate cities to host the Games of the XXX Olympiad and the Paralympic Games in 2012* clearly outlined the assumption of inclusivity in regard to *Olympic identity*. Under the section where "objection to the bid" was to be defined, the official response was, "There is no organised opposition to hosting the Games in London" (p. 3). In fact, this was categorically untrue, as the organized opposition group "No to London 2012" would prove.[14] The following call to action, taken from their website,[15] clearly exemplifies their organized anti-Olympic action during the Olympic bid. It read:

"SAY NO TO LONDON 2012—From February 16–19, 2005, delegates from the International Olympic Committee will be visiting east London, providing an opportunity to expose the misleading and shallow populism of the London bid supporters. This may be one of our few chances to stop the bid in its tracks—the final decision will be made in July 2005. A corporate-sponsored, multi-million pound Olympics in London will be a financial and environmental disaster built on lies told to some of the poorest communities in Britain. It will lead to even more draconian "anti-terror" and public order legislation and be paid for not by the rich or businesses but by Londoners—Our chance to say WE DON'T Back the Bid!"

However, despite sporadic and relatively localized objections and demonstrations (some of which will be explored later) there was no large-scale opting out. This led to the assumption that there was a strong imagined community, which bolstered the *Olympic identity*. The cornerstone of Anderson's concept of imagined community, as discussed earlier, was the invention of the printed word and the subsequent rise of print media, which according to him provided the technological means for the widespread dissemination of national identity. Anderson contends that the concept of national identity is rooted in the banality of human existence, and that newspapers formulate an imagined community that "is visibly rooted in everyday life" (1983, p. 36). I would argue that Anderson's considerations should be applied to contemporary *Olympic identity* formation in a similar but more extended way by examining both the print-media and other means of identity dissemination. In this line, let us now look at the formulation of *Olympic identity* in various contexts.

Rhetorical Living

Following the opening of *that* envelope in 2005, London 2012 became an inevitable occurrence that would change parts of East London forever. What was once a collection of diverse and multi-cultural East and South-East London boroughs was now to be transformed into an *Olympic City*. This city needed to develop an *Olympic identity* that would have to be accessible both to those who lived in the area and to the rest of the nation. This we can call "London 2012," which was—and remains—an ideological creation. In this ideological realm, there were no borders, no segregation, and no vilification. "London 2012" was a fantasy, a Camelot re-imagined, with Lord Sebastian Coe playing King Arthur. Futuristic artist impressions of this new Olympic land entered the public consciousness, utopian images that were bolstered by the conceptualization of *legacy* and of benefit for all.

The heady inference was that the benefits of Olympic delivery would permeate all parts of the nation in a variety of ways. The associated notion was that the 2012 Games were to be a showcase for Great Britain to prove to a global audience the greatness of the nation. This message was repeated by an abundance of agents. Below is a selection of comments made at different stages of Olympic delivery.

- "The Games are already a fantastic advert for Britain, promoting the country as a place to live, to work, to visit and to do business. With the eyes of the world on London in 2012 it is a unique opportunity to strengthen our international reputation" (Lord Sebastian Coe).[16]
- "As London is about to host the 2012 Olympic Games next month, the UK's construction sector could benefit from this summer's excellent completion of the Olympic venue and one of the greatest showcases on the Earth to bid for major international project in the future" (Train4TradeSkills).[17]
- "I am confident that we can derive over £13bn benefit to the UK economy over the next four years as a result of hosting the Games. I am certain that when you add in the benefits from construction the total gain will be even greater. These four weeks in a British summer are going to be like no other four weeks in a British summer. They will be about making the most of our country, being everything it can be, at the centre of the world's attention" (UK Prime Minister, David Cameron).[18]

We have seen that Olympic hosting was supposed to attract enormous investment and consumption during and after the Games, particularly in the tourism and retail sectors (Dunn and McGuirk 1999). During Olympic delivery, the above statements and many others along the same lines were broadcast throughout the British media without contradictory evidence, and were intended to capitalize upon the *concrete* beneficial outcomes of Olympic hosting. The ignored reality was that there was much evidence, such as the tourism example highlighted earlier, emphasizing the dubious nature of such a belief in *concrete* beneficial outcomes (see also Perryman 2012).

The attitude of a variety of stakeholders described above illustrates the all-encompassing emphasis of positivity and national benefit that added a dimension of ownership for those who lived and worked in Britain, which was not limited to British people in any nationalistic sense. This perspective strengthened Games, giving them a national resonance, as opposed to a national identity. I suggest that this inclusive national resonance was vastly different to a segregational national identity, which, according to Guibernau (1996), represents a "socio-historical context within which culture is embedded and the means by which culture is produced, transmitted, and received" (p. 79).

The Olympic delivery needed to temporarily re-imagine Great Britain as an inclusive host of "London 2012" and, in the process, eliminate exclusive aspects of identity. To accomplish this lofty aim, the Olympic deliverers had to create a British *Olympic identity* that had its physical form in East London and its ideological form resonating throughout the British Isles. Specific Olympic logos and themed paraphernalia were crucial to the success of this inclusive, though fleeting and momentary, *Olympic identity*.

The creation of such an inclusive, accessible identity ensured that the British people were able to take ownership of the Games. Thus, the nation could buy into the notion that they too were part of a historic British event, despite the fact that the sporting aspect of the Games was London-centric. The 2012 Olympic delivery adopted a variety of methods to enable Olympic consumption in many different spaces and across many different themes, one clear example of which was the Olympic Torch Relay that transported the Olympic Flame around the British Isles in the months preceding the Games.[19] The invented, highly repeated tradition of the Olympic torch relay was employed to help accomplish such unity; it was another of the manufactured mythologies that helped form the Olympic identity. The relay, which has been utilized by all recent Olympic hosts, is "governed by overtly or tacitly accepted rules and of a ritual or symbolic nature, which seek to inculcate certain values and norms of behaviour by repetition, which automatically implies continuity with the past" (Hobsbawm and Ranger 1983, p. 2). Fundamentally, the pageantry and mythology of the relay was a great example of an inclusive *Olympic identity* that, crucially, used the "resources of history [real and imagined], language, and culture in the process of becoming rather than being. It was less about 'who we are' or 'where we came from,' so much as what we might become" (Hall 1996, p. 4).

Creating Consumable Identity for All

Having clarified how the 2012 *Olympic identity* was based upon *faith*, quite regardless of contradictory evidence, let us now consider how it was processed through Olympic rituals, commercialization, and representation.

The focus was on the spectacular and the mundane, the exceptional and the everyday, the traditional and the contemporary. This was the ethos and agency of the *Olympic identity*. It was an identity experienced in the familiar local environment, with one's friends and families, neighbors, strangers, skin colors, social classes, and religions. It was felt in pubs and bars, in fast-food outlets and supermarkets. It was bought, eaten, driven, spent, drunk, worn, touched, heard, and consumed. It was everywhere.

As a result of the introduction of, and ever-growing dependence upon, 24/7 news (available through 24-hour news reportage on TV and radio stations, the Internet, Twitter, and other forms of social media), access to extremely current but depth-limited information is available at society's fingertips and is relied upon as a valuable source of truth. The application of such technology to the Olympic Movement is most readily apparent in the period immediately preceding the Games. Today, Olympic-related information is presented by the media in abridged forms, where loquaciousness is frequently at a premium and erudition is obsolete, presumably reserved for the off-message Parliamentarian or for the dissenting scholar. It is within the Olympic delivery time frame that the flow of Olympic-related news is relayed, its content merely hinting at the wider political, social, and cultural settings in which they occur.

The notions of knowledge and power are critical in this process. Bourdieu's work *On Television and Journalism*, published in 1998, highlights the means with which television constructs and produces news, information, and debate in abridged forms. Condensing the news into bite-sized snippets, he argues, makes it impossible for journalists to conduct any meaningful analysis; they are constrained by issues of time and effect. Therefore, news-casting is pared back and becomes less concerned with factual depth and more concerned with catching a viewer's attention, which is achieved through the use of buzzwords that disseminate a specific narrative without any substance. One such buzzword for the 2012 Olympics was *legacy*.

This structuring of televised news, Bourdieu argued, has a wide, homogenizing effect upon news purveyors, creating the template for other news disseminators, such as newspapers, to follow. The advent of Twitter, after Bourdieu's death, takes this process further by providing news stories to the globe in 140 characters or less. This significantly affects society's ability to assess critically sociological events, such as local level Olympic delivery impact, in the absence of personal experience. As Bourdieu contends in relation to the homogenization of news, this "sort of game of mirrors reflecting one another produces a formidable effect of mental closure" (1998, p. 24). This mental closure was intrinsic to the discursive narrative of Olympic delivery interpretation and assumption because the media formed the perceptions of 2012 Olympic delivery for those without personal experience, who constituted the vast majority of the global population.

This commodification permeated every strand of everyday life. Familiar, everyday objects that formed part of the affective and cognitive structures of quotidian life, those regular, reliable features around which mundane habits and routines were organized, all became fleetingly Olympic-related. Consequently, *Olympic identity* was embraced, simply by living one's routine existence. The diverse, inclusive, unifying nature of Olympic delivery facilitated the easy consumption of the inclusive *Olympic identity* in its transient, "once-in-a-lifetime," rhetoric, and ideology.

This process brings to mind the themes discussed in Hobsbawm and Ranger's edited volume on *The Invention of Tradition*, where a key argument in relation to the concept of national identity is that the powerful create traditions in order to generate an identity-affirming illusion that indoctrinates the populations with "certain values and norms of behaviour by repetition, which automatically implies continuity with the past" (1983, p. 2). However, my findings raise questions on their suggestion that such identity-affirming events are solely Machiavellian techniques created by a power élite to control the masses for some ulterior motive. To apply the full context of this post-modernist, conspiracy-theorist perspective to the 2012 Games would lend too much credence to the supposition that there exists an underlying controlling motive that uses this "Mega-Event" exclusively for ideological manipulation. However alluring it might be to subscribe to a Machiavellian—or Marxist—caricature where all the Olympic strings are pulled to meet the ends of the ruling classes, it appears that the creation of the Olympic mythology "simply" provided something lacking in sections of contemporary British society—an Olympic-related imagined community (Edensor 2002, p. 68); notably, a sense of belonging and the hope of better things to come in otherwise bleak times.

The *Olympic identity* was an exception to overt displays of nationality and to traditional British apprehension around such displays. This explains why the 2012 Olympic Games managed to unify vast swathes of British society without contradiction and without fear of racism, elitism, regionalism, or classism. The universality of *Olympic identity* was effectively interpreted and claimed by many greatly different social groups, whose enthusiasm was emblematic of the Olympics' broad appeal.

The Olympic Games promised hope, inclusivity, excitement, riches, opportunity, and adventures. It included you, whoever you were, your community, your region, your nation; all were welcome in the *Olympic identity* family. Moreover, once the excitement of the Games was over, those who bought into this identity-affirming Olympic package were free to return to their pre-Games existence full of happy memories stored in their nostalgia banks, ready to be releases at choice moments in the future. For many, the retort to the Marxist critique would be, who cares if it was pseudo-Machiavellian, it was fun while it lasted and it will never happen again!

CHAPTER 10

Conclusion: Extinguishing the Olympic Torch

In this book, I have sought to illustrate the power relations that were at play within the "Olympic schema." In particular, I have highlighted how the ideological superstructure of Olympic sport has been used in the attempt to mobilize the "common consent" of the masses (Gramsci 1971; Rowe 2004).[1] A cursory examination of the numerous Olympic-related literature reveals the relevance of the Games to many aspects of contemporary society including, amongst many others, politics (Espy 1979; Kanin 1981; Burbank, Andranovich, and Heying, 2001), sponsorship (Brown 2000; 2002), tourism (Brown 2007), religion (Rothenbuhler 1989; Guttman 1992), social movements (Armstrong, Hobbs, and Lindsay 2011), capitalist economics (Lenskyj 2000), and terrorism (Charters 1983; Reeve 2001; Toohey and Taylor 2008; Richards, Fussey, and Silke 2010). Indeed, it is conceivable that one would be able to build a life-sized papier-mâché replica of London's Olympic Stadium using just a small selection of such publications. However, none of them deals adequately with life in the shadow of the Olympic Torch. It is hoped that this text has contributed to fill this lacuna.

The appeal of the IOC and the Olympic Games as an academic research subject cannot be disputed; such an appeal is more widely reflected through mainstream non-academic publications. Publications on the Olympics include historical studies of specific Games, such as that conducted by Walters (2006) on the 1936 Nazi Berlin Games, or Kent's (2008) cautionary tale of the 1908 London Olympics. Other publications sought to provide "inside knowledge" on a variety of issues, focusing on behind-the-scenes accounts of the internal ramifications of Olympic bidding and delivery—two examples of such literature are Yarbrough's (2000) portrayal of the

1996 Atlanta Olympics and Lee's (2006) account of the 2012 London Olympic bid.

The wide variety of Olympic-related literature reflects the malleability of the Olympics as a subject of study far beyond the "sporting" domain. Scholars who take what might be called an "Olympic outcome" perspective have provided depersonalized, "before and after" geographical analyses (Preuss 2004; Gold and Gold 2007), illustrating the benefits and pitfalls of Olympics hosting. Others have explored the risks of Olympic hosting— a theme that is receiving growing interest—and the need for the intense security and surveillance of Olympic locales (Boyle and Haggerty 2009; Coaffee, Fussey, and Moore 2011; Cornelissen 2011; Eick 2011; Fussey et al. 2011; Giulianotti 2011; Samatas 2011; Schimmel 2011). Yet, despite such well-publicized risk analyses, a consistent positive Olympic narrative proselytizes the belief that becoming an Olympic host is hugely beneficial, sociologically and economically.

This does not mean that there are no Olympic critics and both academic research (Lenskyj 2000, 2002, 2008; Boykoff 2011) and investigative journalism (Jennings 1996, 2000) provide interesting counterpoints to the more commonplace positive Olympic eulogies. However, from the outset such counterpoints appear to be oriented toward an anti-Olympic perspective, lacking therefore an open-minded academic approach.[2] In contrast to such approaches, my research aimed at providing an objective account and, thus, an informed sociological analysis of London 2012 Olympic history.

In 1871, the French novelist Gustave Flaubert maintained that our general ignorance of history often leads to slandering and vilification of our own age (cited in Scammell 1995). Paradoxically, the Olympic Movement appears to both bolster and contradict Flaubert's assumption, depending on which version of history is read. As each Olympic Games is an episode of a larger Olympic narrative, a single edition of the Games can either be engulfed by history or left to stand-alone for consideration. By ignoring history, the analysis of the contemporary Games may end up supporting Flaubert's assertion because past Olympics—accurately or not—are generally perceived more positively than the current version, which can easily be vilified through nostalgic comparison. On the other hand, any true exploration of the history of the Olympic Movement may discourage the slandering and vilification of the contemporary Games simply because the IOC has too many skeletons in their closet, though they are rarely remembered.

One particularly well publicized example of corruption is represented by the 2002 Salt Lake City Winter Olympics bid, which was surrounded by revelations that up to 20 of the 110 IOC members had been bribed with holidays, jobs, university places for relatives, and cosmetic surgery. During an official

Olympic visit, one IOC member even requested Viagra, a vibrator, and a Violin from the hosts (Jennings and Sambrook 2000; Lenskyj 2000)—faster, higher, and stronger indeed. Another example of malpractice is provided by the case of Barcelona. When the city won the right to host the 1992 Games, reports of corrupt practice in the bidding process were suppressed by the IOC (Jennings 2000). The allegations of corruption, which involved delegates from Toronto, Sweden, Atlanta, Manchester, and Cape Town, remained buried until 1998, when a Swiss member of the IOC publicly proclaimed that prospective host cities often engaged in bribery, and that vote buying and selling was a long-standing practice among IOC members (Christie 1998; Lenskyj 2000). In spite of these revelations of corruption, for many the Barcelona Games remain a "gold standard" of Olympic hosting practice.

In this book, I have argued that Olympic delivery and its evolution are best explored through the ethnographic method and that these aspects of the Olympic process should be considered separately from other forms of the Olympic milieu. This approach allows a critical analysis of Olympic processes, development, implications, and outcomes without having to contend with the often-eclipsing properties of the event itself or its promised *legacy*. Thus, it is possible to separate those involved in Olympic delivery by choice from those involved by circumstance; a separation that, in turn, enables comparison and contrast of the rhetoric and the reality as they unfurl. Consequently, the specific focus of this research was the seven-year Olympic delivery window between 2005 and 2012, when London became *The Olympic City*.[3]

The categorization of London as *Olympic City* manifested itself in numerous ways, which have informed—and will continue to inform—Olympic-related academic analyses for years to come. The specific purpose of this research was to examine, in real-time, the "emergent fissures" (Horne and Manzenreiter 2006) of the 2012 Games by shedding light on the experiential aspects of its delivery. In this regard, and in accordance with some of Silk's (2011) suggestions for an insightful 2012 analysis, this research got "under the skin" of London 2012. The empirical study of the Olympic delivery milieu from a bottom-up ethnographic perspective facilitated a study of Olympic-related passivity and activity, consumption and production, engagement and escapism,

My research focused on the contestations, ambiguities, and contradictions of Olympic delivery and, as such, it provided a reversal of the spectacle (Kellner 2008). It examined the London 2012 Olympic Games in relation to its impact on those who were directly implicated by its delivery, in particular, the local communities. The latter experienced Olympic delivery first-hand, and had a direct stake in its implications, processes, and outcomes. It was through their experiences that the realities of 2012 Olympic delivery became manifest. This study narrates their stories, rephrased in suitably academic prose.[4]

Olympic delivery was considered a facilitator and producer of a kind of identity that was *diverse, fluid,* and *psychosocial*. The outcomes of this trilogy became manifest throughout the Olympic delivery period in a diversity of localized perceptions that included such variances as:

- "The Olympic Games is the worst thing to happen to East London since the Blitz" (AM Community worker, March 2009)
- "The Olympics, it made no difference to my life" (Jermaine, *ExCeLland* resident, July 2012)
- "I can't wait for the Olympics; I love athletics" (Jill, decanted *Stratfordland* resident, May, 2010)
- "It's all so exciting, it's a shame we had to move" (Saul, decanted *Stratfordland* resident, June 2012)
- "2012 is making such a difference to the area; it's definitely a good thing" (Achmed, *Dispersal Zone* resident, January 2012)
- "I wish I hadn't bothered protesting and done something useful, like read a good book" (Maureen, *Stratfordland* resident, September 2010)

These views are indicative of the complex interplay between identity, delivery, and expectations. However, this study was not simply about collating perceptions of Olympic hosting, or of delivery. Crucially, it examined the impact of Olympic delivery on the every-day lives of the local communities by applying Bourdieu's approach to this milieu (Wacquant 1989, p. 50). This involved recognizing and understanding the processes and outcomes of Newham's modification, and how these processes informed perceptions of identity, action, and behavior. The everyday implications of Olympic delivery were addressed through ethnographic cases, showing how these perceptions, actions, and experiences were, to a large extent, guided by and dependent upon the individuals' position and place in society. The Olympic reordering of Newham occurred on the basis of the constraints, the opportunities available to the local communities, and the "access" to them; as a consequence, some local residents were able to benefit more than others. Ethnographic research has shown how the "locals" came to know, define, order, and reorder their locales, some of which evolved greatly during the Olympic delivery, others remained relatively unchanged.

The Evolution of Newham

I began this study by reflecting on the assumption that in the western world the transformative implications of hosting an urban Olympics—as opposed to the use of out-of-town locations like in Sydney 2000 (Lenskyj 2002; Owen

2002)—are only possible in impoverished urban areas; that is, in areas that contain low levels of place-ownership and place-identity. The demographics and deprivation levels of the residents in these locations contribute to the belief that they are ideal recipients of Olympic regeneration. However, many local residents appear to be unable to take full advantage of the Olympic hosting opportunities. Furthermore, to add insult to injury, these areas and their residents are often vilified and denigrated by Olympic media discourse throughout the Olympic bidding and delivery. It follows that the Olympic-related socio-economic enhancement is usually evaluated either via holistic considerations of the Olympic Games, or through a "before and after" demographic comparisons of the Olympic locales. These methods will generally discount the Olympic delivery milieu, thus promoting a positive evaluation of the Olympic *legacy*, while in fact ignoring the reality experienced by those who were supposed to benefit from Olympic hosting—that is, the local hosting community populace, as opposed to the geographic locale.

To this extent, I found particularly useful the application of Auge's (1995) conceptualization of *non-place* to contemporary Newham. Auge argued that a *non-place* is a place of transience that lacks the significance necessary to be considered *place*. He argued that if a *place* can be defined as relational, historical, and concerned with identity, then a space that cannot be defined as such must be a *non-place* (Auge 1995, pp. 77–78). As I have indicated, Olympic delivery Newham was not concerned with holistic identity, nor did Newham have a holistic place-related history. In fact, one may have to go back to the pre-World War II industrial era, well before Newham's formation in 1965, to discover in this locale a sense of *place* as defined by Auge (see, Willmott and Young's study published in 1957), albeit a poor and deprived *place*. As Auge argues, the *non-place* cannot integrate *places of memory* that occurred within its boundaries in former periods. This was clearly the case with contemporary Newham and its industrial past. By the time of Olympic delivery, Newham's identity as an industrial holistic *place* had long become a relic of the past, which had little or no resonance to contemporary Newham life (Hobbs 1988).

To define Newham a *non-place* was to consider it a place of transit and transience, a stop on a journey elsewhere, similar to an airport or a train station—involving just a slightly longer wait (Auge 1995, pp. 29–32). In contrast, the Council mantra of Newham being "a place to live, work and stay" implicitly wanted to address the borough's high demographic churn. Newham mirrors Auge's description of *non-place* as environments where there is an excess of places, identities, relationships, and histories, but none of which are holistically supported or reinforced (Auge 1995, pp. 36–37; Buchanan 1999, p. 280).

Newham's composition perpetuated the *non-place* narrative that defined this locale as a diverse collection of identities, places, relationships, and histories that prevented a holistic identity being formed. This diversity is exemplified by Newham's high streets where Eastern European delis can be found alongside Kurdish cafes and fried chicken shops selling *Halal* meat. The common language in these outlets and among the people who visit and shop in them is *English-Creole*, which perhaps best exemplifies Newham as an English *non-place*. It is in this regard that Newham's character could be inferred as the product of its component parts (Mol 2002, p. 39). It is perhaps through the language uniformity that place-related identities, relations, and histories are formed and asserted (Korpela 1989; Johnston, Gregory, and Smith 1994). The absence of such identity-affirming uniformity would make Newham a "strange entity" (Lefebvre 1991, p. 53); that is, a place that, though aspiring to be "real," fails to produce its "own space" or simply lacks those distinctive qualities that, according to Auge, characterize a *place*.

My research findings suggest that Newham was a livable *non-place*. This categorization appeared to have significant consequences for Olympic delivery. When combined with poverty, crime, and deprivation, it suggested that Newham required widespread urban regeneration in order to remedy this "strange entity" and it social maladies. Accordingly, the 2012 Olympic deliverers chose to denigrate Newham (and other parts of East London) as a *London's Gash* that needed healing. The characteristics of the *non-place*, combined with the borough's statistical portfolio, supported the indication that Olympic hosting would address the underlying social malady of this locale. However, Auge's theorization of *non place* is not sufficient to address the complexities of Olympic delivery. Such complexities and the inconsistencies of the ethnographic reality are better addressed from a perspective that takes into account Bourdieu's work.

This concluding chapter raises some significant questions that transcend the Olympic sporting domain and address its lasting impact on the host communities. In particular, I ask, what are the wider implications of living in a *non-place* and why is it regarded as an ideal host for Olympicization? Are the distinguishing features that made Newham a livable *non-place* (as opposed to the airports, shopping malls, and railway stations that Auge referred to in 1995) only possible through poverty and deprivation, and are these "alluring features" lost through the introduction of wealth? Can there be such a thing as an appealing *non-place* for all social classes whereby the place identity is definable only by the absence of a holistic identity? Can there ever be a livable *non-place* where it is possible to walk the streets alone at night without fear of abuse or crime, and where there is no need for the kind of private security that segregates neighbors from each other? More to the point, do we all, in contemporary Western society, live to some degree in a *non-place*, and is the concept of a holistic *community* losing its relevance to contemporary urban culture? Future research may seek to expand on Auge's conceptualization of *non-place* and ask similar questions in relation to other contemporary urban contexts. Here, let us look at some aspects of the post-Olympics situation.

An Olympic Opiate Hangover: Considering Post-Olympic Newham

This research suggests that an assessment of the Olympic *legacy* cannot be separated from the reality and the long-held perceptions that made Newham attractive to very different people such as the so-called post-place *flaneurs* (King 1993), transnational élites (Friedmann and Wolff 1982), stateless persons (Wallerstein 1993), cosmopolites (Hannerz 1992), and creative classes (Florida 2005). Regardless of definition, these metropolitan migrants appeared actively to seek the nuances of the *non-place* in order to satiate their demand for vibrant, urban life. However, as we have seen, the implications of this migration suggest that this influx appears to threaten precisely the characteristics of the *non place* that is sought in the first instance. This specific migrant population has been directly linked to an increase in the cost of living in the locales they move to. This ultimately permits access only to affluent people, pushing the less economically advantaged to relocate elsewhere (Cole 1987; Hughes 1990; Smith 1996; Ley 2003).

This process leads to the "trendy" place becoming a site of stale cultural monism that metropolitan migrants will in the future seek to escape. The Olympic-related Newham addition to this poverty-diversity-trendiness-reclamation-cultural monism-untrendiness-poverty cycle would require further study. Additionally, future research may seek to explore the implications of the dichotomy of Newham's Olympic regeneration, which drastically modified some parts of the borough while leaving others relatively unscathed. This future research may be conducted during the post-Olympic *legacy* context to consider whether a new strand of *non-place* is emerging and if so to explore its wider implications.

These questions suggest that the evolution of Newham has a long way to go before meaningful evaluations of the impact of the 2012 Olympic Games can be made. However, from the evidence collated during Olympic delivery this study argues that the chances of the Olympic Games being used to "inspire a generation" in the race of life can be improved by the creation of a new model of Olympic delivery. In this regard, an alternative model need not necessarily be vastly different to succeed. For example, it might be sufficient to extend the length of Olympic delivery, or modify the time frame of nominating Olympic hosts perhaps a decade in advance; thus, local people's *habitus* (Bourdieu and Wacquant 1992) may be enabled to evolve at a steadier rate. This small adjustment could have significant repercussions linked to local people having the time to adjust to impending Olympic opportunities. For example, a longer 2012 Olympic delivery window might have encouraged unskilled local people to become more inclined to enter education and training and still be in time to compete for Olympic delivery employment. An extended delivery period would also allow the creation of additional organizations specifically aimed at integrating local people into sustainable Olympic-related employment and at providing greater opportunities for consultation and prescriptive community initiatives.

It might therefore be suggested that Olympic legacies should not take the form of land reclamation, employment, and wealth injection or colonization of urban areas, which as future research may indicate did little to address the sociological issues of Newham. Rather, it could be argued that Olympic *legacy* should focus on education and longer-term investment in deprived areas in order to help address class-related sociological issues through a steady and patient modification of *habitus*, as opposed to the current model that inspired *hysteresis* for many Newham residents (Hardy 2008). This *hysteresis* was justified by the relatively tight time constraints of the Olympic Games and its ability to act as a mitigating spatial action.

Throughout Olympic delivery, this *hysteresis* appeared to be celebrated by all, with the exception of the local communities who only partook once they resigned themselves to the fact that, other than Olympic entertainment, there would be no tangible Olympic benefits for them. This point addresses one of the primary questions of this study—that is, was there a differentiation between local and non-local perceptions of Olympic delivery, and what were the implications of such differentiation? Ultimately, this study has shown that local people did experience Olympic delivery differently from those living elsewhere in Britain. They had to live through Olympic delivery disruption and, while enduring this process, they were rewarded with the same Olympic benefits as the rest of the country; that is, 2012 Olympic sporting enjoyed from afar. While parts of Olympic Newham were modified into entertainment venues reserved to those lucky enough to have an Olympic ticket, other areas of the borough remained relatively untouched.

The unmistakable narrative of London's Olympic delivery was one of divisive reclamation, which used Olympic sport to facilitate "alienation, ruling class ideology, and commodification" (Giulianotti 2005, p. 41). From a Marxist perspective, it could be argued that the 2012 Olympic Games became an opiate to keep the masses in stupefied happiness (Brohm 1978, p. 108) and to reduce potential critical assessments of the delivery realities. The processes followed during 2012 Olympic delivery and the power relations observed during the meetings between the Olympic deliverers and the local communities would support a neo-Marxist conclusion that the ruling capitalist class owned and controlled the means of production and were open to "negotiation" with the purpose of maintaining their hegemony in an oft one-sided intercourse that manufactured common consent without giving the impression of force and domination (Gramsci 1971). Moreover, in this line, sport can be seen as a vehicle to support and transmit ruling bourgeois ideologies on a huge scale through the mass media (Brohm 1978, pp. 47–48). If we accept this line of analysis, we should then ask whether the 2012 Olympics were successfully used to manufacture consent and "class collaboration at every level" (Brohm 1978, 108). The common consensus was that the 2012 Olympics were fundamentally a great success enjoyed by all. What was there to object about?

A Tale of Two Cities

This ethnographic research shows that Olympic delivery was a tale of two imagined cities and of two ways of living. This emerged clearly in the Newham areas that were most affected by the 2012 Games, namely *Stratfordland* and parts of *ExCeLland*. One of these imagined cities was a relic of the past—the city of pre-bid Newham, which no longer existed. The other was a vision of the future—the idealistic post-Games utopian Newham that was to come. Neither of them, however, actually held resonance during Olympic implementation. During Olympic delivery, the Newham locations that could once be considered as evidence of "non-place" were better symbolized as a *differential space* (Lefebvre 1991) where everything seemed to be, in the attendant socio-political milieu, up for grabs or, at least, for renegotiation. This "*differential place of hysteresis*" (Lefebvre 1991; Bourdieu 1984) was a place of negotiation over the post-Games utopia; a process that saw an ever-increasing differentiation between pre-Games Newham and post-Games Newham.

For many residents of pre-bid *Stratfordland*, this process was reminiscent of a sociological bleep test, whereby the agents kept running until they could no longer keep up with the ever-increasing demands of the test and succumbed to an inevitable relocation. Ethnographic research during this intermediate time involved exploring, understanding and defining the communities that represented the *right* and *wrong* fit for both locales, which for many was the result of self-definition according to established *habitus*.

The relations of power at play in this process of "place-identity definition" structured—to a large degree—human behavior in Newham. The position of local actors was determined by the amount and value of the *capital* they possessed.

The new opportunities and potential benefits brought about by the 2012 Games required a constant negotiation and renegotiation of the actors' position. This issue emerged in a variety of ways but is perhaps best exemplified by the Olympic-related employment opportunities from which local residents were left out because they were unable to compete with a highly skilled, motivated, and cheap *Eastern European* workforce. Consequently, Olympic delivery became a space of conflict and competition as agents competed to gain a monopoly in the *species of capital* that was most effective in this field in this period.

Newham's Olympic Blueprint

Pierre Bourdieu's theoretical perspective resonated deeply in this analysis. Bourdieu argued that the answer to the question of inclusion and exclusion is found in the agent's *habitus*. Such *habitus* has been described as a "second sense," a "practical sense," or a "second nature" (cited in Johnson 1993) that equips social actors with a practical "know-how" for social engagement. Thought and action are constrained but not determined by *habitus*, which only provides a blueprint for perception and action. According to Bourdieu, people are not fools and do not act blindly according to *habitus*. Rather, they act on the basis of what they see as common sense; for Newham residents, such common sense translated into the view that Olympic benefits were not accessible to them.

Olympic delivery instigated cross-border economic processes of flows of capital, labor, goods and services, raw materials, and migrant workers; all of which caused *hysteresis* to occur within Newham. This 2012 Olympics delivery milieu was, for some, permeated by a myriad Olympic-related upheavals and disillusionments, notably involving security implementation and the lack of employment opportunities for local people. The opiate-like properties of the impending 2012 Olympic Games (Brohm 1978) shifted the focus away from delivery reality toward the event and the post-Games *legacy*; that is, the utopia that was to come.

This reality has implications for notions of social dominance because *habitus* is homologous to the objective structures of the world. As this study has shown, inequality and the lack of ability to recognize or take advantage of Olympic benefits were prevalent for many pre-Olympic residents during Newham's Olympic delivery. For some, this inequality was invisible; for others, it was mitigated by the transient Olympic milieu. This leads to the conclusion that Olympic delivery maintains the class-associated power relations of the wider capitalistic society, whereby the dominated contribute to their own domination. The dispositions that inclined pre-bid Newham residents to such complicity were the effect of domination, lodged deeply inside their *habitus*. This perspective has enabled a critical analysis of Olympics delivery as a reconfiguration of the generic class struggle, packaged and sold in a way that resonated with both the wider society and at the local level, as a result of Olympic association.

The majority of those who consumed the 2012 Olympic Games delivery did so away from the real, live experience of the Games. They were the "armchair" Olympians who stayed away either because of geographical distance from London or because they were unable to buy a ticket. They consumed a version of reality primarily through the media broadcasts, and for them London's 2012 Olympic Games and its delivery were the "Best Games Ever." One fundamental question that should be asked is, "how many of the millions who attended the events at the Olympic Park actually saw Newham?" Answering this question properly would require a separate research. Here, I can only guess that they were relatively few, as most would have fallen in line with the efficient "corporate kettling" that helped guide some 80% of Olympic visitors from railways stations in Westfield Stratford City to the Olympic Park and back again.

Education, Education, Education: A Taste of Things to Come

Olympic delivery had—temporarily—cleansed, created, isolated, and commoditized Newham's Olympic locales. In these areas, Newham life was not as the long-standing community knew it. This reordered Olympic reality was particularly prominent in *Stratfordland*, where Olympic-related urban regeneration sought to cleanse the locale by removing and masking pre-Olympic signifiers that marked non-Olympic Newham. This had powerful connotations for those who considered as home these vilified spaces of everyday life. This Olympic reordering of Newham instigated a new sense of place where access depended on the ownership of certain characteristics and of considerable amounts of what Bourdieu describes as *species of capital*.

Some theorists argue that whoever "controls public space sets the program for representing society" (Zukin 1998, p. 370). Urban geographer Don Mitchell claims that public spaces can be crucial to the role of socio-spatial negotiation by providing groups and individuals with the geographical location where they can "make their desires and needs known, to represent themselves to others and the state—even if through struggle—as legitimate claimants to public considerations" (2003, pp. 32–33). In the context of Olympic Newham, gentrification was the prime motivation for the evolution of public space; in particular, as Kennedy and Leonard (2001) point out, such evolution was a consequence of

- The involuntary or voluntary displacement of renters, homeowners, and local businesses, such as those living in *Stratfordland*
- Increased real estate values and increased tax revenue
- The deconcentration of poverty
- Changing the cultural fabric of the community
- Changing leadership and power structure within the community
- An increased value put on the neighborhood by outsiders

A crucial component is missing from the above list. This is university-led gentrification, which is going to play a significant role in the reordering of Newham's post-Olympic landscape.[5] Of course, it is hard to argue against increasing educational opportunities; however, the question to ask is whether "university-gentrification," and the related university education, would benefit Newham traditional residents.

It could be argued, following Bourdieu, that an individual's history is intrinsic to guiding life in a particular (though not determinate) direction. This would translate into the pessimistic conclusion that Newham's local communities, like the residents of Carpenters Estate, could not gain significant Olympic *legacy* benefits because they lacked the prerequisite know-how to succeed, or even exist in this *field*. Bourdieu's term *doxa* denotes this know-how, which refers to what is taken for granted within a particular society. Let me stress that doxa is "what goes without saying because it comes without saying" (Bourdieu 1977, pp.167–169); it helps to establish social limits and the sense of one's place in society, which among many Newham's residents was intrinsically linked to pre-Olympic perceptions that Olympic opportunities were "not for us" (Bourdieu 1979, p. 549). As expected, Olympic delivery did create many employment opportunities in Newham, which, however, proved inaccessible to most of the pre-bid community groups. Interestingly, many Newham residents were ambivalent toward the entire Olympic process; they were either pessimistic, and became over disappointed quickly, or did not consider themselves as eligible to beneficial opportunities in the first place.

The postulate that Newham's Olympic *legacy* would predominantly benefit a future populace, as opposed to the pre-Games residents, mirrors similar analyses on other Olympic Games. For example, it is worth mentioning the research of Garcia-Ramon and Albet (2000), who claimed that the greatly lauded Barcelona 1992 Games had always been oriented toward the needs of an upwardly mobile global audience at the expense of locally specific social needs. This perspective was supported by Lenskyj's assertion that the Sydney 2000 Games produced much "real world" evidence[6] that the Olympic Games exacerbate existing social problems, which the Olympic *legacy* did not alleviate (2002, pp. 227–231).

The Olympic Park may well follow a pattern that is already observable in the BV; that is, producing gated communities where the residents reside until the education needs of their children trigger a return to suburbia. The transition toward an Olympic Newham *habitus* resonates more with those who dwell—or at least work—in *The City* than with those who operate in the post-industrial landscape of pre-bid Newham. Interestingly, it was poverty that facilitated Newham's diversity and relatively low price of real estate, which, in turn, made it an appealing location for the childfree bourgeois. These properties are reminiscent of the precursors of many other gentrified urban locales (Jacobs 1996; Lees 2003).[7]

The findings of this study indicate that Newham's communities were happy being who they were and appeared to have little aspiration to change, much to the chagrin of Sir Robin Wales and others who had invested in the Olympic project. The 2012 Olympic delivery would reorder some of the areas that represented pre-Olympic Newham, such as *Stratfordland*, but the larger schema of Newham life would change very little. The poor would remain poor and the unemployed would remain unemployed. Newham's cycle would thus perpetuate itself. Some areas of post-Olympic Newham may welcome a more affluent future populace, which may prove divisive and create future spaces of conflict. This is a reality for future studies to explore. In this regard, post-Olympic Newham promises to be a very interesting laboratory for sociological research—very interesting indeed.

Epilogue

Eventually, Newham's Olympic delivery period ended. The Olympic structures and the related infrastructures were completed. Feelings of hysteresis took a back seat for the duration of this 17-day sporting event. The outcomes of the narratives of fear that attempted to modify the behavior of local people during the Games would be available for scrutiny from the day the Games began; this, however, was beyond the remit of my research. As I stood at Stratford station, in the same place where I stood all those years back, when my research began, I could see behind me the 68 "magical steps"

Figure 10.1 One Day to Go.

Figure 10.2 Olympic Screening.

that led to the Olympic Park and Westfield; they were dominated by a big screen indicating that the Olympics would begin in a few hours.

Over to the left, stood the tower blocks of the Carpenters Estate, now devoid of most of its former residents. The top floor flats were now occupied by television crews waiting to broadcast their "Panasonic" backdrop of the Olympic Park. Conspicuously, each tower was now covered by Olympic-inspired commercials; brand names, logos, and pictures of celebrities covered these 23-stories tower blocks, looming large over all those who walked by. Elsewhere, John Morgan House, a 28-story office block, had become a larger than life BMW advertisement, while a Coca-Cola advert covered the glass walled bridge that linked Stratford and Westfield to the Olympic Park. Newham had, in many respects, been screened; unless one knew where to look, to all intents and purposes, it had become invisible. With a final glance, I turned around and got back on the underground, leaving behind Olympic Stratfordland and Newham—Olympic delivery was over, and it was time for the Games to begin.

Notes

Introduction   In Pursuit of Olympic Gold

1. From Centrebet (Australia), 2012 Host Betting Odds, November 2004-July 2005.
2. I will address the Olympic bidding team in greater detail in chapter 2. For now, let me mention that it included Princess Anne, Lord Sebastian Coe, the Olympic Chief Executive Keith Mills, the Chairman of the British Olympic Association Craig Reedie, the [then] Culture Secretary Tessa Jowell, the [then] Mayor of London Ken Livingstone, and a plethora of British sportsmen and women, such as David Beckham, Kelly Holmes, Sir Steve Redgrave, and Tanni Grey-Thompson, among many others.
3. This was exemplified by the London 2012 Candidate City Bid Bulletin, which stressed the passion and support for the Games (see http://www.london2012.com/documents/bid-publications/bid-bulletin-march-05.pdf).

1   The New(Ham) World

1. More information is available at: http://www.guardian.co.uk/news/datablog/2010/may/25/birth-rate-statistics-england-wales.
2. Information available at: http://www.newham.info/Custom/LEA/Demographics.pdf.
3. The 2007 Index of Multiple Deprivation combines a number of indicators into a single deprivation score for each small area in England. Indicators are: 1) Income; 2) Employment; 3) Health, deprivation and disability; 4) Education, skills and training deprivation; 5) Barriers to housing and services; 6) Crime and Living; and 7) Environment deprivation.
4. Rai, D., Withey, J., Thacker, C., Tampubolo, G., Ogg, J., & Burton, J. (2008). *Newham Household Panel Survey Wave 5 Report*.
5. According to the 2007 English Indices of Multiple Deprivation, Newham ranks second behind Hackney for "rank of extent," which measures the "proportion of a district's population living in the most deprived [areas] in England" (Noble et al. 2008, pp. 81, 86).

6. For more see Ipsos MORI (2008) available at: http://www.ipsos-mori.com/DownloadPublication/1247_srI_localgovt_understanding_london_life_062008.pdf.
7. For more information see: LBN and NHS Newham (2011, p. 84).
8. DCLG Housing Strategy Statistical Appendix data provided by Newham Info under the "housing" theme is available at: http://www.newham.info/IAS/profiles/profile?profileId=44&geoTypeId=6&geoIds=00BB (accessed 13 July 2011).
9. The 2001 census did not take into account the influx of economic migrants; of particular note to this study are white Eastern European construction workers.
10. This document is available at: http://www.newham.info/Custom/LEA/Demographics.pdf.
11. For more information see: GLA Round Low Population Projections (2008).
12. See http://theehp.com/2011/09/30/housing-newham-sets-up-task-force-to-deal-with-super-sheds/.
13. Les Mayhew is part-time Professor of Statistics at Cass Business School. He is managing director of Mayhew Harper Associates Ltd. This research consultancy specialise in the use of large administrative data sets and local governance and community issues.
14. Les Mayhew (2009) *The London Borough of Newham: Counting the Confirmed and Unconfirmed Population*, cited in *Newham, London: Local Economic Assessment 2010 to 2027* (Newham, London, 2010a, 2010b).
15. *The Economist* Bagehot columnists survey the politics of Britain, British life and Britain's place in the world. The column and blog are named after Walter Bagehot, an English journalist who was the editor of *The Economist* from 1861 to 1877. The writers are not explicitly acknowledged. See http://www.economist.com/blogs/bagehot.
16. This report is available at: http://www.aston-mansfield.org.uk/pdf_docs/research/newham-key-statistics.PDF.
17. For a deeper review of the term, its history and its uses see Murray (1990; 1994) and Wacquant (2008).
18. Cited in Aston Mansfield's *Newham Key Statistics* (2011).
19. For more information see: GLA Round Low Population Projections (2008).
20. This Economic Development Strategy sets out Newham Council's vision for the economic prosperity of the borough and provides a framework for the Council to deliver a range of initiatives.
21. More information is available at: http://www.telegraph.co.uk/news/9222709/London-council-accused-of-social-cleansing-as-it-asks-housing-benefit-families-to-move-north.html.
22. "ExCeL London" opened in 2000 as an exhibition and conference centre; it is located to the south of Newham on the northern quay of the Royal Victoria dock. During the Olympics, it would have to host seven events, including Boxing, Wrestling, Judo, Tae Kwon Do, Weight-lifting, Table Tennis and Fencing. The centre would therefore have to be prepared to cater for large numbers of spectators and Olympic visitors.

23. For a definition of spoking see later, chapter 3, page74.
24. To place this into context Russia spans nine time zones, is home to one hundred nationalities but speaks only 150 languages (Sixsmith 2011, p.10).
25. The notion of a Newham identity is problematic, despite great efforts of place branding that includes "Welcome to Newham" signs around the Stratford's new Westfield shopping centre and elsewhere. The borough of Newham was created in April 1965 by merging the long-standing locales of East and West Ham into one borough of the newly formed Greater London, which did little to create a unified identity for those who lived through this transition.
26. Auge's mechanisms of the "non-place" were exemplified by their ability to replace or enhance human interaction, such as the credit card that replaces cash or the electronic ticket barriers that replace conductors.
27. For a more robust review of Bourdieu's three-tiered methodology see Bourdieu and Wacquant 1992, pp. 104–107.

2   The 2012 Transition: Process and Politics

1. The processes of gentrification include the production of the potential gentry, the generation of potentially gentrifiable neighborhoods and the creation of the potentially gentrified. These processes explain why only certain inner-city areas with inexpensive housing opportunities occupied by the 'powerless' become gentrified (see Lees, Slater, and Wyly 2008).
2. The term "glocalization" was popularized by Robertson (1992, pp. 173–174). It describes how global pressures and demands are made to conform to local conditions. These processes include the ways in which global companies customize their products for particular markets and allow for influential outcomes to come from democratic engagements between local and global actors.
3. For more information see: http://www.newham.gov.uk/2012Games/Mayor SirRobinWaleshailsarrivalofthe2012Games.htm?Printable=true.
4. "Live, work and stay" is a Newham Labour council motto that describes the borough as a "place where people want to live, work and stay." This attempted self-fulfilling prophecy Newham mantra that describes the borough as a place within which to "live, work and stay" implicitly addresses the notion of low place ownership addressed earlier. It validates the perceptions that many residents in fact believe the opposite; that is, they "exist, earn and then leave." The following websites provide two interesting and opposing perceptions:
   Rhetoric—http://www.newham.com/live/about_newham/discover _newham/449,10,0,0.html.
   Reality (albeit tinged with bias)—http://www.forestgate.net/a-place-to-live-work-and-stay.
5. The word Olympicization is used to represent Olympics-related regeneration.
6. For more information see: http://www.telegraph.co.uk/sport/olympics/2355352/ IOC-panel-are-ready-to-assess-public-support.html.
7. This 2006 Act is available at: http://www.legislation.gov.uk/ukpga/2006/12/ pdfs/ukpga_20060012_en.pdf. There are historically clear restrictions placed

upon the rights of anti-Olympics protest, such as at Vancouver 2010, where protests and public demonstrations were aggressively minimized and marginalized far away from the global media (Boykoff 2011). Similar restrictions of expression and the control of assembly are enshrined within the *London Olympic Games and Paralympic Games Act* of 2006. Section 22 of this Act enables the police (or those defined as an "enforcement officer") to "enter land or premises on which they reasonably believe a contravention of regulations under section 19 is occurring." Section 19 pertains to the offence of advertising unofficial or unlicensed products and permits authorities to cover or remove advertising. In addition, this Act provides legislative powers to constrain both the bearers *and* producers of placards. The wording of the Act ensures that these measures extend beyond commercial endeavors to encompass political activity. A fundamental tenant of Olympic hosting is delineated by the IOC's Olympic Charter rule 51—section three. This explicitly forbids public protest near Olympic venues, thus overriding centuries-old, enshrined domestic rights and freedoms.

8. The City of London, or the "Square Mile," is a major business and financial center, often referred to simply as the "City." It is a local authority in central London but it is unique in that it is administered by the Corporation of London rather than a standard local authority council. The "City" has a unique status in British local government in that it is part of Greater London for most administrative purposes, but it remains a separate ceremonial county retaining many independent local government powers and civic identity, including its own police force.

9. Most of these boroughs were considered 'deprived' areas. Arguably, the most comprehensive way to measure such deprivation is to consider the Index of Multiple Deprivation (IMD) and contrast these boroughs accordingly. An IMD score indicates deprivation levels taking into account income, employment, health, education and skills, housing, crime and living environment. Each of these areas incorporates sub-sections, which are relationally weighted in terms of their impact on deprivation, with income, employment, and health being deemed the most vital. In a 2007 ranking of 354 English local authorities the Olympic boroughs ranked accordingly (the higher the ranking the more deprived the location): Waltham Forest—twenty-seventh; Greenwich—twenty-fourth; Newham—sixth; Tower Hamlets—third; Hackney—second. For more information, see http://www.communities.gov.uk/documents/communities/pdf/576659.pdf.

10. The ExCeL hosted seven Olympic events (see also chapter 1, n. 22) and, within its five arenas, eighty 2012 Olympic medals were decided.

11. For more information see: http://www.thisislocallondon.co.uk/news/topstories/889199.londons_most_dangerous_streets_revealed/.

12. More statistical information is available at: http://maps.met.police.uk/access.php?area=00BBGU&ct=7&sort=rate&order=d.

13. An example of such an internet site can be found at: http://www.stooly.com/places-to-avoid-living-in-london/.

14. The term "fed" is one of many colloquialisms used to describe the police, others include filth, pigs, old-bill, five-oh, the use of which can be considered an indicator of demographic, although to expand upon this in greater detail would require further research.
15. The term "Poles" was used in this context as a generic reference to all male construction workers of Eastern European origin.
16. Such "payment" was not monetary, but timeoriented. This included different voluntary actions such as sweeping halls in community centers following important meetings, helping out in youth clubs, manning stalls at community fairs, and a host of other such "payments," in exchange for information and permission of access and inclusion.

3 Newham Divide and Document

1. The Olympic Park Legacy Company was a public sector, not-for-profit organization. It was to be responsible for the long-term planning, development, management, and maintenance of the Olympic Park and its facilities after the London 2012 Games, and for delivering the Olympic legacy promises made in the original London 2012 bid. However, the OPLC became part of a Mayoral Development Corporation in 2012, amalgamating the OPLC responsibilities into the Mayor of London's authority. From 1 April 2012, the London Legacy Development Corporation (LLDC) took over the OPLC responsibilities of long-term planning, development, management, and maintenance of the Olympic Park. From October 2012, the LLDC also acquired new powers, including planning powers, for both the Olympic Park and surrounding area (Private correspondence, LLDC, April 2012).
2. An example of such actions was evidenced when in April 2000 AM established a mobile fresh fruit and vegetable initiative in response to members's complaints that some areas of the community, including Cranberry Lane, had little or no access to fresh produce. Eric Samuels, an ordained minister and volunteer co-ordinator of the Newham Food Access Partnership, stated that Cranberry Lane was "a really poor estate. There are more children under ten there per square mile than anywhere else in the country, but it's a food desert. There's only one way in and out of the estate so it takes twenty minutes to get to the nearest shop, which is expensive." With help from the charity, Samuels set up regular trips to Spitalfields market buying fruit and vegetables at wholesale prices then selling them in the estates community centre once a week at the same price. Now he runs eight such "markets" across Newham each week, two of them located in schools. For more information regarding food deserts see Wrigley (2002) or http://www.independent.co.uk/life-style/health-and-families/health-news/special-report-feeding-the-demand-for-healthy-diets-750144.html.
3. Community Service is an Order of the court that is bestowed upon a convicted criminal and used as an alternative to a prison sentence. It is usually required that the recipient carries out between 80 and 300 hours of unpaid

work within 12 months of the date of the order. For more information see: http://www.pkc.gov.uk/Social+care+and+health/Criminal+justice+social+work/Community+Service+Orders/
4. The Thames Gateway stretches east from the London boroughs of Newham, Tower Hamlets and Greenwich for approximately 45 miles and encompasses three regions: London, East and South East England. Its boundary points are between Westferry in Tower Hamlets and the Isle of Sheppey. The Department for Communities and Local Government are responsible for the over-seeing of a project designed to regenerate the area and develop brownfield land, farmland and marsh to increase the economic prosperity. The regeneration of the Thames Gateway development is the latest manifestation of the regeneration of the Thames Estuary, which according to www.communities.gov.uk dates back to 1981. In the years preceding the Olympic Games this project contributed significantly to the improvement of *Stratfordland*'s public transport infrastructure.
5. For a deeper account, see Cohen, P. and Rustin, M.J. (2008). *London's Turning: The Making of Thames Gateway.* Farnham: Ashgate and Poynter, G. (2009). The 2012 Olympic Games and the reshaping of East London, in R. Imrie, L. Lees & M. Raco (eds), *Regenerating London: governance, sustainability and community in a global age* (pp. 131–150). London: Routledge.
6. For a selection of media coverage, see: http://savecarpenters.wordpress.com/media/
7. In 1980 Margaret Thatcher's government introduced legislation – The Housing Act 1980 – which implemented the Right-to-Buy scheme. This was a policy that gave council and housing association tenants a legal right to buy their homes.
8. For more information see: http://www.newham.gov.uk/Regen/GreaterCarpentersNeighbourhoodredevelopmentFAQs.htm#14
9. For more information see: http://www.newham.gov.uk/Regen/GreaterCarpentersNeighbourhoodredevelopmentFAQs.htm#14
10. For more see: http://www.guardian.co.uk/sport/2012/jun/13/london-2012-legacy-battle-newham.
11. For a comprehensive guide to Newham regeneration plans visit: http://www.newham.gov.uk/InformationforBusinesses/RegenerationProjects/RegenerationProjects.htm
12. Carpenters Against Regeneration Plan (CARP) were a group of residents, primarily leaseholders, who lived on the Carpenters Estate. They campaigned on two fronts – idealistically, they were against Carpenters closure; pragmatically, they campaigned for a 'fair deal' if they were re-housed.
13. The TBAG campaign was established to demonstrate against the tower blocks being evacuated and for an improvement in the living conditions there. The TBAG engaged in direct social action that took the form of hanging banners from the outer walls of the tower blocks and attempting to lobby Sir Robin Wales at public events.
14. Private interview—July 2012.

Notes • 171

15. This estate, completed in 2004, was located between the Royal Docks and the River Thames. It was a development undertaken by George Wimpey plc that replaced a 1960s estate (which included the two tower blocks of Barnwood Court) with an "urban village" containing mixed tenure housing, a primary school, a parade of shops, a community hall and an outdoor communal space (that is, a village green). The location was rebranded – from "West Silvertown" to "Britannia Village," which aimed to convey the socio-economic modification exemplified by the transformed physical landscape.
16. In 1989, the Prince of Wales introduced the phrase "urban village" in his publication, *A Vision for Britain* where he outlined his hope for the development of urban villages that would re-introduce vibrant street life (HRH The Prince of Wales 1989, p.4). The pursuit of this ambition led to the formation of the Urban Villages Group (UVG) whose members subscribed to the principles of humane urban environments (Thompson-Fawcett 1996), and to recommendations on how these principles could be applied in new developments (Franklin and Tait 2002, p.257).
17. For more details, see Trevaskis consulting tender document (2006). A copy of this document is available at: http://www.bvra.org.uk/documents/ITTv5.pdf.
18. By closure, Weber (1968, pp. 32–33) described a set of processes whereby a specific collective restricts "access to the opportunities (social or economic) that exist in a given domain"...Its members "draw on certain characteristics of their real or virtual adversaries to try and exclude them from competition. These characteristics may be race, language, confession, place of origin or social background, descent, place of domicile, etc." See also Wacquant (2008) for a different approach to the concept of closure.
19. Sarah Nutall (2009) argued that the complex interplays of an individual's past and present and the formative and informative entanglements of history, people and place shaped contemporary urban margins. This resonates with Bourdieu's notion of *habitus* explored earlier.
20. "In the end, what is it that people reproach youths for? That they occupy the squares, that they sit on the benches or the steps in front of stores...that they stay there talking, laughing, making a racket." Youths, on the other hand, perceive "the street as a mere place of well-being, a neutral ground upon which they can put their mark" (Calogirou 1989, p. 36–37; Bourdieu 1991, p.12; Wacquant 2008, p.189).
21. In the work of Bourdieu (2001), the word *doxa* refers to the practice of accepting oppression without realising that one is being oppressed (see Chapter 4, n. 30).

4 Life in the Shadow of the Olympic Torch

1. For more information see: http://www.olympic.org/commercial-sponsorships.
2. For more information regarding the BOA see: http://www.teamgb.com/about-boa.

3. In agreement with Fussey et al.'s (2011) conclusions, Olympic-related urban regeneration is considered to be "a comprehensive integrated vision and action which leads to the resolution of urban problems and which seeks to bring about lasting change in the economic, social, physical and environmental condition of an area." (Roberts and Sykes 2000, p.17).
4. This—implicit—reward is gained by the victors of the IOC Olympic bidding contest.
5. Docklands was the new name given to the Pool of London; at one time the largest port in the world covering an area of 8½ square miles. For more information see http://www.londondrum.com/cityguide/docklands.php.
6. The London Development Agency (LDA) was a functional body of the Greater London Authority (GLA). It was the Regional Development Agency for Greater London, whose purpose was to drive sustainable London-wide economic growth. The LDA ceased to exist in March 2012.
7. For more information, see: http://news.bbc.co.uk/1/hi/sci/tech/4299714.stm.
8. For more, see: http://news.bbc.co.uk/1/hi/sci/tech/4299714.stm.
9. The ODA was the public body responsible for developing and building the London 2012 Olympic venues and infrastructure. For more information, see http://www.london2012.com/about-us/the-people-delivering-the-games/oda/.
10. In this book, Bourdieu argued that women accepted being dominated by men, seeing this interplay as a matter of course. He refers to this acceptance using the word *doxa*, which refers to the practice of accepting oppression without realising that one is being oppressed.
11. For a full explanation of the ladder and its categorical rings see Burns, Hambleton, and Hoggett (1994).
12. For more information, see: http://www.citizensuk.org/campaigns/citysafe-campaign/.

5 Employment and Capital Gains

1. This document was produced by the *Advance to Deliver* project. The report is available at: http://www.aston-mansfield.org.uk/pdf_docs/research/newham-key-statistics.PDF. For more information on the *Advance to Deliver* project, see: http://www.aston-mansfield.org.uk/a2d.php.
2. The full text is at: http://www.newham.gov.uk/2012Games/AboutThe2012Games/default.htm.
3. The newspaper account is available at: http://www.dailymail.co.uk/news/article-419161/Mayor-Olympic-borough-says-locals-lazy-jobs-project.html.
4. For more information regarding the ESOL program, see: http://www.direct.gov.uk/en/educationandlearning/adultlearning/improvingyourskills/dg_10037499.
5. This information was obtained from a personal interview with an Albanian Shpresa organisation leader, October 2011.
6. This is the official title given to the applicants who succeeded in becoming volunteers. See http://www.direct.gov.uk/en/Nl1/Newsroom/DG_190795.

7. More information is available at: http://epress.lib.uts.edu.au/scholarly-works/bitstream/handle/2100/449/Ourpromise2012.pdf?sequence=2.
8. This is a partnership of 35 state-funded youth and community services within Newham
9. This research was conducted by the Institute of Education, University of London—*Tackling the NEET Problem.*
10. More data regarding NEETs is available at: http://www.ioe.ac.uk/TacklingNEETs.pdf.
11. For more information, see http://www.britannia-village.newham.sch.uk/achievements.html.
12. For more information see: http://www.lda.gov.uk/news-and-events/media-centre/press-releases/2006/major-skills-study-for-the-london-2012-games-gets-underway.aspx.
13. More information is available at: http://www.lda.gov.uk/news-and-events/media-centre/press-releases/2006/major-skills-study-for-the-london-2012-games-gets-underway.aspx.
14. The full newspaper report is available at: http://www.dailymail.co.uk/news/article-419161/Mayor-Olympic-borough-says-locals-lazy-jobs-project.html.

6 The Rings of Exclusion

1. More information is available at: http://www.london2012.com/documents/oda-transport/final-transport-plan/transport-plan-part-2-ch-7-.pdf.
2. The NVSC fulfils the roles that Community Voluntary Services (CVS) forms in other parts of the country; that is, to provide infrastructure support networks for the third sector. A CVS is funded by the local authority; however, the Newham council did not fund a CVS and, consequently, Newham's third sector formed and funded their own equivalent—the NVSC—in 2001.
3. Newham's dispersal zone saw the police 'join forces' with Newham council in order to combat 'anti-social' behavior. The dispersal zone enabled those policing Newham to ban 'groups of troublemakers' from specific locations in the borough for 'anti-social behavior'. Anyone who breached the notice could be arrested and would risk a custodial sentence of up to three months and/or a fine of up to £2,500. Such highly visible punitive solutions to urban problems can be explained by a political desire for public and tabloid popularity (Garland 2000). Wacquant (2001, 2008) argues that such attempts to govern through criminal justice were part of a more general attack on the dispossessed. See also: http://www.newham.gov.uk/YourEnvironment/ReportingAntiSocialBehaviour/DispersalzoneinStratfordtowncentre.htm.

7 Securitization: The Olympic Lockdown?

1. More information on David Cameron's summation is available at: http://www.morethanthegames.co.uk/london-2012/0916184-london-2012-cameron-defends-decision-double-olympic-ceremonies-budget.

2. For more information, see http://www.dailymail.co.uk/sport/olympics/article-2025014/london-olympics-2012-Sebb-Coe-confident-Olympic-safety-despite-london-riots.html.
3. This Olympic Security Review Conference was held at the Ocquirrh Institute in Salt Lake City, Utah. It comprised some 60 participants from the private sector and from local, state, and federal public safety representatives to discuss the security lessons learned from the 2002 Olympics. For more information, see http://leavitt.li.suu.edu/leavitt/?p=578.
4. In this regard, the widening gulf between rich and poor and the increased closure of political élites onto themselves and the media coupled with the increasing distance between the lower class and the dominant institutions of society all breed disaffection and distrust. They converge to undermine the legitimacy of the social order and to redirect hostility toward the specific organization of the state that has come to symbolize its unresponsiveness and naked repressiveness: the police. In the vacuum created by the lack of political linkages and the absence of recognized mediations between marginalized urban populations and a society from which they feel rejected, it is no wonder that relations with the police have everywhere become both salient and bellicose, and that incidents with the "forces of order" are invariably the detonator of the explosions of popular violence that have rocked poor neighborhoods (Cashmore and McLaughlin 1992; Wacquant 2008, pp.31–32).
5. The expression "Broken Britain" was first used by British Prime Minister David Cameron during his 2010 election campaign, which promised to give the police more powers to fight crime and provide deterrents. This theme evolved into Cameron's attack on Britain's "Broken Society" in the aftermath of the 2011 Riots, which was illustrative of his political orientation regarding rights and responsibilities, crime and punishment, and society being unaware, or unconcerned about the consequences of their actions. See: http://www.bbc.co.uk/news/uk-politics-14524834.
6. For more, see http://www.guardian.co.uk/sport/2011/nov/13/us-worried-london-olympics-security-2012.
7. More data is available at: http://www.dailymail.co.uk/sport/olympics/article-2024108/London-riots-Olympic-chiefs-confident-security-2012-Games.html.
8. For more information, see http://www.aim25.ac.uk/cats/118/11487.htm.
9. More data regarding this consultation is available at: http://www.homeoffice.gov.uk/media-centre/press-releases/2012-consultation-wanstead-flats.
10. For more information, see http://www.bbc.co.uk/news/uk-england-london-13985226.
11. For more information, see http://savewansteadflats.org.uk/.
12. See http://news.bbc.co.uk/1/hi/uk/285553.stm for more information.
13. For more data, see http://www.nmp.org.uk/p/about-nmp.html.
14. In 1984, Section 1 of the Police and Criminal Evidence Act (PACE) standardized the power of the police to stop and search for stolen or prohibited articles throughout England and Wales. PACE determined that there must be an

objective basis for police suspicion to stop and search – such as reliable information from the public or an individual "acting suspiciously." The Criminal Justice and Public Order Act of 1994 (Section 60) empowered the police to stop and search members of the public in anticipation of acts of violence. Further legislation in the form of the Terrorism Act of 2000 (Section 44) enabled the police to stop and search persons and vehicles in order to look for articles that could be used in acts of terrorism. Ministry of Justice figures published in October 2007 revealed that black and Asians were more likely to be stopped than whites were. Within London, these figures indicated that, in 2005–2006, black people were more than seven times more likely to be stopped than whites were. This is particularly problematic in boroughs such as Newham. For more information, see http://www.historyextra.com/feature/stop-and-search-what-can-we-learn-history
15. For more information, see http://www.met.police.uk/stopandsearch/what_is.htm.
16. More information is available at: http://www.met.police.uk/stopandsearch/.
17. See: http://www.nmp.org.uk/2012/05/volunteer-to-become-nmp-community-legal.html for more information.
18. Interestingly, during one of the training events it emerged that, in targeting "who," the most likely recipient of these "Bust Cards" would be, CLOs adopted the same stereotyping attitude that the MPS were accused of using for "Stop and Search."

8 Big Game Hunting: Baiting the Hooks

1. The term "Rent Gap" refers to the shortfall between the actual economic return from present land use of an area (capitalized ground rent) and the potential return that it would yield if it were put to its optimal use (potential ground rent). As a rent gap increases, it creates lucrative opportunities for developers, investors, homebuyers, and local governments to orchestrate a shift in land use – for instance, from working-class residential to middle or upper class residential or high-end commercial (Smith 1979; Lees, Slater, and Wyly 2008, p.52).
2. For more examples, see http://www.nestoria.co.uk/britannia-village/flat/sale#dyn:/coord_51.506799,0.025438,51.504128,0.017971/flat/sale/sortby-price_highlow.
3. More examples are available at: http://homes.trovit.co.uk/index.php/cod.ad/type.2/what_d.house%20britannia%20village/id.71691h1yxTt/pos.1/pop.0/.
4. At the time of writing, the Olympic Village is to be converted into 2,818 homes for 6,000 people. Triathlon homes will take over ownership of 1,379 homes; 675 of the latter are intended for social rent. The remaining 1,439 homes will be available to rent or buy on the private market. For more see Meredith (2012).
5. For more details, see http://www.newham.gov.uk/News/2011/September/WestfieldStratfordCityNewhamslastinglegacy.htm?Printable=true.

176 • Notes

6. More data are available at: http://uk.westfield.com/stratfordcityleasing/assets/stratfordcityleasing/news/press-toolkit/Westfield_Stratford_City_Fact_Sheet_May_2011.pdf.
7. For more information, see http://www.newham.gov.uk/News/2011/September/WestfieldStratfordCityNewhamslastinglegacy.htm?Printable=true.
8. Kettling is a tactic used by the police to control large crowds during demonstrations and protests. The success of this tactic depends on restricting or preventing movement. Corporate kettling is defined here as a suggestive, sub-conscious version of this tactic, whereby people, unless otherwise informed, would assume that there was only one direction to follow around Stratfordland. Professor Richard Giulianotti, who conceptualized the expression 'Corporate Kettling', outlined its meaning to me in the vicinity of the Olympic Park during the 2012 events.
9. For more, see http://uk.westfield.com/stratfordcityleasing/assets/stratfordcityleasing/news/press-toolkit/Westfield_Stratford_City_Fact_Sheet_May_2011.pdf.
10. Some 5,000 vehicles could be accommodated there. These parking spaces were not available for public use during the Olympic Games period (June—September 2012). For more information, see http://uk.westfield.com/stratfordcity/getting-here/car-park-closures.
11. More information is available at: http://www.e-architect.co.uk/london/the_shoal_stratford.htm.
12. For more details, see http://www.e-architect.co.uk/london/the_shoal_stratford.htm.
13. Betting shops were considered problematic in Newham. In June 2012, Labour Councilor Neil Wilson proposed a crackdown on the number of betting shops in the borough stating that Newham's streets were "blighted by the prevalence of bookmakers" (York 2012). According to Shadow Minister for Public Health, Diane Abbott (MP for Hackney North and Stoke Newington), this Newham blight was the result of bookmakers targeting poor, deprived areas and exploiting those who lived there. In support of this argument, she stressed that there were three times more betting shops in Newham than in the prosperous borough of Richmond. For more information, see http://www.dianeabbott.org.uk/news/speeches/news.aspx?p=102784. One unintended outcome of Olympic hosting may therefore be seen to be that in certain parts of Newham bookmakers would become less frequent as their customers become more affluent, which may symbolize the true Olympic legacy and the associated reordering of the area (For further illustrations and explanation, see Appendix A – Figures 31–34).
14. The word "CHAV" is an acronym and it is denigratory. It stands for Council Housed and Violent. For a full account of this word and its connotations, see the publication *CHAVS: The Demonization of the Working Class* (Jones 2011).

9 Going for the Gold: The All-Consuming 2012 Ethos

1. For more information see http://www.london2012.com/documents/locog-publications/singapore-presentation-speeches.pdf.

2. For more information, see http://news.bbc.co.uk/onthisday/hi/dates/stories/july/6/newsid_4940000/4940112.stm.
3. For more information, see: http://news.bbc.co.uk/sport1/hi/other_sports/olympics_2012/4654821.stm
4. For more information, see http://webarchive.nationalarchives.gov.uk/+/http://www.culture.gov.uk/images/publications/2012LegacyActionPlan.pdf.
5. For more information, see http://www.guardian.co.uk/sport/2011/mar/28/jeremy-hunt-london-2012-legacy.
6. See: http://www.telegraph.co.uk/sport/olympics/news/8944428/London-2012-Olympics-Sport-England-to-miss-legacy-target-as-Games-fail-to-inspire-youngsters.html.
7. More information regarding this assumption is available at: http://news.bbc.co.uk/1/hi/uk/4656771.stm
8. The ETOA is a trade organisation for European travel companies. As such, it can be relied upon to provide a relatively neutral perspective of Olympic impact on tourism.
9. For more information regarding this suggestion, see: http://members.etoa.org/Pdf/ETOA%20Report%20Olympic.pdf.
10. Gardner, Pickett, and Brewer (2000) have outlined this perspective. "Humans," they say, "are inherently social creatures. We gather in groups the world over and form affectional pair- bonds in every known human society (Brewer and Caporael 1995). Social exclusion is an effective and ubiquitous form of punishment across all age groups and cultures (see Williams 1997 for review), and a lack of positive social relationships has repeatedly been associated with startling decreases in physical and mental wellbeing (for review, see Gardner, Gabriel, and Diekman 2000). Indeed, the need to belong—a need fulfilled only through affiliation with and acceptance from others—is so universally powerful that it has been proposed to be as basic to our psychological makeup as hunger or thirst is to our physical makeup (Baumeister and Leary 1995). Past research has presented ample behavioral [sic] evidence consistent with a need to belong; individuals who are rejected will symbolically or explicitly (Williams and Sommers 1997) attempt to connect themselves to a larger social whole the importance of belonging has been emphasised throughout the history of psychology. The need to belong was stressed by early motivation theorists (e.g., Maslow 1971), and more recently, cogent arguments for its fundamental nature have been presented (Baumeister and Leary 1995). We believe that just as physical hunger increases sensitivity to food cues (Atkinson and McClelland 1948), social hunger increases sensitivity to social cues, implying that an individual's shifting levels of belonging may fundamentally shape the perception and representation of his or her social world" (Gardner, Pickett, and Brewer 2000, pp. 486–495).
11. For more information regarding Sir Robin Wales's opinion see: http://www.guardian.co.uk/uk/2005/aug/08/olympics2012.ukcrime.
12. For a more complete account of these comments see: http://www.theyworkforyou.com/debates/?id=2005-07-06a.404.0.

13. This report is available in full at: http://blogs.metro.co.uk/olympics/london-2012-how-we-won-the-olympic-bid/.
14. The "No to London 2012" group was formed in late 2004. It was a coalition of East London residents, academics, community groups, anti-authoritarian, and social justice campaigners who were concerned about the implications of London bidding to stage the Olympics. Concern regarding London 2012 came from a variety of perspectives that included environmental issues, policing concerns, displacement, and use of public land. In 2005, the group organised demonstrations including that advertised above and a flotilla of canal boats along the river Lea in an attempt to raise awareness for the movement. These demonstrations resulted in local and national media coverage. Following London's award of the 2012 Olympic Games, the group created a forum that aimed to provide a collection of counter-Olympic narratives that indicated the realities of Olympic hosting, this internet resource was named Games Monitor and can be accessed at http://www.gamesmonitor.org.uk/ (Private interview, Carolyn, "No to London 2012" founder member, February 2012).
15. For more information see: http://www.nolondon2012.org/.
16. For more information see: http://www.prnewswire.com/news-releases/london-2012-olympic-and-paralympic-games-showcase-british-industry-and-power-of-sport-as-catalyst-for-social-economic-and-community-change-games-leader-and-1984-la-gold-medallist-seb-coe-tells-american-business-leaders-139466088.html.
17. For more information, see: http://train4tradeskills.wordpress.com/2012/07/02/the-olympic-venue-is-an-excellent-showcase-for-british-construction-industry/.
18. For more information, see http://www.lbc.co.uk/cameron-olympics-will-boost-economy-by-13bn-56837.
19. The torch relay highlighted the transitory re-imagination of Great Britain into London 2012; a highly social construct that appeared to attain quasi-natural resonance. This concept resonated with Sarup's definition of identity, which was delineated as a "mediating concept between the external and the internal, the individual and society...a convenient tool through which to understand many aspects, personal, philosophical, political, of our lives" (1996, p.28).

10 Conclusion: Extinguishing the Olympic Torch

1. In this regard, forms of popular culture, particularly sporting Mega-Events such as the Olympic Games, emerge within a Gramscian framework as crucial battlefields where social values and relations are shaped, represented, and contested. Consequently, the application of Gramsci's concept of hegemony facilitates an exploration of the dynamic framework of the Olympic industry and their actions, motivations, and ideologies. It also enables an analysis of how these are disseminated and perceived throughout Olympic delivery and beyond (see also Hargreaves 1986; Giulianotti 2005).

2. As Lenskyj herself stated in the introduction to her 2008 work *The Best Olympics Ever? Social Impacts of Sydney 2000*, "I make no claim that the book is comprehensive or balanced, or that it employs a traditional scholarly approach. Rather, it is an attempt to examine social inequities generated or exacerbated by Sydney's Olympic preparations from the perspective of disadvantaged people whose voices would not otherwise be heard." (2002, p. 1)
3. This was a title London shared with Beijing between 2005 and 2008 and then with Rio from 2009 until 2012.
4. This prose is supported by a series of photographs provided in Appendix A. In agreement with Les Back's assertions that often words fail to do justice to the vivid nature of everyday life, I included these snapshots of Newham life as a sociological tool to add depth to research (2007, pp.17–18). These photographs illustrate the dichotomy of Newham life during the Olympic delivery and provide a pictorial illustration of the themes discussed throughout this study. They point to the uneasy fit between many of Newham residents' habitus and the rapid evolution of the Newham context during Olympic delivery; they were included to endow the reader with a degree of closeness to the milieu, which could not be offered solely in textual form.
5. In addition to the planned UCL campus on Carpenters Estate, Birkbeck College (University of London) planned to open a new campus in Stratfordland in the autumn of 2013. The University of East London (UEL) also has a recently refurbished their base there (See: http://www.bbk.ac.uk/prospective/stratford/new-campus on Birkbeck College; and http://www.uel.ac.uk/campuses/stratford/ on UEL).
6. Lenskyj defined the real world as Sydney's streets; its low-income neighborhoods, homeless refuges, and its indigenous communities (2002, pp 227–228).
7. Spitalfields, a 250-acre location that borders the London borough of Tower Hamlets and the City of London, is an example of the uneasy meshing of gentrification and diversity within East London. This was explored by Jane Jacobs (1996) who commented that 'the co-presence of Bengali settlers, home-making gentrifiers and megascale developers activated an often conflictual politics of race and nation' (p. 72).

References

Agnew, J. (1998). *Geopolitics: Revisioning World Politics*. London: Routledge.
Albrow, M. (1990). Globalization, knowledge and society: An introduction. In M. Albrow and E. King (eds.), *Globalization, Knowledge and Society*. London: Sage.
Aldous, T. (1992). *Urban Villages: A Concept for Creating Mixed-use Urban Developments on a Sustainable Scale*. London: Urban Village Group.
Aldous, T. (ed.). (1995). *Economics of Urban Villages*. London: Urban Village Forum.
Allan, G. A. (1989). *Friendship, Developing a Sociological Perspective*. New York: Harvester Wheatsheaf.
Amin, A. (2002). Ethnicity and the multicultural city: Living with diversity. *Environment and Planning A, 34*, 959–980.
Anderson, B. (1983). *Imagined Communities: Reflections on the Origin and Spread of Nationalism*. London: Verso.
Anderson, E. (1999). *Code of the Street: Decency, Violence, and the Moral Life of the Inner City*. New York: W. W. Norton.
Armstrong, G. (1998). *Football Hooligans: Knowing the Score*. Oxford: Berg.
Armstrong, G., Hobbs, R., and Lindsay, I. (2011). Calling the shots: The pre-2012 London Olympic contest. *Urban Studies, 48* (15), 3169–3184.
Arnstein, S. (1969). A ladder of citizen participation. *Journal of the American Institute of Planners, 35*, 216–224.
Aston, C. (1983). *A Contemporary Crisis: Political Hostage-taking and the Experience of Western Europe*. Westport, CT: Greenwood Press.
Aston Mansfield. (2011). *A2D: Newham Key Statistics*. Retrieved June 3, 2011, from http://www.aston-mansfield.org.uk/pdf_docs/research/newham-key-statistics.PDF.
Atkinson, M. and Young, K. (2008). *Deviance and Social Control in Sport*. Champaign, IL: Human Kinetics.
Atkinson, R. (2003). Domestication by cappuccino or revenge on urban space? Control and empowerment in the management of public spaces. *Urban Studies, 40*(9), 1211–1245.

Atkinson, R. and Bridge, G. (2005). *Gentrification in a Global Perspective*. London: Routledge.
Atkinson, R. G. and Helms, G. (2007). *Securing an Urban Renaissance: Crime, Community and British Urban Policy*. Bristol: The Policy Press.
Auge, M. (1995). *Non-Places: An Introduction to Supermodernity*. London: Verso.
Auletta, K. (1982). *The Underclass*. New York: Vintage Books.
Back, L. (2007). *The Art of Listening*. New York: Berg.
Bagehot (2012, July 14–20). Scourge of the slums. *The Economist*, 26.
Banfield, E. C. (1970). *The Unheavenly City: The Nature and Future of our Urban Crisis*. Boston: Little, Brown.
Barnard, S., Butler, K., Golding, P. and Maguire, J. (2006). Making the news: The Athens Olympics 2004 and competing ideologies? *Olympika: The International Journal of Olympic Studies, XV*, 35–56.
Barney, R. K., Wenn, S. and Martyn, S. (2002). *Selling the Five Rings: The International Olympic Committee and the Rise of Olympic Commercialism*. Salt Lake City: The University of Utah Press.
Baudrillard, J. (1988). *Selected Writings*. Cambridge: Polity Press.
Bauman, Z. (1998). *Globalization: The Human Consequences*. New York: Columbia University Press.
Baumeister, R. F. and Leary, M. R. (1995). The need to belong: Desire for interpersonal attachments as a fundamental human motive. *Psychological Bulletin, 117*, 497–529.
Beck, U. (1998). *Democracy Without Enemies*. Cambridge: Polity Press.
Berry, B. J. L. (1985). Islands of renewal in seas of decay. In P. E. Peterson (ed.), *The New Urban Reality*. Washington, DC: Brookings.
Billig, M. (1995). *Banal Nationalism*. London: Sage.
Billings, A. C. and Eastman, S. T. (2002). Framing identities: Gender, ethnic, and national parity in network announcing of the 2002 winter Olympics. *Journal of Communication, 53*, 369–386.
Bose, M., and Grant, A. (2005, February 15). IOC panel are ready to assess public support. *The Telegraph*. Retrieved February 15, 2005, from http://www.telegraph.co.uk/sport/olympics/2355352/IOC-panel-are-ready-to-assess-public- support.htm.
Bourdieu, P. (1977/2002). *Outline of a Theory of Practice*. Cambridge: Cambridge University Press.
Bourdieu, P. (1979). *Algeria 1960*. Cambridge: Cambridge University Press.
Bourdieu, P. (1984). *Distinction: A Social Critique of the Judgment of Taste* (R. Nice, Translator). Cambridge, MA: Harvard University Press.
Bourdieu, P. (1986). The forms of capital, in J. Richardson (Ed.), *Handbook of Theory and Research in the Sociology of Education* (pp. 241–258). Connecticut: Greenwood.
Bourdieu, P. (1987). What makes social class? On the theoretical and practical existence of groups. *Berkeley Journal of Sociology, 32*, 1–18.
Bourdieu, P. (1991). *Language and Symbolic Power*. Cambridge: Polity Press.

Bourdieu, P. (1993a). Concluding remarks: For a sociogenic understanding of intellectual works. In C. Calhoun., E. LiPuma and M. Postone (eds), *Bourdieu: Critical Perspectives* (pp. 263–275). Cambridge: Polity Press.
Bourdieu, P. (1993b). *The Field of Cultural Production*. Cambridge: Polity Press.
Bourdieu, P. (1998). *On Television and Journalism* (P. P. Ferguson, Trans.). London: Pluto.
Bourdieu, P. (1999). *The Weight of the World*. Cambridge: Polity Press.
Bourdieu, P. (2000). *Pascalian Meditations*. Cambridge: Polity Press.
Bourdieu, P. (2001). *Masculine Domination*. Cambridge: Polity Press.
Bourdieu, P., and Wacquant, L. (1992). *An Invitation to Reflexive Sociology*. Cambridge: Polity Press.
Boykoff, J. (2011). The anti-Olympics. *New Left Review, 67*(Jan/Feb), 41–59.
Boyle, P. and Haggerty, K. (2009). Spectacular security: Mega-Events and the security complex. *International Political Sociology, 3*, 257–274.
Brewer, M. B. and Caporael, L. R. (1995). Hierachial evolutionary theory: There is an alternative and it's not creationism. *Psychological Inquiry, 6*, 31–34.
Brohm, J. M. (1978). *Sport: A Prison of Measured Time*. London: Ink Links.
Brown, G. (2000). Emerging issues in Olympic sponsorship: Implications for host cities. *Sport Management Review, 3*, 71–92.
Brown, G. (2002). Taking the pulse of Olympic sponsorship. *Event Management, 7*, 177–186.
Brown, G. (2007). Sponsor hospitality at the Olympic Games: An analysis of the implications for Tourism. *International Journal of Travel Research, 9*, 315–327.
Brown, J. B. (2007). *Building Powerful Community Organisations: A Personal Guide to Creating Groups that can Solve Problems and Change the World*. New York: Long Hand Press.
Buchanan, I. (1999). Non-places: Space in the age of supermodernity. *Social Semiotics, 9*(3), 393–398.
Buck, N., Gordon, I., Hall, P., Harloe, M., and Kleinman, M. (2002). *Working Capital: Life and Labour in Contemporary London*. London: Routledge.
Burbank, M., Andranovich, G., and Heying, C. H. (2001). *Olympic Dreams: The Impact of MegaEvents on Local Politics*. Boulder, CO: Lynne Rienner Publishers.
Burns, D., Hambleton, R. and Hoggett, P. (1994). *The Politics of Decentralisation: Revitalising Local Democracy*. Basingstoke: Macmillan.
Butler, T. and Robson, G. (2001). Social capital and neighbourhood change in London: A comparison of three South London neighbourhoods. *Urban Studies, 38*, 2145–2162.
Calhoun, C., LiPuma, E. and Postone, M. (eds.) (1993). *Bourdieu: Critical Perspectives*. Cambridge: Polity Press.
Calogirou, C. (1989). Sauver son honneur: Rapports sociaux en milieu urbain defavorise. In L. Wacquant, *Urban outcasts: A comparative sociology of advanced marginality*. Cambridge: Polity Press.
Cashmore, E. and McLaughlin, E. (eds.) (1992). *Out of Order: Policing Black People*. London: Routledge.

Castells, M. (1991). *The Information City: Information Technology, Economic Restructuring and Urban-Regional Process.* Oxford: Basil Blackwell.
The Centre on Housing Rights and Evictions (COHRE). (2007). *Mega-Events, Olympic Games and Housing Rights: Opportunities for the Olympic Movement and Others.* Geneva, Switzerland: COHRE.
Chalip, L. and Costa, C.A. (2005). Sport event tourism and the destination brand: Towards a general theory. *Sport in Society,* 8(2), 218–237.
Charters, D. (1983). Terrorism and the 1984 Olympics. *Conflict Quarterly,* 3(4), 37–47.
Christie, J. (1998). IOC vows to expel voting members who took bribes. *The Globe and Mail,* December 14, p.2.
Clark, J., Dyson, A., and Millward, A. (1999). *Housing and Schooling: A Case-Study in Joined up Problems.* York: York Publishing Services.
Clarke, J. and Critcher, C. (1985). *The Devil Makes Work.* London: Macmillan.
Cloke, P., Philo, C., and Sadler, D. (1991). *Approaching Human Geography: An Introduction to Contemporary Theoretical Debates.* London: Paul Chapman.
Coaffee, J. (2009). Protecting the urban: The dangers of planning for terrorism. *Theory, Culture & Society,* 26(7/8), 343–355.
Coaffee, J., Fussey, P., and Moore, C. (2011). Laminated security for London 2012: Enhancing security infrastructure to defend Mega sporting Events. *Urban Studies,* 48(15), 3311–3327.
Coe, S. (2009). *The Winning Mind: My Inside Track on Great Leadership.* London: Headline.
Cohen, P. and Rustin, M.J. (2008). *London's Turning: The Making of Thames Gateway.* Farnham: Ashgate.
Cole, D. (1987). Artists and urban development. *Geographical Review,* 77, 391–407.
Cornelissen, S. (2011). Mega Event securitisation in a third world setting: Glocal processes and ramifications during the 2010 FIFA World Cup. *Urban Studies,* 48(15), 3221–3240.
Crow, G. and Allen, G. (1994). *Community Life: An Introduction to Local Social Relations.* Hemel Hempstead: Harvester Wheatsheaf.
Curtis, L. A. (1985). *American Violence and Public Policy: An Update of the National Commission on the Causes and Prevention of Violence.* New Haven, CT: Yale University Press.
Davis, M. (1990). *City of Quartz.* London: Verso.
Day, G., and Murdoch, J. (1993). Locality and community: Coming to terms with place. *Sociological Review,* 41(1), 82–111.
Dench, G., Gavron, K., and Young, M. (2006). *The New East End: Kinship, Race and Conflict.* London: Profile.
Department of Communities and Local Government. (2007a). *The English Indices of Deprivation 2007: Summary.* Retrieved April 10, 2010, from http://www.communities.gov.uk/documents/communities/pdf/576659.pdf.
Department of Communities and Local Government. (2007b). *The English Indices of Deprivation 2007.* London: HMSO.

Department for Culture, Media and Sport/Strategy Unit Report. (2002). *Game Plan: A Strategy for Delivering Government's Sport and Physical Activity Objectives.* Retrieved, July 5, 2008, from http://www.sportdevelopment.org.uk/html/gameplan.html.

Department for Culture, Media and Sport. (2007). *Our Promises for 2012: How the UK Will Benefit from the Olympic Games and Paralympic Games.* Retrieved January 8, 2010, from http://epress.lib.uts.edu.au/dspace/bitstream/handle/2100/449/Ourpromise2012.pdf?sequence=2.

Department for Culture, Media and Sport. (2008). *Before, During and After: Making the Most of the London 2012 Games.* Retrieved January 1, 2010, from http://webarchive.nationalarchives.gov.uk/+/http://www.culture.gov.uk/images/publication s/2012LegacyActionPlan. pdf.

Dowding, K., Dunleavy, P., King, D. and Margetts, H. (1995). Rational choice and community power structures. *Political Studies, 43*, 265–277.

Duneier, M. (1999). *Sidewalk.* New York: Farrar, Straus and Giroux.

Dunn, K. M. and McGuirk, P. (1999). Hallmark events, In R. Cashman and A. Hughes (eds.), *Staging the Olympics: The Event and its Impact* (pp. 18–34). Sydney: University of New South Wales Press.

Durkheim, E. (1964). *The Division of Labour in Society.* London: Macmillan Free Press. (Original work published 1893).

Echanove, M., and Srivastava, R. (2010). *What We See: Advancing the Observations of Jane Jacobs.* New York: New Village Press.

Edensor, T. (2002). *National Identity, Popular Culture and Everyday Life.* Oxford: Berg.

Eick, V. (2011). Lack of legacy? Shadows of surveillance after the 2006 World Cup in Germany. *Urban Studies, 48*(15), 3329–3346.

Eisinger, P. (2000). The politics of bread and circuses: Building the city for the visitor class. *Urban Affairs Review, 36*, 872–884.

Elder, C., Pratt, A. and Ellis, C. (2006). Running race: Reconciliation, nationalism and the Sydney Olympic Games. *International Review for the Sociology of Sport, 41*(2), 181–200.

Espy, R. (1979). *The Politics of the Olympic Games.* Berkeley: University of California Press.

Essex, S., and Chalkley, B. (1998). Olympic Games: Catalyst of urban change. *Leisure Studies, 17*(3), 187–206.

European Tour Operators Association. (2006). *Olympic Report.* Retrieved July 5, 2011, from http://www.etoa.org/docs/olympic-report-2006/2006_etoa-olympic-report.pdf?sfvrsn=2.

Eyquem, M. T. (1976). The founder of the modern Games. In M. M. Killanin and J. Rodda (eds.), *The Olympic Games: 80 Years of People, Events and Records* (pp. 138–143). New York: Collier Books.

Fainstein, S. S., Gordon, I., and Harloe, M. (eds.) (1992). *Divided Cities: New York and London in the Contemporary World.* Oxford: Basil Blackwell.

Ferguson, N. (2003). *Empire: How Britain Made the Modern World.* London: Allen Lane.

Florida, R. (2002). *The Rise of the Creative Class*. New York: Basic Books.
Florida, R. (2005). *The Flight of the Creative Class: The New Global Competition for Talent*. New York: Harper Collins.
Foster, P. (2011). London riots: China raises questions over safety of 2012 Olympic Games. *The Telegraph*. Retrieved August 9, 2011, from http://www.telegraph.co.uk/news/uknews/crime/8690809/London-riots-China-raises- questions -over-safety-of-2012-Olympic-Games.html.
Franklin, B. and Tait, M. (2002). Constructing an image: The urban village concept in the UK. *Planning Theory, 1*, 250–272.
Fraser, N. (2012). *Over the Border: The Other East End*. London: Function Books.
Friedmann, J. and Wolff, G. (1982). World city formation: An agenda for research and action. *International Journal of Urban and Regional Research, 6*, 309–344.
Fussey, P., Coafee, J., Armstrong, G., and Hobbs, D. (2011). *Securing and Sustaining the Olympic City: Reconfiguring London for 2012 and Beyond*. Aldershot: Ashgate.
Garcia-Ramon, M.D. and Albet, A. (2000). Pre-Olympic and post-Olympic Barcelona, a model for urban regeneration today? *Environment and Planning A, 32*(8), 1331–1334.
Gardner, W. L., Pickett, C. L., and Brewer, M. B. (2000). Social exclusion and selective memory: How the need to belong influences memory for social events. *Personality and Social Psychology Bulletin, 26*, 486–496.
Garland, D. (2000). The cultures of high crime societies: Some preconditions of recent law and order policies. *British Journal of Criminology, 40*, 347–375.
Giulianotti, R. (2005). *Sport: A Critical Sociology*. Cambridge: Polity Press.
Giulianotti, R. (2011). Sport Mega Events, urban football carnivals and securitised commodification: The case of the English Premier League. *Urban Studies, 48*(15), 3293–3310.
Giulianotti, R. and Klauser, F. (2011). Introduction: Security and surveillance at sport Mega Events. *Urban Studies, 48*(15), 3157–3168.
Gold, J. R. and Gold, M. M. (eds.) (2007). *Olympic Cities: City Agendas, Planning, and the World's Games, 1896–2012*. Oxon: Routledge.
Greater London Authority. (2008). *Data Management and Analysis Group: GLA 2008 Round Demographic Projections*. Retrieved June 1, 2011, from http://legacy.london.gov.uk/gla/publications/factsandfigures/DMAG-briefing2009–02- round-projections.pdf.
Gramsci, A. (1971). *Selections From the Prison Notebooks*. London: Lawrence and Wishart.
Grenfell, M. (ed.). (2008). *Pierre Bourdieu: Key Concepts*. Durham: Acumen.
Guibernau, M. (1996). *Nationalisms: The Nation-state and Nationalism in the Twenty-first Century*. Cambridge: Polity Press.
Guttman, A. (1992). *The Olympics: History of the Modern Games*. Chicago: University of Illinois Press.
Hardy, C. (2008). Hysteresis. In M. Grenfell (ed.). *Pierre Bourdieu: Key Concepts* (pp. 131–148). Durham: Acumen.
Harvey, D. (1989). *The Condition of Postmodernity: An Inquiry into the Origins of Cultural Change*. Oxford: Basil Blackwell.

Harvey, D. (2005). *A Brief History of Neo-liberalism.* Oxford: Oxford University Press.
Hall, D. E. (1996). Bambi on top. *Children's Literature Association Quarterly, 21(3),* 120–125.
Hall, S. (1993). Culture, community, nation. *Cultural Studies, 7,* 349–363.
Hall, S. (2012). *City, Street and Citizen: The Measure of the Ordinary.* Oxon: Routledge.
Hannerz, U. (1992). Cosmopolitans and locals in world culture. In M. Featherstone (ed.). *Global culture: Nationalism, Globalism and Modernity* (pp. 237–251). London: Sage.
Hansard. (2005). *House of Commons Debates: London 2012 Olympic Bid.* Retrieved May 8, 2012, from http://www.theyworkforyou.com/debates/?id=2005-07-06a.404.0.
Hargreaves, J. A. (1986). *Sport, Power and Culture.* Cambridge: Polity Press.
Hargreaves, J. (2000). *Freedom for Catalonia? Catalan Nationalism, Spanish Identity and the Barcelona Olympic Games.* Cambridge: Cambridge University Press.
Harker, R., Mahar, C., and Wilkes, C. (1990). *An Introduction to the Work of Pierre Bourdieu: The Practice of Theory.* London: Macmillan.
Haylett, C. (2001). Modernization, welfare and third way politics: Limits to theorising thirds? *Transactions of the Institute of British Geographers, 26*(1), 43–56.
Haylett, C. (2003). Culture, class and urban policy: reconsidering equality. *Antipode, 35*(1), 55–73.
Her Majesty's Inspectorate of Constabulary. (2006). *Inspection of Newham BCU Metropolitan Police Service.* London: HMIC London and the BTP Office.
Herbert, S. (2005). The trapdoor of community. *Annals of Association of American Geographers, 95*(4), 850–865.
Hill, D. (2011). London riots: Pressure grows to show that the 2012 Olympics will be safe. *The Guardian.* Retrieved August 9, 2011, from http://www.guardian.co.uk/uk/davehillblog/2011/aug/09/london-riots-2012-olympic- safety-fears.
Hill, D. (2012). London 2012 legacy: The battle begins on a Newham estate. *The Guardian.* Retrieved June 13, 2012, from http://www.guardian.co.uk/sport/2012/jun/13/london-2012-legacy-battle-newham.
Hill, D. M. (1994). *Citizens and Cities: Urban Policy in the 1990s.* Hemel Hempstead: Harvester Wheatsheaf.
Hirschi, T. (1969). *Causes of Delinquency.* Berkeley: University of California Press.
Hobbs, D. (1988). *Doing the Business: Entrepreneurship, the Working Class and Detectives in the East End of London.* Oxford: Clarendon.
Hoberman, J. (2004). Sporting nationalism in an age of globalization. In J. Bale and M. K. Christiansen (eds.), *Post Olympism: Questioning Sport in the Twenty-first Century* (pp. 177–188). Oxford: Berg.
Hobsbawm, E. J. and Ranger, T. (eds.). (1983). *The Invention of Tradition.* Cambridge: Cambridge University Press.
Hodgson, A., Spours, K., and Stone, J. (2009). Preface. In The Learning and Skills Network. *Tackling the NEETs Problem: Supporting Local Authorities in Reducing Young People Not in Employment, Education and Training* (p. vi–vii).

Holcomb, H. B. and Beauregard, R. A. (1981). *Revitalizing Cities*. Washington, DC: Association of American Geographers.

Hope, T. (1999). Privatopia on trial? Property guardianship in the suburbs. *Crime Prevention Studies, 10*, 15–45.

Hope, T. (2001). Community, crime prevention in Britain: A strategic overview. *Criminal Justice, 1*(4), 421–439.

Hopkins, N. and Norton-Taylor, R. (2011). US officials worried about security at London 2012 Olympics. *The Guardian*. Retrieved November 13, 2011, from http://www.guardian.co.uk/sport/2011/nov/13/us-worried-london-olympics-security-2012.

Horne, J. and Manzenreiter, W. (2006). *Sports Mega Events: Social Scientific Analyses of a Global Phenomenon*. Malden, MA: Blackwell.

HRH The Prince of Wales. (1989). *A Vision of Britain: A Personal View of Architecture*. London: Doubleday.

Hughes, R. (1990). *Nothing if Not Critical: Selected Essays on Art*. New York: Knopf.

Imrie, R., Lees, L., and Raco, M. (2009). *Regenerating London: Governance, Sustainability and Community in a Global City*. London: Routledge.

Ipsos MORI, Social Research Institute. (2008). *Understanding London Life: Report Prepared for Capital Ambition*. Retrieved September 10, 2009 from http://www.ipsos-mori.com/DownloadPublication/1247_srI_localgovt_understanding_london_life_062008.pdf.

Jacobs, J. (1961). *The Death and Life of Great American Cities*. New York: Vintage Books.

Jacobs, J. (1996). *Edge of Empire: Postcolonialism and the City*. London: Routledge.

Jackson, S. and Andrews, D. (2005). *Sport, Culture and Advertising: Identities, Commodities and the Politics of Representation*. London: Routledge.

Jennings, A. (1996). *The New Lords of the Rings: Olympic Corruption and How to Buy Gold Medals*. London: Pocket Books.

Jennings, A. (2000). *The Great Olympic Swindle*. London: Simon & Schuster.

Jennings, A. and Sambrook, C. (2000). *The Great Olympic Swindle: When the World Wanted its Games Back*. London: Simon & Schuster.

Johnson, R. (1993). Editor's introduction. In R. Johnson (ed.), *The Field of Cultural Production: Essays on Art and Literature*. Cambridge: Polity Press.

Johnston, R.J., Gregory, D. and Smith, D.M. (eds.). (1994). *The Dictionary of Human Geography* (3rd ed.). Oxford: Blackwell.

Johnstone, C. (2004). Crime, disorder and urban renaissance. In C. Johnstone and M. Whitehead (eds.), *New horizons in British urban policy: Perspectives on New Labour's urban renaissance*. Aldershot: Ashgate.

Jones, O. (2011). *Chavs: The Demonization of the Working Class*. London: Verso.

Jones, P. and Wilks-Heeg, S. (2004). Capitalising culture: Liverpool 2008. *Local Economy, 19*(4), 341–360.

Kanin, D. B. (1981). *A Political History of the Olympic Games*. Boulder, CO: Westview Press.

Kellner, D. (2008). *Globalization and Media Spectacle: From 9/11 to the Iraq War*. Retrieved March, 1 2012, from http://www.thefreelibrary.com/ Globalization+and+ media+spectacle%3A+from+9%2F11+to+the+Iraq+wa r-a0197106153.
Kennedy, M. and Leonard, P. (2001). *Dealing with Neighborhood Change: A Primer on Gentrification and Policy Choices*. Washington: The Brookings Institution.
Kent, G. (2008). *Olympic Follies: The Madness and Mayhem of the 1908 London Games a Cautionary Tale*. London: JR Books.
King, A. (2000). Thinking with Bourdieu against Bourdieu: A practical critique of the habitus. *Sociological Theory*, *18*(3), 417–433.
King, A. D. (1993). Identity and difference: The internationalization of capital and the globalization of culture. In P. L. Knox (ed.), *The Restless Urban Landscape*. Englewood Cliffs, NJ: Prentice-Hall.
Kleidman, R. and Rochon, T. R. (1997). *Dilemmas of Organisation in Peace Campaigns*. Boulder, CO: Lynne Rienner.
Korpela, K. M. (1989). Place-identity as a product of environmental self-regulation. *Journal of Environmental Psychology*, *9*, 241–256.
Lee, M. (2006). *The Race for the 2012 Olympics: The Inside Story of How London Won the Bid*. London: Virgin Books Ltd.
Lees, L. (2003). Visions of urban renaissance: The urban task force report and the urban white paper. In R. Imrie and M. Raco (eds.), *Urban renaissance? New Labour, Community and Urban Policy*. Bristol: The Policy Press.
Lees, L., Slater, T. and Wyly, E. (eds.). (2008). *The Gentrification Reader*. Oxon: Routledge.
Lefebvre, H. (1991). *The Production of Space* (D. Nicholson-Smith, Trans.). Oxford: Blackwell.
Lenk, H. (1979). *Social Philosophy of Athletics: A Pluralistic and Practice-orientated Philosophical Analysis of Top Level Amateur Sport*. Champaign, IL: Stipes.
Lenk, H. (1984). The essence of Olympic man: Toward an Olympic philosophy and anthropology. *International Journal of Physical Education*, *21*, 9–14.
Lenskyj, H. J. (2000). *Inside the Olympic Industry: Power, Politics and Activism*. Albany, NY: State University of New York Press.
Lenskyj, H. J. (2002). *The Best Olympics Ever? Social Impacts of Sydney 2000*. Albany: State University of New York Press.
Lenskyj, H. J. (2004). Making the world safe for global capital: The Sydney 2000 Olympics and beyond. In J. Bale and M. K. Christensen (eds.), *Post-Olympism? Questioning Ssport in the Twenty-first Century* (pp. 135–146). Oxford: Berg.
Lenskyj, H.J. (2008). *Olympic Industry Resistance: Challenging Olympic Power and Propaganda*. Albany: State University of New York Press.
Lesly, P. (1974). *The People Factor: Managing the Human Climate*. Homewood, IL: Richard D. Irwin.
Levacic, R. and Woods, P. (2002). Raising school performance in the league tables (part 1): Disentangling the effects of social disadvantage. *British Educational Research Journal*, *28*(2), 208–226.

Lewis, P. (2012). Police face racism scandal after black man records abuse. *The Guardian*. Retrieved March 30, 2012, from http://www.guardian.co.uk/uk/2012/mar/30/police-racism-black-man-abuse.

Ley, D. (1980). Liberal ideology and the postindustrial city. *Annals of the Association of American Geographers, 70*, 238–258.

Ley, D. (1994). The downtown eastside: One hundred years of struggle. In S. Hasson and D. Ley (eds.), *Neighbourhood Organizations and the Welfare State*. Toronto: University of Toronto Press.

Ley, D. (1996). *The New Middle Class and the Remaking of the Central City*. Oxford: Oxford University Press.

Ley, D. (2003). Artists, aesthetics and the field of gentrification. *Urban Studies, 40*(12), 2527–2544.

Liebow, E. (1967). *Tally's Corner: A Study of Negro Streetcorner Men*. Boston, MA: Little, Brown.

Lipton, M. (1976). *Why Poor People Stay Poor*. Cambridge, Mass: Harvard University Press.

Livingstone, K. (2011). *Ken Livingstone: You Can't Say That*. London: Faber and Faber.

Lydall, R. (2004). East End strikes gold. *London Evening Standard*, November 10. p.12.

MacAloon, J. (1981). *The Great Symbol: Pierre de Coubertin and the Origins of the Modern Olympic Games*. Chicago: University of Chicago Press.

MacAloon, J. (1992). The ethnographic imperative in comparative Olympic research. *Sociology of Sport Journal, 9*, 104–130.

MacAloon, J. (2006). The theory of the spectacle: Reviewing Olympic ethnography. In A. Tomlinson and C. Young (eds.). *National Identity and Global Sports Events* (pp. 15–40). Albany, NY: SUNY Press.

MacNeill, M. (1996). Networks: Producing Olympic ice hockey for a national television audience. *Sociology of Sport Journal, 13*, 103–124.

Maguire, J., Butler, K., Barnard, S., and Golding, P. (2008).Olympism and consumption: An analysis of advertising in the British media coverage of the 2004 Athens Olympic Games. *Sociology of Sport Journal, 25*(2), 167–186.

Marrs, C. (2003). The benefits of believing (London's 2012 Olympic bid and its potential catalyst for regeneration). *Regeneration & Renewal*, 13 June 2003, p.23.

Maslow, A. H. (1971). *The Farther Reaches of Human Nature*. New York: Viking.

Mathews, G. (2011). *Ghetto at the Center of the World*. London: University of Chicago Press.

Meredith, D. (2012). The Olympic legacy: Creating a new community for London in Stratford. *The Guardian*. Retrieved July 19, 2012, from http://www.guardian.co.uk/housing-network/2012/jul/19/olympic-legacy-social-housing- east-village.

Mitchell, D. (2003). *The Right to the City: Social Justice and the Fight for Public Space*. New York: The Guilford Press.

Mol, A. (2002). *The Body Multiple*. Durham, NC: Duke University Press.

Mollenkopf, J. H., and Castells, M. (eds.). (1991). *Dual City: Restructuring New York*. New York: Russell Sage Foundation.

Monroe, S. and Goldman, P. (1988). *Brothers: Black and Poor – A True Story of Courage and Survival*. New York: William Morrow.
Mooney, G. (2004). Cultural policy and urban transformation? Critical reflections on Glasgow, European city of culture 1990. *Local Economy, 19*(4), 327–340.
Moragas, M. D., Belen, A., and Puig, N. (eds.). (2000). *Volunteers, Global Society, and the Olympic Movement*. Lausanne: Olympic Museum Press.
Murray, C. (1990). *The Emerging British Underclass*. London: IEA.
Murray, C. (1994). *Underclass: The crisis deepens*. London: IEA.
Newham Language Shop. (2005). *Newham Council Language Survey*. Retrieved May 1, 2006, from http://www.languageshop.org.uk/.
Newham London. (2010a). *Newham, London: Local Economic Assessment 2010 to 2027*. Retrieved January 15, 2012, from http://www.newham.info/Custom/LEA/Demographics.pdf.
Newham London. (2010b). *Newham, London: Economic Development Strategy 2010 to 2027*. Retrieved January 15, 2012, from http://www.newham.gov.uk/NR/rdonlyres/A04F1BA2-4015-43AA-AE1D-D3F8E9FE93B8/0/NewhamEconomicDevelopmentStrategy2010.pdf.
Norton-Taylor, R. (2012). London tower block residents lose bid to challenge Olympic missiles. *The Guardian*. Retrieved July 10, 2012, from http://www.guardian.co.uk/sport/2012/jul/10/residents-tower-government-olympic- missiles.
Nutall, S. (2009). *Entanglement: Literary and Cultural Reflections on Post-apartheid*. Johannesburg: Wits University Press.
O'Ceallaigh, J. (2011). Olympics visitors guide. *The Telegraph*. July 26. Retrieved July 26, 2011, from http://www.telegraph.co.uk/travel/destinations/europe/uk/london/8663143/Olympics-Visitors-Guide.html.
Office for National Statistics. (2007). *Index of Multiple Deprivation*. Retrieved August 6, 2009, from http://data.gov.uk/dataset/index_of_multiple_deprivation_imd_2007.
Office for National Statistics. (2008). *Annual Population Survey 2008*. Retrieved August 3, 2009, from http://www.ons.gov.uk/ons/search/index.html?pageSize=50&sortBy=none&sortDirection=none&newquery=annual+population+survey+2008.
Omi, M. and Winant, H. (1994). *Racial Formation in the United States: From the 1960s to the 1990s*. New York: Routledge.
Oquirrh Institute. (2003). *The 2002 Winter Games: Security Lessons Applied to Homeland Security*. Salt Lake City: Oquirrh Institute.
Owen, K. A. (2002). The Sydney 2000 Olympics and urban entrepreneurialism Local variations in urban governance. *Australian Geographical Studies, 40*(3), 323–336.
Pardo, I. (1996). *Managing Existence in Naples: Morality, Action and Structure*. Cambridge: University of Cambridge Press.
Pardo, I. and Prato, G. B. (eds.). (2012). *Anthropology in the City: Methodology and Theory*. Farnham: Ashgate Publishing Limited.
Park, R. E. (1967). *On Social Control and Collective Behavior*. Chicago, IL: University of Chicago Press.

Payne, M. (2005). *Olympic Turnaround: How the Olympic Games Stepped Back From the Brink of Extinction to Become the World's Best Known Brand and a Multi-billion Dollar Global Franchise*. Twyford, UK: London Business Press.

Perryman, M. (2012). *Why the Olympics Aren't Good for Us, and How they can be*. London: OR Books.

Pitt, J. (1977). *Gentrification in Islington*. London: Barnsbury People's Forum.

Poplin, D. E. (1979). *Communities: A Survey of Theories and Methods of Research*. New York: Macmillan.

Poulantzas, N. (1973). *Political Power and Social Claims*. London: Sherd & Ward.

Poynter, G. (2009). The 2012 Olympic Games and the reshaping of East London. In R. Imrie, L. Lees, and M. Raco (eds.), *Regenerating London: Governance, Sustainability and Community in a Global Age* (pp. 131–150). London: Routledge.

Power, A. (1987). *Property before People: The Management of Twentieth-century Council Housing*. London: Unwin.

Power, A. (1996). Area-based poverty and residential empowerment. *Urban Studies*, 33, 1535–1564.

Power, A. and Turnstall, R. (1991). *Swimming Against the Tide: Polarisation or Progress on 20 Unpopular Council Estates, 1980–1995*. York: Joseph Rowntree Foundation.

Preuss, H. (2004). *The Economics of Staging the Olympics: A Comparison of the Games 1972–2008*. Cheltenham: Edward Elgar Publishing Ltd.

Preuss, H., Gemeinder, K. and Segun, B. (2008). Ambush marketing in China: Counterbalancing Olympic sponsorship efforts. *Asian Business & Management*, 7, 243–263.

Proshansky, H. M., Fabian, A. K., and Kaminoff, R. (1983). Place-identity: Physical world socialization of the self. *Journal of Environmental Psychology*, 3, 57–83.

Raco, M. (2003). Remaking place and securitising space: Urban regeneration and the strategies, tactics and practises of policing in the UK. *Urban Studies*, 40(9), 1869–1887.

Raco, M. (2007). Securing sustainable communities: Citizenship, safety and sustainability in the new planning. *European and Regional Studies*, 14(4), 305–320.

Rai, D., Withey, J., Thacker, C., Tampubolo, G., Ogg, J., and Burton, J. (2008). *Newham Household Panel Survey Wave 5 Report*. London: London Borough of Newham.

Rayner, G. (2011). 7/7 inquest: London woefully unprepared for terrorist attack on 2012 Olympics, warns coroner. *The Telegraph*. Retrieved May 6, 2011, from http://www.telegraph.co.uk/news/uknews/terrorism-in-the-uk/8498250/77-inquest-London-woefully-unprepared-for-terrorist-attack-on-2012-Olympics-warns-coroner.html.

Real, M. R. (1996). The post-modern Olympics: Technology and the commodification of the Olympic movement. *Quest*, 48, 9–24.

Reckless, W. C. (1973). *American Criminology: New Directions*. New York: Appleton Century Crofts.

Reckless, W., Dinitz, S., and Kay, B. (1957). The self component in potential delinquency. *American Sociological Review*, 22, 566–570.

Reckless, W. C. and Dinitz, S. (1967). Pioneering with the self-concept as a vulnerability factor in delinquency. *Journal of Criminal Law, Criminology and Police Science*, 58, 515–523.
Reeve, S. (2001). *One Day in September: The Full Story of the 1972 Munich Olympics Massacre and the Israeli Revenge Operation 'Wrath of God'*. New York: Arcade Publishing.
Richards, A., Fussey, P., and Silke, A. (eds.). (2010). *Terrorism and the Olympic Lessons for 2012 and Beyond*. London: Routledge.
Ritchie, I. (2002). Cool rings: Olympic ideology and the symbolic consumption of global sport. In K. B. Wamsley, R. K. Barney, and S. G. Marts (eds.), *The Global Nexus Engaged: Sixth International symposium for Olympic research* (pp. 61–70). London, ON: University of Western Ontario.
Roberts, P. and Sykes, H. (eds.) (2000). *Urban Regeneration: A Handbook*. London: Sage.
Robertson, R. (1992). *Globalization: Social Theory and Global Culture*. London: Sage.
Robson, G. and Butler, T. (2001). Coming to terms with London: Middle-class communities in a global city. *International Journal of Urban and Regional Research*, 25, 70–86.
Robson, G. and Butler, T. (2004). *London Calling: The Middle Classes and the Remaking of Inner London*. Oxford: Berg.
Roche, M. (2000). *Mega-Events and Modernity: Olympics and Expos in the Growth of Global Culture*. New York: Routledge.
Rollock, N. (2009). *The Stephen Lawrence Inquiry 10 Years on: An Analysis of the Literature*. London: Runnymeade.
Rose, D. (2004). Discourses and experiences of social mix in gentrifying neighbourhoods: A Montréal case study. *Canadian Journal of Urban Research*, 13(2), 278–316.
Rothenbuhler, E.W. (1989). Values and symbols in public orientations to the Olympic event. *Critical Studies in Mass Communication*, 6, 138–157.
Rowe, D. (2004). Antonio Gramsci: Sport, hegemony and the national-popular. In R. Giulianotti (ed.), *Sport and modern social theorists* (pp. 97–110). Basingstoke: Palgrave Macmillan.
Rowe, D., McKay, J. and Miller, T. (1998). Come together: Sport, nationalism and media image. In L. Wenner (ed.). *Mediasport* (pp. 119–133). New York: Routledge.
Russell, J. A., and Ward, L. M. (1982). Environmental psychology. *Annual Review of Psychology*, 33, 651–688.
Ryan, P. (2002). Olympic security: The relevance to homeland security, in *The 2002 Olympic Winter Games: Security Lessons Applied to Homeland Security*, the Oquirrh Institute, Salt Lake City: The Ocquirrh Institute.
Samatas, M. (2011). Surveillance in Athens 2004 and Beijing 2008: A comparison of the Olympic surveillance modalities and legacies in two different Olympic host regimes. *Urban Studies*, 48(15), 3347–3366.

Sampson, R. (2009). Disparity and diversity in the city: Social (dis)order revisited. *British Journal of Sociology, 60*, 1–31.
Sanders, P. (1989). *The Simple Annals: The History of Essex and East End Family.* Gloucester: Alan Sutton.
Sarup, M. (1996). *Identity, Culture and the Postmodern World.* Edinburgh: Edinburgh University Press.
Sassen, S. (1991). *The Global City: New York, London, Tokyo.* Princeton: Princeton University Press.
Sassen, S. (2001). The global city: Strategic site/new frontier. *American Studies, 41*, 79–95.
Sawhill, I.V. (1989). The underclass: An overview. *The Public Interest, 96*, 3–15.
Scammell, M. (1995). *Designer Politics: How Elections Are Won.* Houndmills, Baskingstoke: Macmillan.
Scherer, J., Sam, M., and Batty, R. (2005). Sporting sign wars: Advertising and the contested terrain of sporting events and venues. *International Journal of Sport Management and Marketing, 1*, 17–36.
Schiller, B. (2004). *The Economics of Poverty and Discrimination.* Upper Saddle River, NJ: Pearson.
Schimmel, K. S. (2011). From "violence complacent" to "terrorist-ready": Post-9/11 framing of the US Super Bowl. *Urban Studies, 48*(15), 3277–3293.
Seabrook, J. (1984). *The Idea of Neighbourhood.* London: Pluto.
Segrave, J. (1988). Toward a definition of Olympism. In J. Segrave and D. Chu (eds.), *The Olympic Games in transition* (pp. 149–161). Champaign, IL: Human Kinetics.
Sennett, R. (2006). *The Culture of the New Capitalism.* London: Yale University Press.
Shaw, C. (2008). *Five Ring Circus: Myths and Realities of the Olympic Games.* Gabriola Island, B.C.: New Society Publishers.
Sibley, D. (1995). *Geographies of Exclusion: Society and Difference in the West.* London: Routledge.
Silk, M. (2011). Towards a sociological analysis of London 2012. *Sociology, 45*(5), 733–748.
Silk, M., Andrews, D.L. and Cole, C.L. (2005). Corporate nationalism(s): The spatial dimensions of sporting capital. In M. Silk, D. Andrews, and C. L. Cole (eds.), *Sport and corporate nationalisms* (pp. 1–13). Oxford: Berg.
Sixsmith, M. (2011). *Russia: A 1,000 Year Chronicle of the Wild East.* London: Ebury Publishing.
Slater, J. (1998). Changing partners: The relationship between the mass media and the Olympic Games. In R. K. Barney, K. B. Wamsley, S. G. Martyn, and G. H. MacDonald (eds.), *Fourth International Symposium for Olympic Research* (pp. 49–69). London, ON: University of Western Ontario.
Slater, T., Curran, W. and Lees, L. (2004). Gentrification research: New directions & critical scholarship. *Environment & Planning A, 36*, 1141–1150.
Smith, N. (1979). Toward a theory of gentrification. In L. Lees, T. Slater, and E. Wyly (eds.), *The Gentrification Reader.* Oxon: Routledge.

Smith, N. (1996). *The New Urban Frontier.* New York: Routledge.
Smith, N. (1998). Giuliani time: The revanchist 1990s. *Social Text, 57,* 1–20.
Smith, N. (2002). New globalism, new urbanism: Gentrification as global urban strategy. *Antipode, 34,* 427–449.
Smith, S. and Schaffer, K. (2000). *The Olympics at the Millennium: Performance, Politics and the Games.* New Brunswick, NJ: Rutgers University Press.
Soja, E. (2000). *Postmetropolis: Critical Studies of Cities and Regions.* Oxford: Blackwell.
Sport England (2003). *Young People and Sport in England: Trends in Participation 1996–2006.* Retrieved, July 5, 2008, from http://www.sportengland.org/index/get_resources/research/understanding_participation.htm,
Srinivasa, S. (2006). *The Power Law of Information: Life in a Connected World.* London: Sage.
Stacey, M. (1969). The myth of community studies. *British Journal of Sociology, 20*(2), 134–147.
Stenson, K. (2001). Reconstructing the Government of crime. In G. Wickham and G. Pavlich (eds.), *Rethinking Law, Society and Governance: Foucault's Bequest.* Oxford: Hart.
Stevenson, D. (1997). Olympic arts: Sydney 2000 and the cultural Olympiad. *International Review for the Sociology of Sport, 32*(3), 227–238.
Stokols, D. (1990). Instrumental and spiritual views of people-environment relations. *American Psychologist, 45,* 641–646.
Suttles, G. D. (1972). *The Social Construction of Communities.* Chicago: University of Chicago Press.
Swyngedouw, E., Moulaert, F. and Rodrigues, A. (2002). Neoliberal urbanization in Europe: Large-scale urban development projects and new urban policy. *Antipode, 34*(3), 542–577.
Taylor, C. (1999). To follow a rule. In R. Shusterman (ed.), *Bourdieu: A Critical Reader.* Oxford: Blackwell.
Thompson-Fawcett, M. (1996). The urbanist revision of development. *Urban Design International,* 1(4), 301–322.
Toohey, K. and Taylor, T. (2008). Mega events, fear, and risk: Terrorism at the Olympic Games. *Terrorism, 22*(4), 451–469.
Townsend, M. (2012). Stop and search racial profiling by police on the increase, claims study. *The Guardian.* Retrieved January 14, 2012, from http://www.guardian.co.uk/law/2012/jan/14/stop-search-racial-profiling-police.
Trevaskis Consulting. (2006). *Britannia Village, Wesley Avenue, London, E16: Invitation to Tender for the Appointment of Managing Agents.* Retrieved January 4, 2012, from http://www.bvra.org.uk/documents/ITTv5.pdf.
Urry, J. (2000). *Sociology Beyond Societies: Mobilities for the Twenty-first Century.* London: Routledge.
Van Maanen, J. (1979). The fact of fiction in organizational ethnography. *Administrative Science Quarterly, 24,* 539–549.
Van Weesep, J. (1984). Condominium conversation in Amsterdam: Boon or burden. *Urban Geography, 5,* 165–177.

Venkatesh, S. (2008). *Gang Leader for a Day*. New York: Penguin Press.
Walters, G. (2006). *Berlin Games: How Hitler Stole the Olympics*. London: John Murray.
Wacquant, L. (1989). Towards a reflexive sociology: A workshop with Pierre Bourdieu. *Sociological Theory*, 7(1), 26–63.
Wacquant, L. (1993). Urban outcasts: Stigma and division in the black American ghetto and French urban periphery. *International Journal of Urban and Regional Research*, 365–83.
Wacquant, L. (1999). *Prisons of Poverty*. Minneapolis, MS: University of Minnesota Press.
Wacquant, L. (2008). *Urban Outcasts: A Comparative Sociology of Advanced Marginality*. Cambridge: Polity Press.
Wacquant, L. (2009). *Punishing the Poor: The Neoliberal Government of Social Insecurity*. Durham, NC: Duke University Press.
Wallerstein, N. (1993). Empowerment and health: The theory and practice of community change. *Community Development Journal*, 28(3), 218–227.
Wallman, S. (1984). *Eight London Households*. London: Routledge.
Wamsley, K. B. (2004). Laying Olympism to rest. In J. Bale, and M. K. Christiansen (eds.), *Post Olympism: Questioning sport in the twenty-first century* (pp. 367–84). Oxford: Berg.
Webb, J., Schirato, T. and Danaher, G. (2002). *Understanding Bourdieu*. Sydney: Allen and Unwin.
Weber, M. (1968). *Economy and Society*. Berkeley: University of California Press.
Wensing, E. H., and Bruce, T. (2003). Bending the rules: Media representations of gender during an international sporting event. *International Review for the Sociology of Sport*, 38(4), 387–396.
Whitson, D. (1998). Olympic sport, global media and cultural diversity. In R. K. Barney, K. B. Wamsley, S. G. Martyn, and G. H. MacDonald (eds.), *Fourth international symposium for Olympic research* (pp. 1–9). London, ON: University of Western Ontario.
Whyte, W.F. (1943). *Street Corner Society: The Social Structure of an Italian Slum*. Chicago: University of Chicago Press.
Wilkins, L. (1991). *Punishment, and Crime and Market Forces*. Aldershot: Dartmouth.
Williams, K. D. (1997). Social ostracism. In R. Kowalski (ed.), *Aversive Interpersonal Behaviors*. New York: Plenum.
Williams, K. D. and Sommers, K. L. (1997). Social ostracism by one's coworkers: Does rejection lead to loafing or compensation. *Personality and Social Psychology Bulletin*, 23, 693–706.
Willmott, P. (1987). *Friendship Networks and Social Support*. London: Policy Studies Institute.
Willmott, P. and Young, M. (1957). *Family and Kinship in East London*. London: Routledge.

Woods, P. and Levacic, R. (2002). Raising school performance in the league tables (part 2): Barriers to responsiveness in three disadvantaged schools. *British Educational Research Journal, 28*(2), 227–247.

Wray-Bliss, E. (2002). Interpretation – appropriation: (Making) an example of labour process theory. *Organizational Research Methods, 5*(1), 80–103.

Wyly, E. and Hammel, D. (2005). Mapping neo-liberal American urbanism. In R. Atkinson and G. Bridge (eds.), *Gentrification in a Global Context: The New Urban Colonialism* (pp. 18–38). London: Routledge.

Yarbrough C.R. (2000). *And They Call Them Games: An Inside View of the 1996 Olympics*. Macon, GA: Mercer University Press.

York, M. (2012). Newham council war on betting shops. *Newham Recorder*. Retrieved June 4, 2012, from http://www.newhamrecorder.co.uk/newham-life/organisations/newham_council_war_on_betting_shops_1_1396659.

Youle, E. (2011). London riots: Police stop and search blamed for tension that sparked Tottenham riots. *London 24*. Retrieved August 10, 2011, from http://www.london24.com/news/crime/london_riots_police_stop_and_search_blamed_for_tension_that_sparked_tottenham_riots_1_990635.

Young, I. (1990). *Justice and the Politics of Difference*. Princeton, NJ: Princeton University Press.

Zakus, D. H. (1992). The International Olympic Committee: Tragedy, farce and hypocrisy. *Sociology of Sport, 9*, 340–353.

Zukin, S. (1995). *The Cultures of Cities*. Oxford: Blackwell.

Zukin, S. (1998). Urban lifestyles: Diversity and standardization in space of consumption. *Urban Studies, 35*(5/6), 825–839.

Index

activism
  activists, 40, 111
  protesting, 3, 73–4, 152, 168, 176
affordable housing, 67–8
Albanians, 3, 85, 115, 172
Anderson, Benedict, 37, 143
Anderson, Elijah, 33, 53, 60
Andrew, Altman, 26–7, 31, 38
Armstrong, Gary, 32, 38, 55, 149, 181, 186
Aston Mansfield, 10, 41, 70, 79–80, 84, 107, 111, 152, 166, 169, 172, 181
Athens Olympics, The, 28, 182, 190, 193
Atlanta Olympics, The, 107–8, 150–1
Auge, Marc
  Auge, Marc, 18–21, 153–5, 167, 182
  non-place, 19–21, 153–5, 157, 167

Barcelona Olympics, The, 28–9, 151, 161, 186–7
Bourdieu, Pierre
  Bourdieu, Pierre, 2, 13, 18, 21–2, 50, 57, 63, 75–6, 89–90, 93–5, 99–100, 120, 123, 146, 152, 154, 156–60, 167, 171–2, 182–3, 186–7, 189, 196
  habitus, 2, 22, 55, 57, 88–9, 94, 99, 121, 156, 158–9, 179, 189
  hysteresis, 2, 99, 123, 156–8, 161, 186

Britannia Village, 50–61, 90–3, 120–1, 130, 133, 161
British Olympic Association (BOA), The, 64–6, 171

CARP, 49–50, 170
Carpenters Estate, 32, 42–6, 48–50, 81, 87, 160, 163, 170, 179
Coe, Sebastian, 68, 76, 107, 137–8, 143–4, 165, 174, 184
community consultation, 23, 27, 33–4, 37, 41, 70, 72–3, 75–8, 102, 110–11, 119, 126, 156, 174
crime
  crime, 10–14, 32, 52–3, 55, 57, 59, 84, 90, 108, 114, 154, 165, 168, 174, 182, 186, 188, 195–7
  criminal, 14, 53, 114, 169–70, 173–5, 188, 193
  criminality, 10, 13–15, 51–3, 58–9, 90
  criminalization, 108

Department for Culture, Media and Sport (DCMS), The, 88, 138–9, 142

Eastern Europeans, 16, 49, 58, 80–5, 95, 154, 166, 169
employment
  employment, 1, 6, 12, 14–15, 18, 26, 34, 42, 46, 59, 67–9, 71, 75,

employment—*Continued*
　78–96, 99, 120, 123, 126, 129,
　　150, 156, 158, 160, 165, 168,
　　172–3, 187
　unemployment, 14, 56–7, 80, 86–8,
　　90, 93, 95–6, 161
Ethical Olympics, The, 68–9, 75, 78
ethnography
　Dispersal Zone, 18, 39–40, 102, 152
　ethnography, 1, 18, 31–3, 38–9, 42,
　　52, 54, 60, 88, 151–2, 154, 157,
　　190, 195
　ExCeLland, 39, 41, 50, 90, 102, 112,
　　127, 132
　fieldwork, 7–8, 10, 14, 16, 23, 32,
　　35, 55, 60, 72, 74–6, 82, 84, 90,
　　93, 102
　Stratfordland, 39, 41–2, 53, 99, 102,
　　128, 152, 157, 160, 163, 176, 179
ExCeL, 18, 31, 39, 50, 166, 168

Fussey, Pete, 23, 38, 95, 99, 107,
　149–50, 172, 184, 186, 193

gangs, 3, 12–15, 33, 92, 128, 133
Giulianotti, Richard, 97, 108, 110, 150,
　156, 176, 178, 186, 193
globalization, 10, 24, 181, 187, 189, 195
glocalization, 24, 167
government, 30, 139, 142, 170, 184–5,
　195–6
Gramsci, Antonio, 78, 149, 157, 178,
　186, 193
Greater London Authority (GLA), The,
　9, 15, 73, 166, 172, 186

Hackney, 29–30, 165, 168, 176
Harvey, David, 24, 53, 122, 186–7
hegemony, 65, 69, 72, 74, 76–8, 89, 97,
　135, 157, 178, 193
Hobbs, Dick, 7, 32, 38, 149, 153, 181,
　186–7
homes, 6, 9, 12, 14, 17–18, 28, 42, 44,
　49, 53, 55, 60, 68–9, 116, 132,
　170, 175

hope, 10, 33, 51, 58, 60, 68, 90, 96, 99,
　106, 127, 147, 171, 188
housing, 6, 9, 16–17, 28, 39, 43–4, 51,
　54, 56–7, 67, 90, 120, 133, 165–8,
　170–1, 184, 190, 192
Hungarians, 10–11, 13

immigration, 17, 19, 81–2, 85, 132
International Olympic Committee
　(IOC), The, 24–5, 27, 29, 31, 37,
　63–6, 109, 137, 149–51, 167–8,
　172, 182, 184

Lefebvre, Henri, 18–19, 21, 154,
　157, 189
legacy
　legacy, 1, 18, 23, 26, 38, 41, 56,
　　65–6, 68–9, 76, 80, 97, 123–4,
　　127, 132, 139, 142, 146, 151,
　　155–6, 158, 161, 169–70, 176–7,
　　185–7, 190, 193
　Legacy Action Plan, 177, 185
Lenskyj, Helen Jefferson, 2–3, 108,
　149–52, 161, 179, 189
Lewisham, 29
Leyton, 68
Livingstone, Ken, 65–6, 68, 165, 190
London 7/7 bombings, The, 109
London 2012 Olympic bid, The, 2–3,
　18, 22–4, 26–8, 31, 34, 37, 41,
　46, 64–9, 86, 137, 142–4, 149–51,
　153, 157, 159–61, 165, 169, 172,
　178, 187, 189–91
London Development Agency (LDA),
　The, 66, 68–9, 93, 172–3
London Legacy Development
　Corporation (LLDC), The, 41, 169
London Organising Committee for the
　Olympic Games (LOCOG), The,
　41, 87, 102–3, 105, 107, 109, 176
London's Gash, 26, 31, 38, 120, 154

Manchester, 65–6, 100, 124, 151
marginalization, 7, 14, 27, 78, 100,
　168, 174

Marxism, 33, 63, 147, 156–7
media, 2, 5, 13, 18, 33–8, 42, 50–1, 64, 70, 81, 87–8, 98, 100, 104–5, 108, 113, 116, 119, 136, 139, 141–4, 146, 153, 157, 159, 168, 170, 173–4, 178, 185, 189–90, 193–4, 196
methodology, 1, 18, 21–2, 32–3, 35, 39–40, 42, 51, 139, 151, 167, 191

NEETs, 14, 90–1, 173, 187
Newham
    Newham Council, 5, 7, 9, 15, 17, 43–4, 46–7, 60, 66, 76, 80, 93, 95, 111, 116, 125, 132, 153, 166–8, 170, 173, 176, 191–2, 197
    Newham Young People's Project (NYPP), 41, 89, 115–16

Olympic Delivery, 1–3, 10, 14, 18, 20–3, 25–8, 30–2, 36–43, 45–6, 50, 61, 67–70, 72–81, 84–5, 87, 89, 93–100, 103–4, 106, 115, 117, 119–24, 126–30, 133, 135–6, 139, 141–7, 149, 151–61, 163, 178–9
Olympic Delivery Authority (ODA), The, 69–75, 77, 101, 172
Olympic Games, The, 1–3, 6, 18, 23–31, 37–9, 41–3, 46, 49–50, 63–9, 73, 76, 79–80, 85–9, 93–105, 107–11, 113, 115–17, 119–22, 124–7, 129, 132, 135–47, 149–53, 155–61, 163, 165, 167–70, 172–4, 176–8, 183–97
Olympic hosting, 1–3, 5, 18–19, 23–9, 31, 37–42, 46, 50, 64–8, 87–8, 94, 97–8, 107–8, 129, 136–40, 142, 144–5, 150–4, 165–6, 168–9, 176, 178, 183, 193
Olympic identity, 76, 89, 97, 100, 135–6, 139–43, 145–7
Olympic Park Legacy Company (OPLC), The, 26, 30–1, 38, 41, 169

Olympicization, 27, 35, 154, 167
Olympism, 23, 27, 63–4, 136, 187, 189–90, 194, 196

Paralympic Games, The, 27, 31, 94, 110, 141–2, 168, 178, 185
policing
    Metropolitan Police Service (MPS), The, 32, 110–12, 114–15, 175
    police, 13, 17, 32, 34, 58, 60, 87, 91, 97, 103, 105–6, 109–17, 128, 168–9, 173–6, 187, 190, 193, 195, 197
    policing, 6, 28, 37, 97, 101, 103, 108, 110–17, 120, 173, 178, 183, 192
policy, 3, 25, 27–8, 41, 44, 51–3, 57–8, 60–1, 67, 84, 101–2, 108, 170, 182, 184, 186–9, 191, 195–6
politics
    political, 3, 18, 25, 28, 37, 39, 50, 54–5, 60, 65–7, 72–3, 80, 95, 97, 117, 123, 136–7, 141, 146, 157, 168, 173–4, 178, 181, 183, 185, 188
    politicians, 17, 26, 28, 37, 47, 51, 60–1, 81, 96, 119, 136–7, 142
    politicking, 23
    politics, 23, 40, 117, 139, 149, 166–7, 174, 179, 181, 183, 185, 187–9, 194–5, 197
poverty, 3, 5–7, 16, 29, 31, 43–4, 120, 154–5, 160–1, 192, 194, 196
power, 3, 13, 15, 37, 44, 50, 52, 69, 73–8, 89, 100, 106, 136–7, 139, 146–7, 149, 157–60, 174, 178, 182, 185, 187, 189, 192, 195

race
    race, 18–19, 53, 60, 65, 81, 95, 136–7, 141, 155, 171, 179, 184–5, 189
    racism, 14, 29, 49, 80, 91, 111–15, 147, 190, 195
regeneration
    gentrification, 16–17, 24, 46, 52, 119–21, 125, 133, 160–1, 167, 179, 189–90, 193–5

regeneration—*Continued*
regeneration, 1–2, 6, 16, 18, 23–7, 30–2, 42, 46, 49–53, 65–6, 68, 80, 93, 96, 119–20, 122–4, 126–8, 130, 132–4, 142, 153–5, 159, 167, 170, 172, 186, 190, 192–3
renewal, 30, 121, 129, 133, 182, 190
reordering, 121–3, 127–8, 152, 159–61, 176
transformation, 1, 5, 9, 18, 21–2, 26, 30, 42–3, 69, 86, 89, 122, 125, 134, 138, 143, 152, 171, 191
regulation, 17, 23, 27, 31, 69, 89, 103–5, 168, 189
residents, 3, 5–7, 9–11, 13, 15–16, 23, 26, 28, 34–5, 39, 42–60, 71, 78–81, 85–6, 88–9, 91–2, 95–6, 99, 101, 111–13, 116, 119–23, 125, 127–30, 152–3, 156–61, 163, 167, 170, 178–9, 191

safety, 14, 47, 53, 57–9, 109–11, 114, 116, 133, 140–1, 174, 186–7, 189, 192
Samaranch, Juan Antonio, 25–6
security
securitization, 3, 23, 31, 53, 57, 59, 97–9, 101, 104–9, 111, 113–17, 127, 173, 184, 186, 192
security, 3, 28, 32, 41–2, 45–6, 52–4, 56–60, 71, 77–8, 91, 96–9, 101, 103–11, 113, 115–17, 121, 130, 150, 154, 158, 174, 183–4, 186, 188, 191–3
segregation, 3, 46, 54, 57, 95–6, 98–9, 121, 123–4, 136, 140–1, 143–4, 154
Singapore, 65, 137, 176
sport, 1–3, 18, 28, 32, 63, 65–9, 80, 88, 97–8, 100, 136–40, 142, 145, 149–50, 154, 156–7, 161, 167, 170, 174, 177–8, 181–91, 193–7
stadia, 26, 43, 50, 76, 149

surveillance, 13, 54, 58, 108, 128, 150, 185–6, 193
sustainability, 29, 51, 53, 56, 138, 156, 170, 172, 181, 188, 192
Sydney Olympics, The, 26, 29, 152, 161, 179, 185, 189, 191, 195–6

terrorism, 98, 107–9, 112, 114–15, 149, 175, 184, 192–5
The East London Citizens Organisation (TELCO), 67–78
Tottenham, 112, 197
tourism, 25, 29, 98, 123, 139–40, 144, 149, 177, 183–4
Tower Hamlets, 29–30, 168, 170, 179
tradition, 14, 19–20, 27, 30, 53, 60, 85–6, 100, 108, 125, 129, 136, 145, 147, 160, 179, 187
training, 1, 14, 41, 86–8, 90, 94–5, 116–17, 156, 165, 175, 187
Transport For London (TFL), 41, 102–3

venues, 1, 25, 39, 41, 50, 87, 100–1, 109–10, 133, 144, 156, 168, 172, 178, 194
vilification, 26–7, 31, 43, 53–4, 58–9, 82, 85, 88, 92, 125, 128, 143, 150, 153, 159
violence, 10–12, 14, 52, 91–2, 95, 114, 127–8, 133, 136, 174–6, 181, 184, 194
volunteerism, 8, 28, 52, 67, 69, 72, 85–9, 102, 105, 117, 160, 169, 172–3, 175

Wacquant, Loic, 12, 22, 28, 51, 54, 57, 61, 95, 100, 105, 152, 156, 166–7, 171, 173–4, 183, 196
Wales, Robin, 17–18, 25–6, 45, 47, 50, 80–1, 86, 90, 122–3, 125, 142, 161, 165, 170–1, 174, 177, 185, 188
Wanstead Flats, 103, 110–11

CPI Antony Rowe
Chippenham, UK
2016-12-27 14:41